Level D

Developing Math & Thinking Skills

Mathematical Reasoning™ products available in print or eBook form.

- Beginning 1 • Beginning 2
- Level A • Level B • Level C • Level D
- Level E • Level F • Level G • Understanding Pre-Algebra
- Understanding Geometry • Understanding Algebra I
- Grades 2-4 Supplement • Grades 4-6 Supplement
- Middle School Supplement (Grades 7-9)

Written by
Carolyn Anderson

Graphic Design by
Karla Garrett • Annette Langenstein

© 2014, 2009
THE CRITICAL THINKING CO.™
(Bright Minds™)
www.CriticalThinking.com
Phone: 800-458-4849 • Fax: 541-756-1758
1991 Sherman Ave., Suite 200 • North Bend • OR 97459
ISBN 978-1-60144-161-4

ABOUT THE AUTHOR

Carolyn Anderson holds graduate degrees in mathematics and education. She taught for more than 20 years in the North Kansas City School District and is currently an Associate Professor of Mathematics at Park University. There she teaches mathematics and math method courses for early childhood and elementary teachers.

Carolyn spent nearly ten years as managing editor of *Math Magic*, a national math magazine and math enrichment developer. She has written educational material for whole numbers, decimals, money, metric system, geometry, and trigonometry. Carolyn has authored a book of math mazes and several math puzzle books. She has been a speaker at numerous conferences on integrating technology into math curriculum and developing summer enrichment programs.

Carolyn has been nominated numerous times for the North Kansas City School District teacher of the year. In 1993 she won the KCI/Northland Regional Chamber Excellence in Education Award. Also, she was recognized as the outstanding math alumni of the year at Central Missouri State University. In 1999 she was the winner of the Larry Markt "above and beyond" award.

Carolyn believes it is important to structure classes for success and good material is a key component of that.

TABLE OF CONTENTS

NCTM Standards

Skills	Number and Operations	Algebra	Geometry	Measurement	Data Analysis and Probability
Adding Whole Numbers	6, 8, 13, 17, 33, 43, 55, 57, 73, 89, 102, 124, 125, 126, 148, 149, 159, 195, 199, 209, 230, 231, 252, 266, 276, 296, 297, 306, 307	9, 35, 89, 148, 149, 150, 200, 252, 254, 274, 297	167, 192, 290, 314	42, 44, 68, 69, 78, 144, 145, 176, 178, 179, 180, 243, 244, 246, 247, 284, 291, 331	14, 17, 43, 45, 88, 188, 193, 201, 202, 204, 205, 219, 239, 241, 270, 271, 287, 288, 289, 321
Analyze	1, 87, 173, 184, 188, 193, 230, 231, 254, 265, 288, 296	36, 37, 43, 131, 146, 147, 169, 252, 254, 296, 348, 349	19, 20, 280	308	10, 45, 88, 204, 205, 289, 321
Angle			162, 163, 164, 165, 166, 167, 260, 314		167, 192, 214, 225
Area		245		178, 179, 180, 244, 291	
Bar Graph				239, 241	10, 45, 88, 287, 289
Calendar		121		68, 69, 122, 248, 304	
Capacity				78, 79, 238, 242, 328, 330, 331	331
Congruence	110	63	11, 46, 66, 67, 181, 214, 283		
Coordinate System			72, 206, 282, 316		
Count	1, 16, 34, 124, 125, 126, 201, 266, 301				
Data Collection					205, 239, 240, 241, 268, 269, 270
Decimals	22, 23, 24, 25, 30, 38, 39, 73,74, 227, 229, 292, 293, 294, 295, 331, 332, 333, 334	36, 37, 230, 231		309, 310, 311, 312, 313	26, 27
Dividing Whole Numbers	97, 100, 103, 104, 105, 117, 151, 153, 156, 157, 170, 171, 172, 212, 213, 279, 298, 299, 323, 324, 337, 339	92, 93, 94, 95, 98, 99, 101, 152, 154, 158, 198, 252, 297, 322, 338			173, 265

NCTM Standards (Cont.)

NCTM Standards

Skills	Number and Operations	Algebra	Geometry	Measurement	Data Analysis and Probability
Equations	89, 104, 105, 148, 149, 150	15, 35, 56, 57, 96, 98, 99, 101, 148, 149, 170, 171, 195, 200, 252, 274, 297, 346	k		
Equivalence	110, 111, 132, 133, 220		130		292
Estimation	13, 14, 29, 47, 168, 269, 306, 307, 321, 339			284, 285	321
Expanded Notation	4, 5, 16, 118, 253, 272				
Fractions	107, 108, 109, 110, 111, 112, 113, 128, 129, 132, 133, 134, 136, 137, 138, 139, 140, 141, 142, 143, 219, 220, 221, 233, 234, 325, 326	131, 135, 155	114, 130	114, 223, 286, 335	261, 320
Graph			21, 160, 161, 225, 259		10, 45, 88, 204, 205, 239, 240, 241, 271, 287, 288, 289, 321
Inequalities	32, 38, 39, 86, 106, 119, 127, 134, 221, 275, 305				
Length	144, 145		176, 177	42, 44, 70, 223, 224, 238, 242, 284, 285, 286, 327, 329, 335, 336	
Likelihood/Prediction					80, 81, 82, 194, 268, 269, 270, 320
Line Graph					204, 271, 287, 321
Money	22, 23, 24, 25, 27, 29, 30, 38, 39, 73, 74, 227, 228, 229, 232, 294, 295, 332, 333, 334	36, 37, 230, 231, 293, 331			292
Multiplying Whole Numbers	55, 57, 58, 59, 60, 61, 62, 110, 116, 156, 157, 158, 159, 170, 171, 186, 187, 189, 190, 191, 196, 197, 200, 211, 212, 235, 236, 237, 262, 263, 264, 278, 317, 319	56, 65, 89, 101, 104, 105, 252, 297	83, 84, 85		87, 154, 222, 318

NCTM Standards (Cont.)

NCTM Standards

NCTM Standards (Cont.)

NCTM Standards

Skills	Number and Operations	Algebra	Geometry	Measurement	Data Analysis and Probability
Temperature				76, 77, 243	271
Time	144, 145	121		48, 49, 53, 68, 69, 120, 122, 248, 302, 303, 304	
Variable		35, 101, 200, 252, 274			
Vocabulary	1, 2, 3, 12, 13, 17, 18, 22, 29, 32, 36, 47, 50, 55, 56, 75, 83, 84, 86, 92, 98, 100, 102, 104, 106, 107, 108, 110, 111, 112, 116, 118, 119, 127, 128, 132, 141, 148, 156, 195, 202, 212, 213, 220, 221, 222, 233, 253, 256, 281, 292, 298		11, 19, 21, 40, 41, 46, 63, 66, 67, 71, 72, 160, 162, 163, 164, 165, 206, 207, 208, 214, 215, 216, 217, 218, 225, 226, 244, 246, 250, 259, 260, 282, 283, 316, 341, 343, 345	42, 44, 48, 68, 69, 70, 76, 77, 78, 79, 121, 174, 176, 178, 182, 183, 238, 242, 243, 290, 291, 302, 304, 327, 328, 329, 330	80, 188, 193, 204, 271
Weight		308		182, 183, 238, 242, 328, 330	
Word Form	2, 3, 16, 118, 253, 255, 272, 273				
Word Problems	19, 26, 27, 86, 87, 90, 91, 92, 93, 98, 99, 108, 109, 113, 130, 149, 173, 184, 185, 195, 198, 202, 203, 213, 219, 265, 293, 295, 298, 305, 318, 322, 331, 338, 340, 346, 347	14, 15, 17, 18, 36, 37, 43, 114, 131, 135, 155, 169, 230, 231, 296	41, 71, 83, 84, 85, 162, 163, 165, 166, 206, 207, 216, 225, 251, 259, 260, 282, 314, 315, 316, 348, 349	68, 69, 70, 120, 122, 144, 145, 175, 177, 180, 182, 183, 238, 242, 243, 245, 247, 290, 291, 304, 327, 328, 329, 330	10, 45, 80, 81, 82, 88, 146, 147, 188, 193, 194, 204, 205, 248, 271, 287, 289, 320, 321

About This Book

Teaching and practicing third grade math concepts and skills has never been easier! This unique all-in-one book allows the teacher to learn right along with the student—no lesson preparation needed! This will save you hours of time. Each section introduces a specific topic, followed by appropriate practice and application activities. Students enjoy the colorful, engaging challenges of the varying activities!

How to Use This Book

This book is a cooperative experience between you and your student. The highly effective activities teach third grade math skills and concepts—and some fourth grade math standards. The skills and concepts presented spiral throughout the book. This means that you will see a topic dealt with for a few pages and then a gap before it is covered again. We do that so the student has multiple opportunities to think about and apply the skill/concept.

Our suggestion is that you proceed through the book page by page. A student who successfully finishes *Mathematical Reasoning™* Level D will know and be able to apply the mathematics skills and concepts taught to most third-graders and some skills not typically taught until fourth grade.

All the books in this series are designed to make students think critically. Students who have worked in one or more of the previous books are likely to find to this book challenging, but not too challenging. Students who did not use one or more of the previous books are likely to find this book more challenging, but should eventually catch up and benefit from the exposure to mathematical reasoning.

Teaching Suggestions

Important: Keep learning fun and you will have an energetic student who looks forward to each lesson. Work around a student's attention span.

There is no one correct way to teach the skills presented in this book. Have fun figuring out different ways to relate the skills to the student's daily life.

The activities in this book are written to the standards of the National Council of Teachers of Mathematics (NCTM).

General Comments

NCTM-suggested strands of Number and Operations, Algebra, Geometry, Measurement, and Data Analysis and Probability are the main categories presented at this level. These strands are subdivided into related skills that can be seen in the left column of the Table of Contents beginning on page iii. We encourage you to look carefully at each area and find innovative ways to strengthen the connection between the various strands and the everyday life of the child.

Mathematical knowledge and its application is becoming an increasingly critical requirement for successful participation in our society. The foundations for this success are embedded within the activities of this book. These are the stepping-stones upon which each child's future will be built. Each topic is important and deserves careful consideration by parents, teachers, and students.

Even numbers have a 0, 2, 4, 6, or 8 in the ones place.
Odd numbers have a 1, 3, 5, 7, or 9 in the ones place.

1	2	3	4	5	6	7	8	9	10
11	12	13	14	15	16	17	18	19	20
21	22	23	24	25	26	27	28	29	30
31	32	33	34	35	36	37	38	39	40
41	42	43	44	45	46	47	48	49	50
51	52	53	54	55	56	57	58	59	60
61	62	63	64	65	66	67	68	69	70
71	72	73	74	75	76	77	78	79	80
81	82	83	84	85	86	87	88	89	90
91	92	93	94	95	96	97	98	99	100

Examples

Even	Odd
2	1
14	17
76	53
88	99
100	105

Look at the 1 – 100 chart and answer the following questions.

1. What is the first even number? _____

2. What is the tenth even number? _____

3. What is the first odd number? _____

4. What is the tenth odd number? _____

5. The second number is _____ (even or odd).

6. The third number is _____ (even or odd).

7. The fourth number is _____ (even or odd).

8. The sum of two even numbers is _____ (even or odd).

9. The sum of two odd numbers is _____ (even or odd).

10. The sum of an even and odd number is _____ (even or odd).

Number Words

one	two	three	four	five
six	seven	eight	nine	ten
eleven	twelve	twenty	thirty	forty
fifty	sixty	seventy	eighty	ninety
hundred	thousand			

Use words from the choice box to write each numeral in its word form. Do not use the word "and".

Standard	Word Form
39	thirty-nine
101	
228	
952	
64	
639	
45	
148	

When you write a check, the amount in word form is on the second line.

Standard Form

Word Form

No. 99

Pay to the order of ___Bob Jones___ $ _130_

One hundred thirty _____ dollars

First National Bank
Anytown, USA

Signed ___Ann Brown___

Fill in the blanks to complete these checks.

Write a check to a charity.

No. 101

Pay to the order of _____ $ _____

_____ dollars

First National Bank
Anytown, USA   Signed _____

Write a check to a friend.

No. 102

Pay to the order of _____ $ _____

_____ dollars

First National Bank
Anytown, USA   Signed _____

Write a check to a store.

No. 103

Pay to the order of _____ $ _____

_____ dollars

First National Bank
Anytown, USA   Signed _____

Thousands	Hundreds	Tens	Ones
1	2	1	3

= 1,000 + 200 + 10 + 3
(Expanded Notation)

Write the number shown in expanded notation.

1. Don saved $1,623.
   1,623 in expanded notation = $\underline{1,000 + 600 + 20 + 3}$

2. Julie drove 2,376 miles.
   2,376 in expanded notation = _____

3. Brian had 706 pieces of
   candy. 706 in expanded notation = _____

4. The school had 349 students.
   349 in expanded notation = _____

5. The mountain was 5,280 feet
   high. 5,280 in expanded notation = _____

6. The plane flew at a height
   of 9,865 feet. 9,865 in
   expanded notation = _____

7. The amount of units below
   in expanded notation = _____

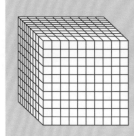 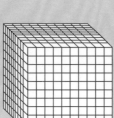 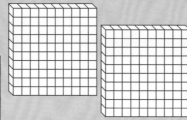 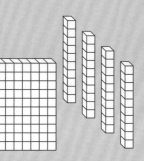

Note: To make reading easier, a comma is placed between the thousand digit and the hundred digit.

World's Tallest Buildings	Built	Height
1st Burj Khalifa, Dubai, United Arab Emirates	2010	2,717 ft
2nd Taipei 101, Taipei, Taiwan	2004	1,667 ft
3rd Petronas 1, Kaula Lumpur, Malaysia	1974	1,483 ft
4th Sears Tower, Chicago, Illinois	1974	1,451 ft
5th Jin Mao Building, Shanghai, China	1999	1,381 ft
6th Two International Finance Centre, Hong Kong	2003	1,362 ft
7th CITIC Plaza, Guangzhou, China	1996	1,283 ft
8th Shun Ming Square, Shenzhen, China	1996	1,260 ft

The table shows the world's tallest buildings. Write the height of each building (tallest first) in expanded form and word form.

1st $2,000 + 700 + 17$

two thousand, seven hundred seventeen

2nd ___

3rd ___

4th ___

5th ___

6th ___

7th ___

8th ___

Note: To make reading easier, a comma is placed between the thousand digit and the hundred digit.

46 + 58 =

$$\begin{array}{r} \overset{\text{tens}}{}\overset{\text{ones}}{} \\ \overset{1}{4}\,6 \\ +\ 5\,8 \\ \hline 1\,0\,4 \end{array}$$

Line up the ones and tens. Begin adding in the ones column and do not keep more than 9 in that column. Regroup when needed.

Find the sums. Shade in each matching answer on the sidewalk below to see which dog gets to eat first.

a   49   b   63   c   94   d   55   e   81
     + 32   + 28   + 17   + 46   + 40

f   67   g   84   h   99   i   41   j   86
     +25   + 18   + 13   + 52   + 36

k   26 + 47 = _____   l   29 + 74 = _____

m   68 + 15 = _____   n   91 + 22 = _____

o   85 + 38 = _____   p   64 + 29 = _____

123	113	133	93	102	92	112	121	81
93	83	103	73	122	82	101	111	91

The answer to a subtraction problem is called the **difference**.

Find the difference.

a
```
  9    11    14     7     3    18    12     9     8
- 6   - 5   - 6   - 5   - 2   - 9   - 5   - 5   - 3
```

b
```
  7    11     6    14     7    10     8    17    13
- 3   - 4   - 3   - 5   - 2   - 9   - 6   - 9   - 7
```

c
```
 10    12    11     6     7    10    12    15    16
- 8   - 3   - 5   - 1   - 4   - 9   - 8   - 7   - 9
```

d
```
  4     9     6     9    11     8    18    14    13
- 3   - 5   - 1   - 2   - 8   - 6   - 9   - 8   - 5
```

e
```
 17     3    14     9    12    15    12    10    11
- 8   - 1   - 7   - 8   - 6   - 7   - 8   - 7   - 6
```

What does each row of answers have in common?
Answer: The digits 1 through 9 are in each row.

Add the ones and regroup (13 ones=1 ten 3 ones).
Add the tens and regroup (14 tens = 1 hundred 4 tens).
Add the hundreds. Regroup when necessary.

```
   H T O                      H T O
    1 1
    2 9 7      OR              2 9 7
 +  1 4 6                   +  1 4 6
 _____                 _____
    4 4 3                      1 3      (7 + 6)
                              1 3 0     (90 + 40)
                              3 0 0     (200 + 100)
                             _____
                              4 4 3
```

Find each sum, then draw an arrow on the target of the matching answer below.

a   892   b   436   c   367   d   276
    + 127   + 219   + 821   + 924

e   527   f   829   g   744   h   392
    + 684   + 921   + 156   + 687

i   239 + 215 + 488 = _____

j   161 + 346 + 123 + 271 = _____

If you added correctly, all but one target below was hit.

901   1079   1211   655   911   1200   900   1019   1750   942   1188

Addition Table

+	0	1	2	3	4	5	6	7	8	9
0	0	1	2	3	4	5	6	7	8	9
1	1	2	3	4	5	6	7	8	9	10
2	2	3	4	5	6	7	8	9	10	11
3	3	4	5	6	7	8	9	10	11	12
4	4	5	6	7	8	9	10	11	12	13
5	5	6	7	8	9	10	11	12	13	14
6	6	7	8	9	10	11	12	13	14	15
7	7	8	9	10	11	12	13	14	15	16
8	8	9	10	11	12	13	14	15	16	17
9	9	10	11	12	13	14	15	16	17	18

Properties of Addition

Zero Property: $a + 0 = a$

$$8 + 0 = 8$$

Commutative Property: $a + b = b + a$

$$2 + 7 = 7 + 2$$

Associative Property:

$$a + (b + c) = (a + b) + c$$
$$5 + (4 + 3) = (5 + 4) + 3$$

The zero property states that when zero is added to any number it will remain unchanged.

The commutative property states that changing the order of the addition does not change the sum.

The associative property states that when adding three numbers, the order of the addition does not matter.

Fill in the blanks.

1. $9 + 7 = \underline{} + 9$

2. $8 + 0 = \underline{}$

3. $6 + (5 + 2) = (6 + \underline{}) + 2$

4. $2 + 4 = 4 + \underline{}$

5. $25 = \underline{} + 0$

6. $9 + (\underline{} + 7) = (9 + 11) + 7$

7. $\underline{} + 17 = 17 + 6$

8. $0 + 0 = \underline{}$

9. $3 + 100 = 100 + \underline{}$

10. $6 + (5 + 8) = (\underline{} + 5) + 8$

11. $35 + 19 = 19 + 35$ illustrates the _____ property.

12. $10 + (20 + 8) = (10 + 20) + 8$ illustrates the _____ property.

13. $100 + 0 = 100$ illustrates the _____ property.

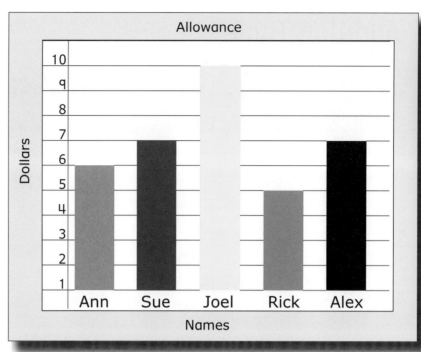

Allowance

Dollars

10
9
8
7
6
5
4
3
2
1

Ann   Sue   Joel   Rick   Alex

Names

1. Who has the greatest allowance? _____

2. Who has the least allowance? _____

3. What is the difference between the least
   and greatest allowance? _____

4. List everyone with an allowance of more than $5.

   _____

5. List everyone with an allowance under $6.

   _____

6. Whose allowance is $5 less than $10?

   _____

1. Find and color each in the figure.

2. Find and color each in the figure.

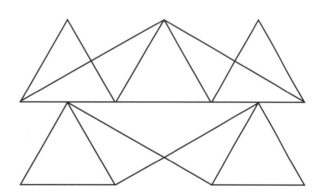

Congruent figures have the same shape and size.
Write the correct letter.

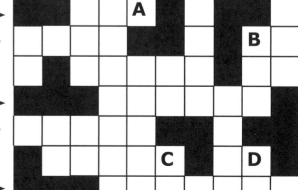

3. _____ is congruent to this shape.

4. _____ is congruent to this shape.

5. _____ is congruent to this shape.

Rounding is used to estimate.

To round to the nearest ten, find the closest ten. If the number is halfway or more, round to the greater ten.

42 rounded to the nearest ten is 40.

40 41 42 43 44 45 46 47 48 49 50

65 rounded to the nearest ten is 70.

60 61 62 63 64 65 66 67 68 69 70

To round to the nearest hundred, find the closest hundred. If the number is halfway or more, round to the greater hundred.

145 rounded to the nearest hundred is 100.

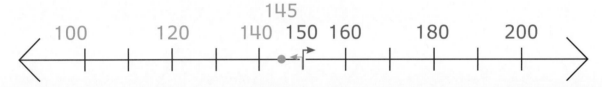

145
100 120 140 150 160 180 200

Round to the nearest ten.

c 81 _____
a 19 _____
s 45 _____
u 33 _____
o 8   _____

Round to the nearest hundred.

n 378 _____
t 198 _____
f 250 _____
h 704 _____
b 477 _____

Solve the riddle by writing the matching letter of each answer below. What does one bread crumb and another bread crumb equal?

‾20 ‾500 ‾30 ‾400 ‾80 ‾700 ‾10 ‾300 ‾20 ‾400 ‾200 ‾50

Estimating gives an approximate answer.

Round each number to the nearest **ten,** then sum.

Round each number to the nearest **hundred,** then sum.

OR

```
  88 →    90
+ 21 → + 20
 109     110
```
Actual   Estimate

```
 164 →   200
+115 → +100
 279     300
```
Actual   Estimate

Round each number to the nearest ten, then find the sum.

Actual	Estimated	Actual	Estimated	Actual	Estimated
a 21 + 92	____ ____	b 42 + 83	____ ____	c 59 + 39	____ ____
d 125 +199	____ ____	e 50 + 68	____ ____	f 19 + 45	____ ____

Round each number to the nearest hundred, then find the sum.

g 829 +105	____ ____	h 929 +952	____ ____	i 199 +249	____ ____
j 85 + 45	____ ____	k 803 +219	____ ____	l 215 +108	____ ____

Use the 8 numbers in the notebook to answer questions 1 and 2.

1. Find two numbers whose estimated sum is 130.

    _____ _____

2. Write and solve your own estimation problem using 2 of the numbers.

    _____

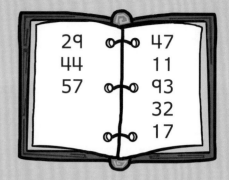

29	47
44	11
57	93
	32
	17

3. Round each row to the nearest ten. Add the estimated sums from each row to estimate the number of runners in the race.

The Big Race

nearest ten

   20

_____

   _____

   _____

_____

_____

+ _____

Estimated number of runners in the race = _____

Llamas are very intelligent, and are also good pack animals. They are often used to carry water and supplies into the mountains where there are no roads.

It is a holiday and Jake is up early getting his pet llama, Larry ready for their family camping trip. Larry must carry all the water to their campsite.

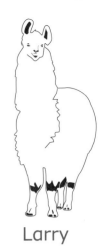

Larry

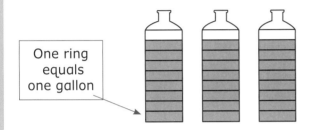

One ring equals one gallon

Add up the number of gallons to find about how many gallons of water Larry will carry.

Write an addition number sentence for the problem.

_____ + _____ + _____ = _____

Complete and color the picture.

By age 10, most children have worn down about 735 crayons. Color 735 small squares.

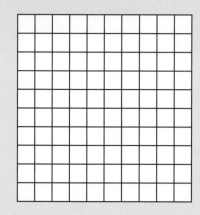
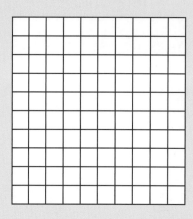

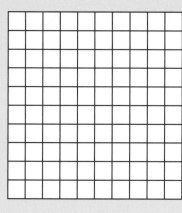
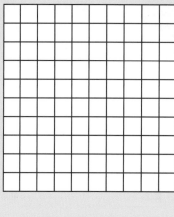
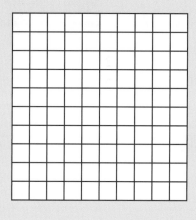

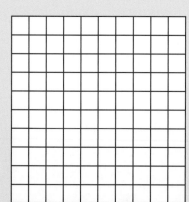
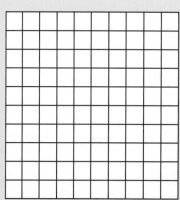
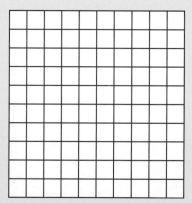

1. Write 735 in expanded notation. _____ + _____ + _____

2. Write 735 in word form. _____

_____

These words can help you identify an addition problem:

- add
- sum
- plus
- total
- altogether

Parts of an Addition Problem

$$5 + 6 = 11$$

addends   sum

For each word problem, write a number sentence and solve.

1. Joe has 34 baseball cards. If his brother has 39 baseball cards, how many baseball cards do they have altogether?

   _____ + _____ = _____

2. Sara ate a pizza slice with 689 calories and drank a soda with 160 calories for lunch. Total her lunch calories.

   _____ + _____ = _____

3. Write your own addition word problem about the picture. Use sum, add, or plus in your problem.

   _____

   _____

   _____ + _____ = _____

Dogs

Cats

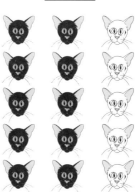

These words can help you identify a subtraction problem.

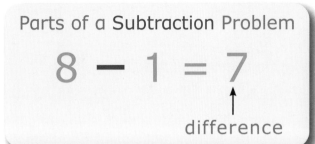

Parts of a Subtraction Problem

8 – 1 = 7

↑
difference

- subtract
- difference
- take-away
- less
- left

For each word problem, write a number sentence and solve.

1. John is 21 years old and his brother James is 14 years old. What is the difference in their ages?

    _____ – _____ = _____

2. Nathan has $69. If he buys a $43 video game, how much money will he have left?

    _____ – _____ = _____

3. Write your own subtraction word problem about the picture. Use less, take-away, or left in your problem.

    _____

    _____

    _____ – _____ = _____

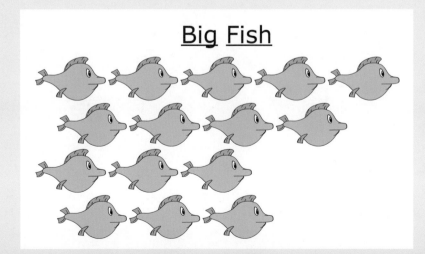

Big Fish

Polygons are closed figures made up of line segments.

 A 3-sided polygon is called a triangle.

 A 4-sided polygon is called a quadrilateral.

 A 5-sided polygon is called a pentagon.

 A 6-sided polygon is called a hexagon.

A 8-sided polygon is called an octagon.

Complete the triangle.

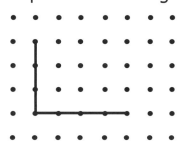

Complete the quadrilateral.

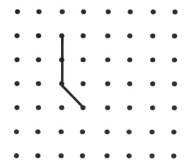

Complete the pentagon.

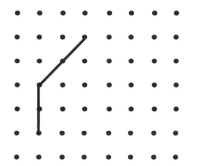

Complete the hexagon.

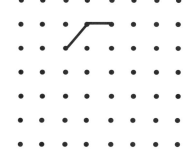

Complete the octagon.

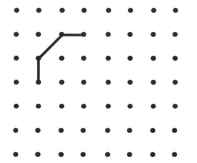

Draw a polygon.
Number of sides = _____

Draw two different examples of each polygon below.

Triangle

Quadrilateral

Pentagon

Hexagon

Octagon

Parallel lines are always the same distance apart and will never meet.

 Perpendicular lines meet at right angles.

1. Draw a line segment parallel to the one given.

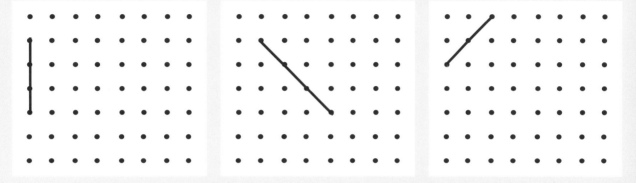

2. Draw a line segment perpendicular to the one given.

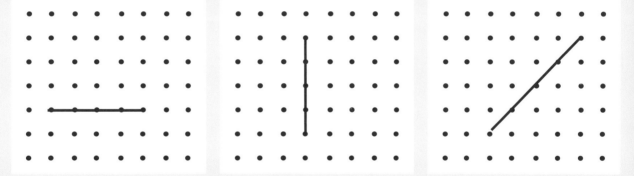

Complete the square, then answer the questions.

3. How many pairs of parallel lines are made with the lines of this square?

_____

4. How many pairs of perpendicular lines are made with the lines of this square?

_____

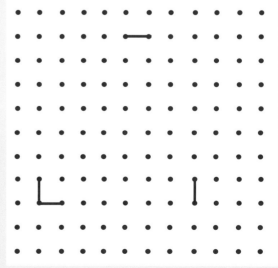

The $ symbol means dollars (money). For example, one dollar is written $1.

To show part of a dollar, we use a decimal point. A decimal point (.) is used to show a part of a whole.

Examples

Twenty-five cents is written $.25.

Fifty cents  is written $.50.

One dollar and twenty-five cents  is written $1.25.

Five dollars and ten cents  is written $5.10.

Two dollars and one cent  is written $2.01.

Draw a line segment to connect each group of money with the matching written amount.

1

$1.35

2

$2.50

3

$ .75

4

$1.20

5

$2.35

Write the amount shown in each picture. Always use a decimal point and dollar sign.

$2.50

1.

2.

$.85
_____

_____

3.

4.

_____

_____

5.

6.

_____

_____

7.

_____

8.

_____

9.

_____

10.

_____

11.

_____

12.

_____

Be sure to line the
decimals up before
you add.

$$\begin{array}{r} {\scriptstyle 1 \quad 1} \\ \$1.89 \\ +1.99 \\ \hline \$3.88 \end{array}$$

Menu

Taco	$1.49
Enchilada	$1.89
Quesadilla	$2.50
Burrito	$2.00
Chips	$1.99
Drink	$1.00

$$\begin{array}{r} \$1.49 \\ 1.99 \\ +1.00 \\ \hline \$4.48 \end{array}$$

Use a number sentence to total each bill, then cross
out the matching answers on the next page.

a   taco, chips, and drink

$ _____ . _____

$ _____ . _____

$ _____ . _____

b   2 enchiladas and 1 drink

$ _____ . _____

$ _____ . _____

$ _____ . _____

c   burrito, chips, and drink

$ _____ . _____

$ _____ . _____

$ _____ . _____

d   2 tacos, chips, and 1 drink

$ _____ . _____

$ _____ . _____

$ _____ . _____

$ _____ . _____

e   2 enchiladas, 1 drink, and
     chips

     $.

     $.

     $.

     $_____.

f   3 burritos and a quesadilla

     $.

     $.

     $.

     $_____.

g   2 tacos, 2 burritos, and
     a drink

     $

     $

     $

     $

     $_____

h   2 tacos, 2 quesadillas, and
     2 drinks

$4.48	$8.98	$5.97	$9.98	$4.99
$7.98	$4.78	$6.67	$8.50	$6.77

*Teaching note: Check to make sure students have marked their answers with dollar
             signs "$."

Continue the patterns.

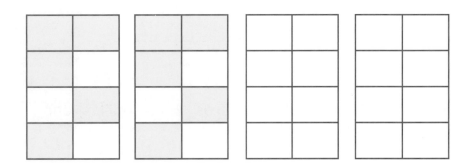

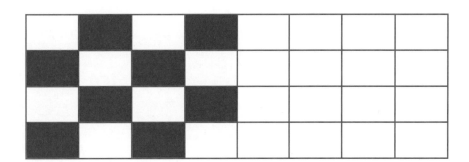

2, 4, 6, 8, ___, ___, ___

1, 3, 5, 7, ___, ___, ___

1, 2, 4, 7, 11, 16, ___, ___, ___

1, 1, 2, 3, 5, 8, 13, ___, ___, ___

Estimating gives an approximate answer.

Estimate the sum of $4.89 + $1.28 to the nearest dollar.

Actual		Estimated
$4.89	⟶	$5.
+ $1.28	⟶	+ $1.
$6.17		$6.

5-Up Rule

To estimate, use the 5-Up Rule. If the digit in the first place to the right of the decimal is 5, 6, 7, 8, or 9, round up to the next dollar amount. If the digit in the first place to the right of the decimal is 0, 1, 2, 3, or 4, round to the dollar amount.

When rounding always use the 5-Up Rule. If rounding to the nearest dollar, then round 50 or more cents to a **dollar** (100 cents) and 49 or fewer cents to **zero**.

Round each amount to the nearest dollar.

_____ Actual

_____ Estimated

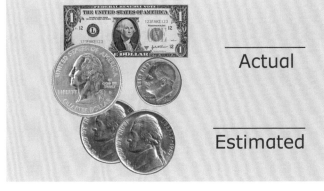

_____ Actual

_____ Estimated

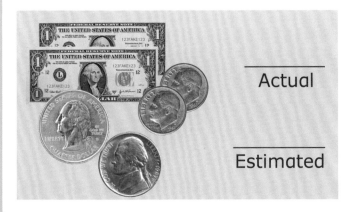

_____ Actual

_____ Estimated

_____ Actual

_____ Estimated

Add Tune-Up

Find the sum.

1.
	23	85	93	87	36
	+ 14	+ 36	+ 59	+ 65	+ 36

2.
	53	76	36	87	32
	+ 49	+ 83	+ 19	+ 64	+ 91

3.
	38	31	45	31	69
	21	14	62	42	38
	+ 43	+ 92	+ 13	+ 83	+ 49

4.
	21	14	35	49	44
	34	76	14	77	30
	+ 65	+ 37	+ 88	+ 65	+ 81

```
 35              3 tens and 5 ones
- 12   OR  minus  1 ten  and 2 ones   OR
 23              2 tens and 3 ones
```

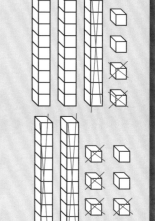

```
 28              2 tens and 8 one
- 26   OR  minus  2 tens and 6 ones   OR
  2                      2 ones
```

Find each difference.

```
  52      46      68      95      88      71      56
- 31    - 23    - 24    - 63    - 18    - 50    - 21
```

Find each difference, then write the letter of the matching answer below to solve the riddle.

```
k   46     i   89     h   67     c   54
  - 24       - 55       - 44       - 23


s   68     t   49     o   39     e   58
  - 53       - 20       - 21       - 42
```

What did the gingerbread man have on his bed?

___ ___ ___ ___ ___ ___   ___ ___ ___ ___ ___ ___
31 18 18 22 34 16   15 23 16 16 29 15

Ordering

Symbol	Meaning	Example	
<	**less than**	2 < 3	2 is **less than** 3
>	**greater than**	5 > 1	5 is **greater than** 1
=	**equal**	2 = 2	2 is **equal** to 2

Note: The arrow always points to the smaller number.

Place <, >, or = in the blank to make a true statement.

a   b   c

    8 __ 2   19 __ 12   22 __ 29

d   e   f

  521 __ 509   43 __ 39   801 __ 810

g   h   i

   50 __ 39   152 __ 160   21 __ 21

j   k   l

$8.35 __ $8.40   29¢ __ 31¢ $1 __ $.89

m   n   o

   5¢ __ 50¢   18 - 7 __ 9 + 2   28 - 19 __ 13 + 7

Find the sums and place the answers in order under each skater (smallest to the largest).

a
$$\begin{array}{r} 75 \\ + 39 \\ \hline \end{array}$$

b
$$\begin{array}{r} 67 \\ + 45 \\ \hline \end{array}$$

c
$$\begin{array}{r} 123 \\ + 149 \\ \hline \end{array}$$

d
$$\begin{array}{r} 83 \\ + 251 \\ \hline \end{array}$$

e
$$\begin{array}{r} 59 \\ + 64 \\ \hline \end{array}$$

f
$$\begin{array}{r} 394 \\ + 83 \\ \hline \end{array}$$

g
$$\begin{array}{r} 75 \\ + 75 \\ \hline \end{array}$$

h
$$\begin{array}{r} 289 \\ + 123 \\ \hline \end{array}$$

i
$$\begin{array}{r} 307 \\ + 179 \\ \hline \end{array}$$

j
$$\begin{array}{r} 231 \\ + 92 \\ \hline \end{array}$$

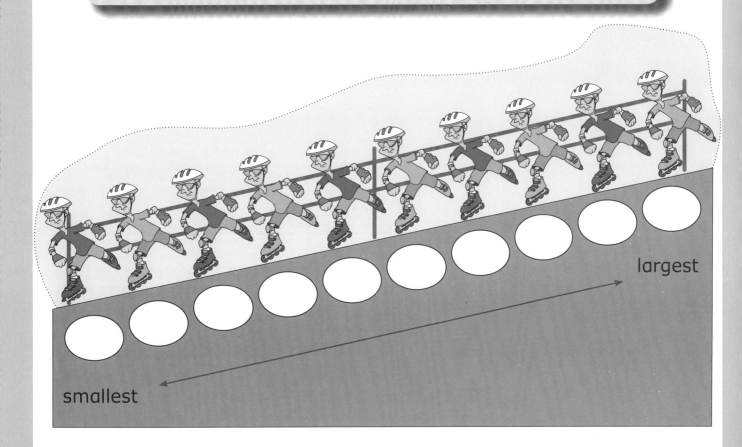

largest

smallest

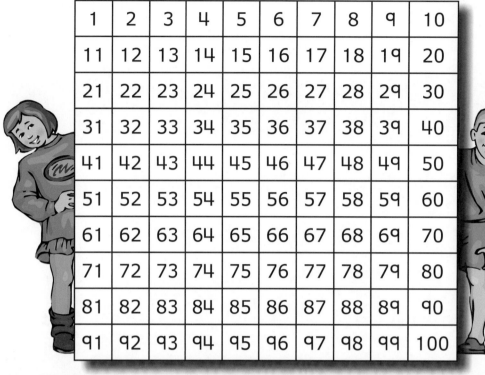

1	2	3	4	5	6	7	8	9	10
11	12	13	14	15	16	17	18	19	20
21	22	23	24	25	26	27	28	29	30
31	32	33	34	35	36	37	38	39	40
41	42	43	44	45	46	47	48	49	50
51	52	53	54	55	56	57	58	59	60
61	62	63	64	65	66	67	68	69	70
71	72	73	74	75	76	77	78	79	80
81	82	83	84	85	86	87	88	89	90
91	92	93	94	95	96	97	98	99	100

Notice the placement of the numbers in the 1 to 100 chart.
Fill in the missing numbers in the blank squares below
using the given number as a clue.

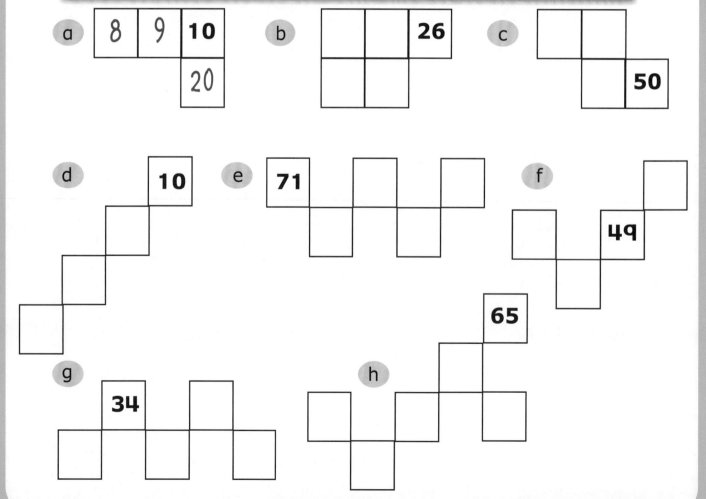

Write in the missing answers to make true number sentences. Then write the matching letter of each answer below to read the message.

8 − 2 = A

1 + _5_ = A

A = _6_

8 + 9 = B

19 - ___ = B

B = ___

5 + 6 = C

14 - ___ = C

C = ___

20 − 5 = D

7 + ___ = D

D = ___

8 + 8 = E

18 - ___ = E

E = ___

15 − 6 = F

2 + ___ = F

F = ___

21 − 3 = G

9 + ___ = G

G = ___

16 + 9 = H

30 − ___ = H

H = ___

11 − 3 = I

20 − ___ = I

I = ___

7 + 7 = J

19 − ___ = J

J = ___

13 - 6 = K

2 + ___ = K

K = ___

9 + 1 = L

22 − ___ = L

L = ___

18 − 13 = M

1 + ___ = M

M = ___

22 − 3 = N

8 + ___ = N

N = ___

21 − 8 = O

7 + ___ = O

O = ___

Message:

___ ___ ___ ___   ___ ___ ___
18   13   13   15   14   13   17

List the coins used to make the total.

$ .25
  .01
+ .01
$ .27

$ .25 quarter	$ .10 dime	$ .05 nickel	$ .01 penny

a   3 coins total 27¢

b   4 coins total 52¢

c   5 coins total 41¢

d   4 coins total 37¢

e   6 coins total 50¢

$ .25 quarter	$ .10 dime	$ .05 nickel	$ .01 penny
1			2

$ .25 quarter	$ .10 dime	$ .05 nickel	$ .01 penny

f   4 coins total 80¢

g   9 coins total 99¢

h   4 coins total $1.00

i   7 coins total 67¢

j   6 coins total 81¢

$ .25 $ .10 $ .05 $ .01

quarter   dime   nickel   penny

Count each group of coins and write the amount. Place a <, >, or = in the center blank to make a true statement.

a $ .51      >    $ .44

b   _____      _____      _____

c   _____      _____      _____

d   _____      _____   _____   _____

$ .25 $ .10 $ .05 $ .01

quarter   dime   nickel   penny

e _____  _____  _____

f _____  _____  _____

g _____  _____  _____

h _____  _____  _____

Polygons

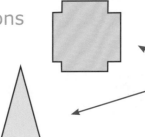

Not Polygons

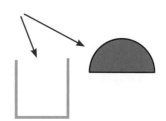

A Polygon is a closed figure made with line segments.

Polygons can be named by their number of sides.

A triangle is a 3-sided polygon.

A quadrilateral is a 4-sided polygon.

A pentagon is a 5-sided polygon.

A hexagon is a 6-sided polygon.

An octagon is an 8-sided polygon.

Name the following polygons.

 _____   _____   _____

 _____   _____   _____

Draw a polygon and write its name.

_____

A 3-sided polygon is called a triangle.

Triangles with sides of 3 different lengths are called scalene triangles.

Triangles with 2 equal length sides are called isosceles triangles.

Triangles with 3 equal length sides are called equilateral triangles.

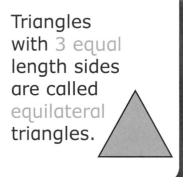

1. Write the letter of all the scalene triangles. _____

2. Write the letter of all the isosceles triangles. _____

3. Write the letter of all the equilateral triangles. _____

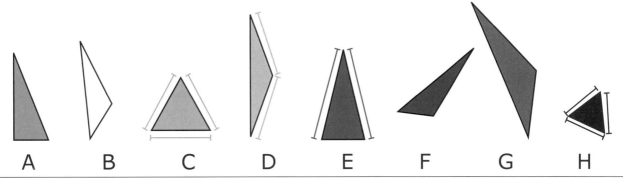

A   B   C   D   E   F   G   H

Use the dots to complete each triangle.

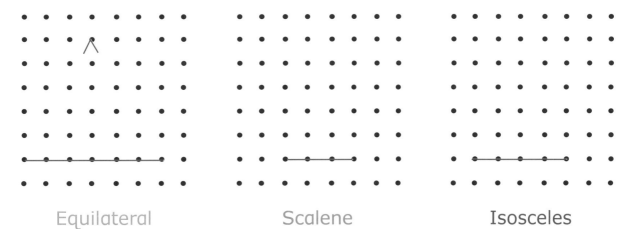

Equilateral   Scalene   Isosceles

A centimeter (cm) is a unit used to measure length. The 14 centimeter ruler below shows a single centimeter is about the width of your little finger.

Estimate the length of the lines in centimeters. Then use a ruler to actually measure to the nearest centimeter.

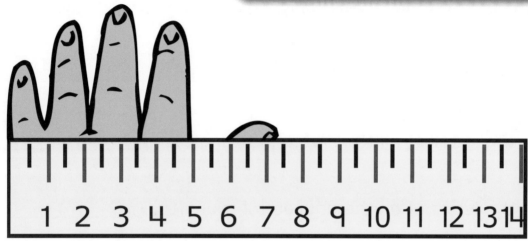

1.

2.

3.

4.

5.

6.

7.

Number	Estimated Length	Actual Length
1		
2		
3		
4		
5		
6		
7		

DISCOVER THE MYSTERY

1		2		3		4		5		6		7		8		9		10	
11		12		13		14		15		16		17		18		19		20	
21		22		23		24		25		26		27		28		29		30	
31		32		33		34		35		36		37		38		39		40	
41		42		43		44		45		46		47		48		49		50	
51		52		53		54		55		56		57		58		59		60	
61		62		63		64		65		66		67		68		69		70	
71		72		73		74		75		76		77		78		79		80	
81		82		83		84		85		86		87		88		89		90	
91		92		93		94		95		96		97		98		99		100	

1.   Pick any 2-digit number.   41

2.   Add up the 2 digits.   4 + 1 = 5

3.   Subtract.   41 - 5 = 36

4.   Find the subtraction answer in the chart.

5.   To the right of that number will be a blue square.

Repeat steps 1 – 5. Notice the answer to the subtraction will always have a blue square to the right of it. Why does that happen? _____

An inch (in.) is a unit used to measure length. An inch is approximately the length of a small paper clip.

Measure the six objects below to the nearest inch and match the answers to see the message.

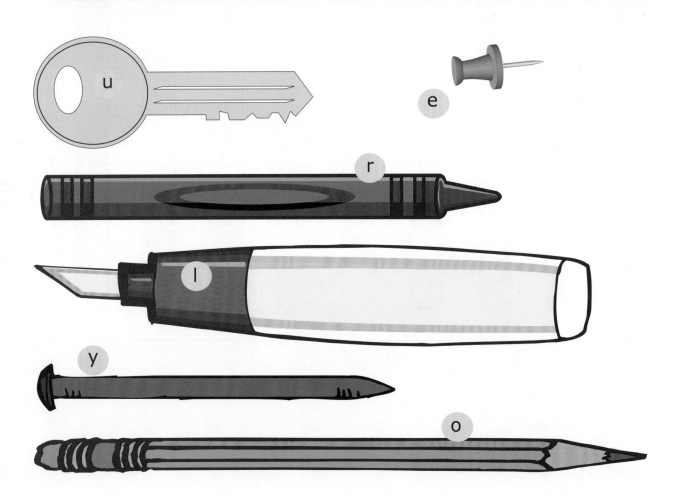

$\overline{\text{4 in.}}$ $\overline{\text{7 in.}}$ $\overline{\text{3 in.}}$ $\overline{\text{5 in.}}$ $\overline{\text{3 in.}}$ $\overline{\text{6 in.}}$ $\overline{\text{1 in.}}$

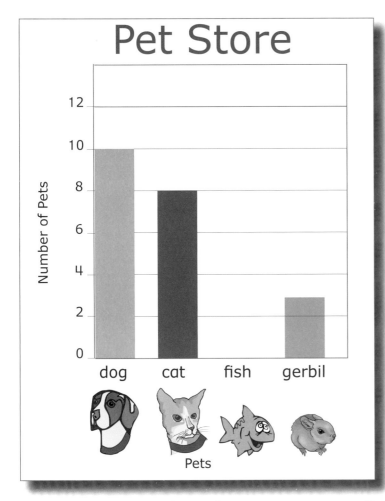

The chart shows the number of pets at the pet store.

1. Which pet does the store have the most of?

    _____

2. Which pet does the store have the least of?

    _____

3. How many gerbils live at the store?

    _____

4. The store sells 2 dogs, 3 cats, no fish, and 1 gerbil. Make a new chart below to show the pets in the store. Remember to write a title and labels.

Congruent shapes are equal in size and shape.

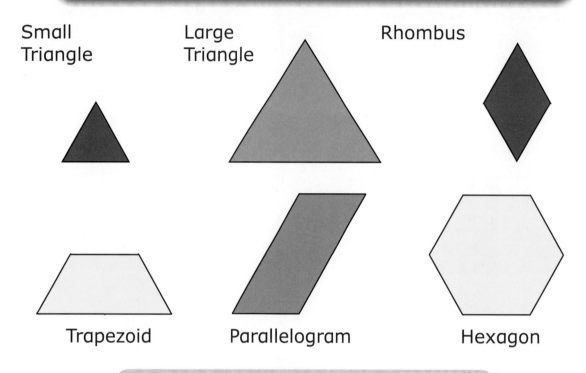

Small
Triangle

Large
Triangle

Rhombus

Trapezoid

Parallelogram

Hexagon

Draw and shade six congruent shapes
to match the shapes above.

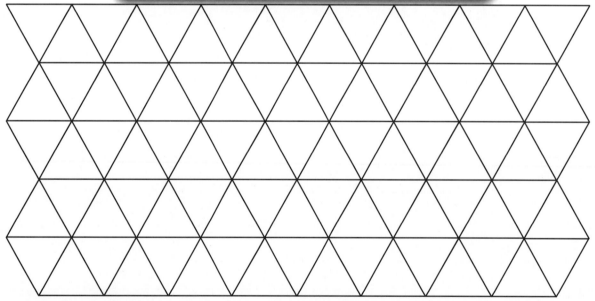

Of the six figures above, name the shapes that are
quadrilaterals.

_____

_____

Rounding to Estimate the Difference

Estimating helps you get a quick idea about the difference. Round each number so you can get a quick estimate of the answer.

Estimate: 63 – 49

63 – **49** rounds to **60 – 50** (estimated difference is 10).
↓   ↓
60   –   50

Estimate: 457 – 51

457 – **51** rounds to **500 – 50** (estimated difference is 450).
↓   ↓
500   –   50

Circle the correct answer.

1. What is the best estimate for 56 – 14?

   40   50   60   70

2. What is the best estimate for 61 – 9?

   30   40   50   60

3. What is the best estimate for 210 – 109?

   100   200   300   400

4. What is the best estimate for 351 – 162?

   100   200   300   400

5. What is the best estimate for 790 – 659?

   100   200   300   400

The hands and numbers on a clock face tell what time it is.

In one hour, the hour hand (shorter hand) moves from one number to the next. Every hour the minute hand (longer hand) moves 60 minutes.

Read: one twenty

or twenty minutes after one

or forty minutes before two

Write: 1 : 20

hour   minutes

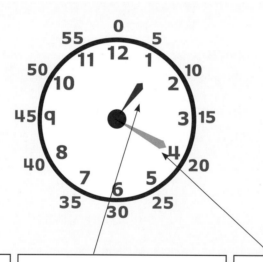

The symbol : is called a colon. The colon separates the hours from the minutes. The number on the left side of the colon tells the hour and the number on the right side tells the minutes.

In the clock above, the hour hand is not pointing exactly at the 1. It has moved a little towards the 2. As the minute hand moves all the way around the clock, the hour hand moves from one hour to the next.

The minute hand is pointing to the 20, so you know it is 20 minutes past the hour. Instead of saying the number of minutes after the hour, you can say the number of minutes to the next hour.

Read and write each time.

1.

Read: _three thirty-five_

Write: _3:35_

2.

Read: _____

Write: _____

3.

Read: _____

Write: _____

4.

How many minutes between

the times? _____

The answer to a subtraction problem is the difference.

Line up the ones, tens, and hundreds. Begin with the ones column. Regroup when necessary.

$$783 - 54 = \begin{array}{r} \text{H T O} \\ 7\,8\!\!\!/\,{}^1\!3 \\ -\ \ 5\ 4 \\ \hline 7\ 2\ 9 \end{array} \quad \text{OR} \quad \begin{array}{r} {}^{70}\ \ \ \ {}^{13} \\ 700 + 8\!\!\!/\,0 + 3\!\!\!/ \\ 50 + 4 \\ \hline 700 + 20 + 9 = 729 \end{array}$$

Subtract, then cross out the matching answer below.

a   529
  – 239
    290

b   207
  – 94

c   921
  – 732

d   856
  – 237

e   428
  – 217

f   403
  – 184

g   927
  – 816

h   463
  – 146

i   831
  – 290

j   392
  – 176

k   523
  – 398

l   239
  – 121

m   655
  – 274

n   821
  – 209

o   712
  – 587

125	216	371	211	612	541
619	381	317	189	289	118
111	135	113	125	219	290

Look for a pattern. Draw figures in the blanks to continue the pattern.

1. _____ _____ _____

2. _____ _____

3. 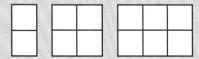 _____ _____ _____

4. _____ _____ _____

5. _____ _____

6. 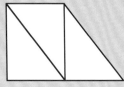 _____ _____

Look for a pattern.

Write numbers in the blanks to continue the pattern.

a　1, 2, 3, 4, 5, 6, 7, ___, ___, ___

b　1, 12, 123, 1234, _____, _____, _____

c　1, 2, 4, 7, 11, 16, 22, ____, ____, ____

d　1, 6, 11, 16, 21, 26, ____, ____, ____

e　1, 2, 2, 3, 3, 3, 4, 4, 4, 4, 5, ____, ____, ____

f　100, 99, 98, 97, 96, 95, ____, ____, ____

g　1, 2, 4, 5, 7, 8, 10, 11, 13, 14, ____, ____, ____

h　1, 3, 5, 7, 9, 11, 13, 15, 17, ____, ____, ____

i　1, 1, 2, 2, 3, 3, 4, 4, ____, ____, ____, ____

j　2, 8, 14, ____, 26, ____, 38, ____

1. _____

2.  _____

3.  _____

4.  _____

5.  _____

6.  _____

7.  _____

8.  _____

9.  _____

Write the letter of the clock below that matches the time on the digital clock above.

a

b

c

d

e

f

g

h

i

Find the difference and connect the matching answers in order below to see something all wet.

a   17
   − 9

b   16
   − 7

c   20
   − 17

d   14
   − 7

e   19
   − 13

f   10
   − 5

g   18
   − 3

h   11
   − 9

i   8
   − 7

j   12
   − 8

k   19
   − 8

l   17
   − 5

m   20
   − 10

n   19
   − 6

o   21
   − 7

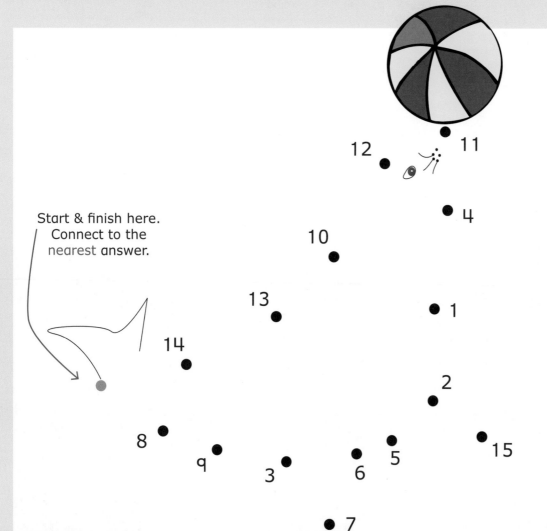

Start & finish here.
Connect to the
nearest answer.

Multiplication is a fast way to add.

2 × 3 means adding two threes,   3 + 3 = 6

3 × 2 means adding three twos,   2 + 2 + 2 = 6

Fill in the blanks.

3 + 3 + 3 + 3   is the same as __4__ × 3   = __12__

5 + 5 + 5   is the same as _____ × 5   = _____

4 + 4   is the same as _____ × 4   = _____

8 + 8 + 8   is the same as _____ × 8   = _____

2 + 2 + 2   is the same as _____ × 2   = _____

9 + 9   is the same as _____ × 9   = _____

1 + 1 + 1 + 1 + 1   is the same as _____ × 1   = _____

7 + 7 + 7   is the same as _____ × 7   = _____

5 + 5 + 5   is the same as _____ × 5   = _____

10 + 10 + 10 + 10   is the same as _____ × 10   = _____

6 + 6   is the same as _____ × 6   = _____

2 × 3 = 6
factors   product

Multiplication is commutative, which means the order of the factors produce the same product.

$$2 × 3 = 6 \text{ and } 3 × 2 = 6$$

Fill in the blanks to make each number sentence true.

6 × 2 = _____   and   2 × 6 = _____

4 × 5 = _____   and   5 × _____ = 20

3 × 4 = _____   and   _____ × 3 = 12

9 × _____ = 18   and   2 × _____ = 18

7 × 3 = _____   and   _____ × 7 = _____

_____ × 8 = 24   and   8 × _____ = 24

1 × _____ = 5   and   5 × _____ = _____

_____ × 5 = 25   and   5 × _____ = _____

6 × 4 = _____   and   _____ × _____ = 24

Complete each number sentence, then draw a line segment to connect each multiplication sentence with its matching addition sentence.

2 × 5 = _10___

3 × 3 = _____

4 × 4 = _____

7 × 3 = _____

2 × 9 = _____

5 × 5 = _____

6 × 1 = _____

4 × 6 = _____

4 + 4 + 4 + 4 = _____

9 + 9 = _____

3 + 3 + 3 = _____

5 + 5 = _10___

5 + 5 + 5 + 5 + 5 = _____

7 + 7 + 7 = _____

6 + 6 + 6 + 6 = _____

1 + 1 + 1 + 1 + 1 + 1 = _____

Multiplication Chart

x	0	1	2	3	4	5	6	7	8	9
0	0	0	0	0	0	0	0	0	0	0
1	0	1	2	3	4	5	6	7	8	9
2	0	2	4	6	8	10	12	14	16	18
3	0	3	6	9	12	15	18	21	24	27
4	0	4	8	12	16	20	24	28	32	36
5	0	5	10	15	20	25	30	35	40	45

2 × 5 means 2 addends of 5   5 + 5 = 10

5 × 2 means 5 addends of 2   2 + 2 + 2 + 2 + 2 = 10

Remember order does not matter in multiplication (commutative property of multiplication). Use the multiplication chart to check your answers.

a 3   5   4   2   5   4
  × 5   × 3   × 4   × 9   × 8   × 7

b 9   5   4   5   4   3
  × 4   × 6   × 5   × 7   × 6   × 8

c 2   5   7   3   5   2
  × 6   × 6   × 4   × 4   × 9   × 0

Continue the pattern.

d 0, 4, 8, 12, 16, ____, ____, ____, ____, ____, ____

e 0, 5, 10, 15, 20, ____, ____, ____, ____, ____, ____

Use the multiplication chart to check your answers.

a

$$\begin{array}{r} 5 \\ \times\ 2 \\ \hline \end{array}$$
$$\begin{array}{r} 2 \\ \times\ 5 \\ \hline \end{array}$$
$$\begin{array}{r} 7 \\ \times\ 1 \\ \hline \end{array}$$
$$\begin{array}{r} 1 \\ \times\ 7 \\ \hline \end{array}$$
$$\begin{array}{r} 5 \\ \times\ 3 \\ \hline \end{array}$$

b

$$\begin{array}{r} 9 \\ \times\ 4 \\ \hline \end{array}$$
$$\begin{array}{r} 8 \\ \times\ 2 \\ \hline \end{array}$$
$$\begin{array}{r} 3 \\ \times\ 7 \\ \hline \end{array}$$
$$\begin{array}{r} 6 \\ \times\ 2 \\ \hline \end{array}$$
$$\begin{array}{r} 8 \\ \times\ 1 \\ \hline \end{array}$$

c

$$\begin{array}{r} 9 \\ \times\ 3 \\ \hline \end{array}$$
$$\begin{array}{r} 2 \\ \times\ 7 \\ \hline \end{array}$$
$$\begin{array}{r} 8 \\ \times\ 3 \\ \hline \end{array}$$
$$\begin{array}{r} 3 \\ \times\ 2 \\ \hline \end{array}$$
$$\begin{array}{r} 6 \\ \times\ 4 \\ \hline \end{array}$$

d

$$\begin{array}{r} 6 \\ \times\ 1 \\ \hline \end{array}$$
$$\begin{array}{r} 9 \\ \times\ 3 \\ \hline \end{array}$$
$$\begin{array}{r} 6 \\ \times\ 3 \\ \hline \end{array}$$
$$\begin{array}{r} 4 \\ \times\ 2 \\ \hline \end{array}$$
$$\begin{array}{r} 4 \\ \times\ 5 \\ \hline \end{array}$$

×	0	1	2	3	4	5	6	7	8	9
0	0	0	0	0	0	0	0	0	0	0
1	0	1	2	3	4	5	6	7	8	9
2	0	2	4	6	8	10	12	14	16	18
3	0	3	6	9	12	15	18	21	24	27
4	0	4	8	12	16	20	24	28	32	36
5	0	5	10	15	20	25	30	35	40	45
6	0	6	12	18	24	30	36	42	48	54
7	0	7	14	21	28	35	42	49	56	63

$$6 \times 7 = 42$$
factors   product

×	0	1	2	3	4	5	6	7	8	9
0	0	0	0	0	0	0	0	0	0	0
1	0	1	2	3	4	5	6	7	8	9
2	0	2	4	6	8	10	12	14	16	18
3	0	3	6	9	12	15	18	21	24	27
4	0	4	8	12	16	20	24	28	32	36
5	0	5	10	15	20	25	30	35	40	45
6	0	6	12	18	24	30	36	42	48	54
7	0	7	14	21	28	35	42	49	56	63

The answer to a multiplication problem is called the product. Find the products. Use the multiplication chart to check your answers.

a
$$\begin{array}{r} 7 \\ \times\ 9 \\ \hline \end{array}$$
$$\begin{array}{r} 7 \\ \times\ 6 \\ \hline \end{array}$$
$$\begin{array}{r} 9 \\ \times\ 7 \\ \hline \end{array}$$
$$\begin{array}{r} 6 \\ \times\ 8 \\ \hline \end{array}$$
$$\begin{array}{r} 2 \\ \times\ 6 \\ \hline \end{array}$$
$$\begin{array}{r} 7 \\ \times\ 2 \\ \hline \end{array}$$

b
$$\begin{array}{r} 7 \\ \times\ 8 \\ \hline \end{array}$$
$$\begin{array}{r} 6 \\ \times\ 6 \\ \hline \end{array}$$
$$\begin{array}{r} 7 \\ \times\ 7 \\ \hline \end{array}$$
$$\begin{array}{r} 4 \\ \times\ 9 \\ \hline \end{array}$$
$$\begin{array}{r} 7 \\ \times\ 5 \\ \hline \end{array}$$
$$\begin{array}{r} 6 \\ \times\ 3 \\ \hline \end{array}$$

c
$$\begin{array}{r} 6 \\ \times\ 4 \\ \hline \end{array}$$
$$\begin{array}{r} 5 \\ \times\ 6 \\ \hline \end{array}$$
$$\begin{array}{r} 1 \\ \times\ 7 \\ \hline \end{array}$$
$$\begin{array}{r} 7 \\ \times\ 0 \\ \hline \end{array}$$
$$\begin{array}{r} 7 \\ \times\ 9 \\ \hline \end{array}$$
$$\begin{array}{r} 2 \\ \times\ 6 \\ \hline \end{array}$$

Continue the pattern.

d   0, 6, 12, 18, 24, _____, _____, _____, _____, _____, _____

e   0, 7, 14, 21, 28, _____, _____, _____, _____, _____, _____

x	0	1	2	3	4	5	6	7	8	9
0	0	0	0	0	0	0	0	0	0	0
1	0	1	2	3	4	5	6	7	8	9
2	0	2	4	6	8	10	12	14	16	18
3	0	3	6	9	12	15	18	21	24	27
4	0	4	8	12	16	20	24	28	32	36
5	0	5	10	15	20	25	30	35	40	45
6	0	6	12	18	24	30	36	42	48	54
7	0	7	14	21	28	35	42	49	56	63
8	0	8	16	24	32	40	48	56	64	72
9	0	9	18	27	36	45	54	63	(72)	81

Find the products. Use the multiplication chart to check your answers.

a

$$\begin{array}{r} 8 \\ \times\ 5 \\ \hline \end{array}$$
$$\begin{array}{r} 5 \\ \times\ 8 \\ \hline \end{array}$$
$$\begin{array}{r} 9 \\ \times\ 8 \\ \hline \end{array}$$
$$\begin{array}{r} 8 \\ \times\ 8 \\ \hline \end{array}$$
$$\begin{array}{r} 9 \\ \times\ 9 \\ \hline \end{array}$$
$$\begin{array}{r} 6 \\ \times\ 8 \\ \hline \end{array}$$

b

$$\begin{array}{r} 9 \\ \times\ 3 \\ \hline \end{array}$$
$$\begin{array}{r} 8 \\ \times\ 7 \\ \hline \end{array}$$
$$\begin{array}{r} 4 \\ \times\ 2 \\ \hline \end{array}$$
$$\begin{array}{r} 5 \\ \times\ 7 \\ \hline \end{array}$$
$$\begin{array}{r} 3 \\ \times\ 4 \\ \hline \end{array}$$
$$\begin{array}{r} 2 \\ \times\ 8 \\ \hline \end{array}$$

c

$$\begin{array}{r} 4 \\ \times\ 9 \\ \hline \end{array}$$
$$\begin{array}{r} 8 \\ \times\ 3 \\ \hline \end{array}$$
$$\begin{array}{r} 5 \\ \times\ 9 \\ \hline \end{array}$$
$$\begin{array}{r} 8 \\ \times\ 4 \\ \hline \end{array}$$
$$\begin{array}{r} 9 \\ \times\ 1 \\ \hline \end{array}$$
$$\begin{array}{r} 8 \\ \times\ 0 \\ \hline \end{array}$$

Continue the pattern.

d   0, 8, 16, 24, 32, _____, _____, _____, _____, _____, _____

e   0, 9, 18, 27, 36, _____, _____, _____, _____, _____, _____

×	0	1	2	3	4	5	6	7	8	9
0	0	0	0	0	0	0	0	0	0	0
1	0	1	2	3	4	5	6	7	8	9
2	0	2	4	6	8	10	12	14	16	18
3	0	3	6	9	12	15	18	21	24	27
4	0	4	8	12	16	20	24	28	32	36
5	0	5	10	15	20	25	30	35	40	45
6	0	6	12	18	24	30	36	42	48	54
7	0	7	14	21	28	35	42	49	56	63
8	0	8	16	24	32	40	48	56	64	72
9	0	9	18	27	36	45	54	63	72	81

Find the products. Use the multiplication chart to check your answers.

a
```
    8        7        3        4        6        9
  × 2      × 4      × 2      × 9      × 1      × 0
```

b
```
    5        9        2        5        8        7
  × 8      × 4      × 3      × 9      × 2      × 4
```

c
```
    5        6        7        9        8        7
  × 4      × 9      × 8      × 9      × 8      × 6
```

d
```
    7        6        6        4        6        2
  × 7      × 6      × 3      × 8      × 4      × 5
```

e
```
    9        7        8        9        7        5
  × 1      × 0      × 6      × 6      × 8      × 7
```

A line of symmetry is an imaginary line that divides a figure into two equal halves. If you fold a figure along a line of symmetry, both sides match (both sides are congruent). Some figures have one or more lines of symmetry while others have no lines of symmetry.

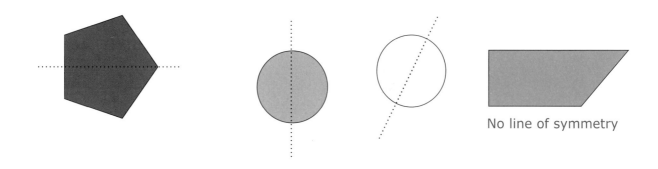

No line of symmetry

Draw a line of symmetry (when possible) for the following shapes.

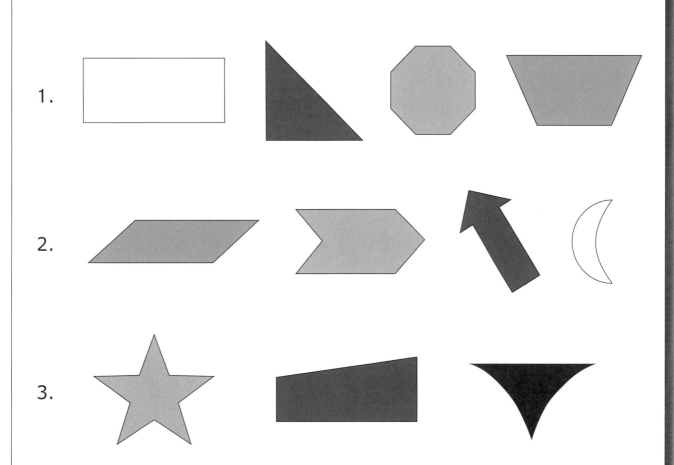

1.

2.

3.

Complete the pictures. Make the right side the same as the left. The line shown is the line of symmetry.

Multiplication Table

×	0	1	2	3	4	5	6	7	8	9
0	0	0	0	0	0	0	0	0	0	0
1	0	1	2	3	4	5	6	7	8	9
2	0	2	4	6	8	10	12	14	16	18
3	0	3	6	9	12	15	18	21	24	27
4	0	4	8	12	16	20	24	28	32	36
5	0	5	10	15	20	25	30	35	40	45
6	0	6	12	18	24	30	36	42	48	54
7	0	7	14	21	28	35	42	49	56	63
8	0	8	16	24	32	40	48	56	64	72
9	0	9	18	27	36	45	54	63	72	81

Properties of Multiplication

Identity Property: $a \times 1 = a$

$6 \times 1 = 6$

Commutative Property: $a \times b = b \times a$

$3 \times 8 = 8 \times 3$

Associative Property:

$a \times (b \times c) = (a \times b) \times c$

$5 \times (2 \times 4) = (5 \times 2) \times 4$

The identity property states that when any number is multiplied by one it will remain unchanged.

The commutative property states that changing the order of the multiplication does not change the product.

The associative property states that when multiplying three numbers together, the order of the multiplication does not matter.

Fill in the blanks.

1. $8 \times 6 = \underline{} \times 8$

2. $100 \times 1 = \underline{}$

3. $4 \times (5 \times 3) = (4 \times \underline{}) \times 3$

4. $2 \times 12 = 12 \times \underline{}$

5. $50 = \underline{} \times 1$

6. $5 \times (\underline{} \times 2) = (5 \times 6) \times 2$

7. $\underline{} \times 17 = 17 \times 20$

8. $0 \times 1 = \underline{}$

9. $20 \times 9 = 9 \times \underline{}$

10. $4 \times (2 \times 6) = (\underline{} \times 2) \times 6$

11. $6 \times (4 \times 2) = (6 \times 4) \times 2$ illustrates the _____ property.

12. $100 \times 1 = 100$ illustrates the _____ property.

13. $9 \times 8 = 8 \times 9$ illustrates the _____ property.

Congruent shapes are equal in size and shape.

This figure 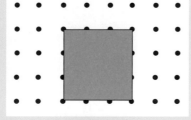 is congruent with this figure.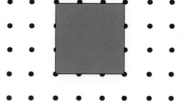

This figure 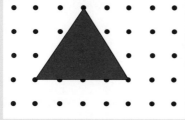 is congruent with this figure.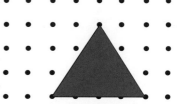

This figure 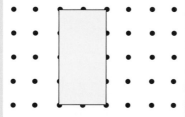 is congruent with this figure.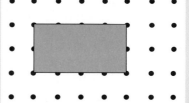

Complete the drawing to form two congruent figures.

 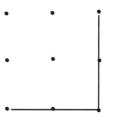 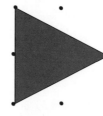 

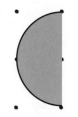 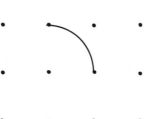  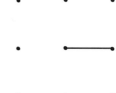

   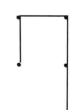

Congruent shapes (figures) are equal in size and shape.

 congruent
figures

 noncongruent
figures

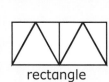
rectangle

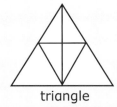
triangle

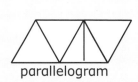
parallelogram

hexagon

Draw and shade a congruent figure for every design above.

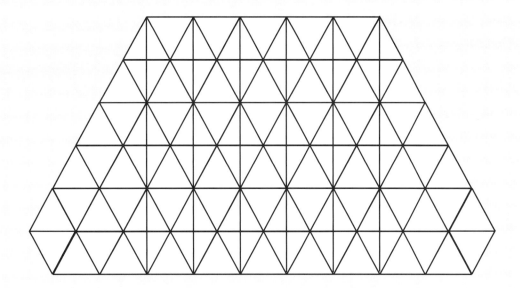

Shade 3 different pairs of congruent figures below.

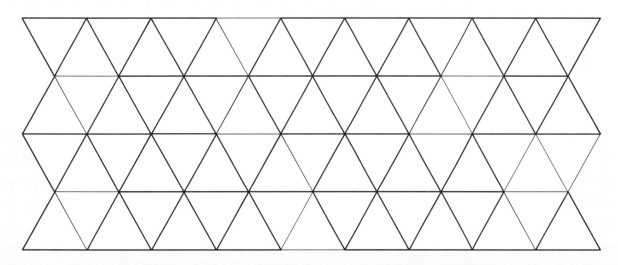

Units of Time
7 days = 1 week
52 weeks = 1 year
12 months = 1 year

January

Sun.	Mon.	Tue.	Wed.	Thu.	Fri.	Sat.
			1	2	3	4
5	6	7	8	9	10	11
12	13	14	15	16	17	18
19	20	21	22	23	24	25
26	27	28	29	30	31	

February

Sun.	Mon.	Tue.	Wed.	Thu.	Fri.	Sat.
						1
2	3	4	5	6	7	8
9	10	11	12	13	14	15
16	17	18	19	20	21	22
23	24	25	26	27	28	

March

Sun.	Mon.	Tue.	Wed.	Thu.	Fri.	Sat.
						1
2	3	4	5	6	7	8
9	10	11	12	13	14	15
16	17	18	19	20	21	22
23	24	25	26	27	28	29
30	31					

Use the calendars on the right to answer the following questions.

1. What date is three weeks after February 27?

   _____

2. What date is two weeks 5 days later than January 28?

   _____

3. What date is 5 weeks 1 day after January 31?

   _____

4. Bryan worked on his science project for 3 weeks 6 days. If he started on March 1st, when did he finish?

   _____

5. Robert went on vacation from January 13th to March 16th. How many weeks was he on vacation?

   _____

6. How many days are there from February 1st to March 20th?

   _____

7. How many weeks equal 28 days?

   _____

Units of Age
12 months = 1 year
365 days = 1 year

1. If the current date is in 2010, what year will it be in 12 months?

    _____

2. If you lived in a house for 3 years, how many months have you lived in the house?

    _____

3. John is 12 years 3 months old. If his sister is 2 years 9 months older, how old is his sister?

    _____

4. Sue was 8 years 5 months old at the start of the school year. If the school year is 9 months long, how old is Sue at the end of the school year?

    _____

5. If Nathan is 9 years 11 months old, how old will he be in one month?

    _____

6. Baby Maria is 1 year 6 months old. How many months old is she?

    _____

Table of Measures
1 foot = 12 inches
1 yard = 3 feet = 36 inches
1 mile = 5,280 feet

 A paper clip is about 1 inch long.

A piece of notebook paper is about 1 foot long.

 A baseball bat is about 1 yard long.

You can walk 1 mile in about 20 minutes.

Complete the following sentences by writing inches, feet, yards, or miles in the blank.

1.   The length of a pencil is about 7 _____.

2.   The length of a bulletin board is about 3 _____.

3.   The length of a car is about 12 _____.

4.   The length of a wallet is about 8 _____.

5.   The distance between Chicago and New York is about 700 _____.

6.   The length of your thumb is about 2 _____.

7.   The height of a one-story building is about 10 _____.

8.   The length of a football field is 100 _____.

Horizontal lines are lines that run parallel to the horizon. The purple line is a horizonal line.
Vertical lines are lines that run perpendicular to the horizon. The green line is a vertical line.

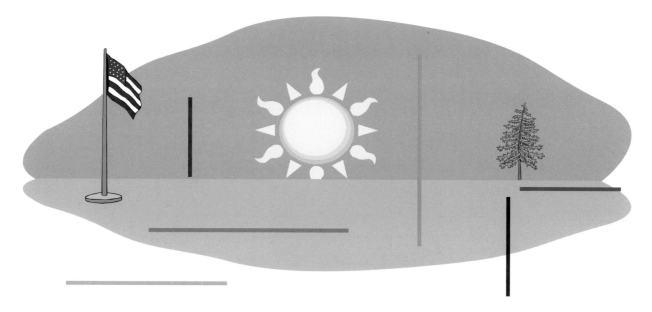

1. Name the other two vertical lines. _____ _____

2. Name the other two horizontal lines. _____ _____

Use the choice box to make each sentence true.

| green | vertical |
| horizontal | blue |

1. The red line and the _____ line are _____ lines.

2. The _____ line is a _____ line that touches the two vertical lines.

Horizontal and vertical lines make up a grid. A point on a grid can be found using an ordered pair of numbers written within parentheses ( ).

Using the grid below, write the letter of the point named by each ordered pair to answer the riddle.

Example: **M** is located at (1,2) where 1 is units to the right and 2 is units up.

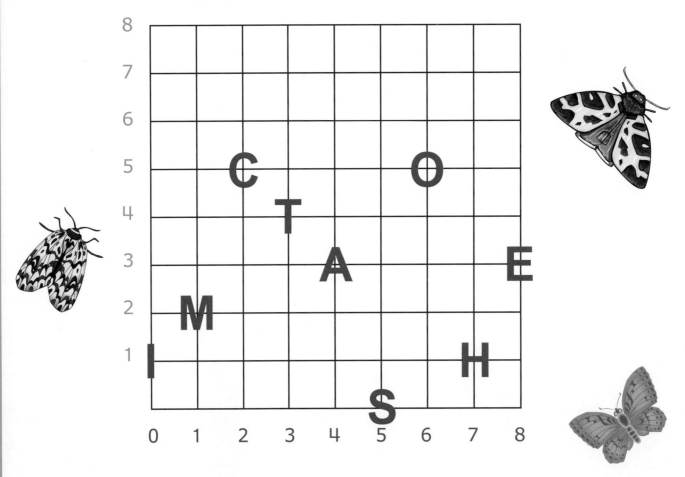

What do moths study in school?

M ___ ___ ___ ___ ___ ___ ___ ___ ___ ___

(1,2) (6,5) (3,4) (7,1) (8,3) (1,2) (4,3) (3,4) (0,1) (2,5) (5,0)

$2.23 + $.74 =
$$\begin{array}{r} \$2.23 \\ +.74 \\ \hline \$2.97 \end{array}$$

$1.46 + $4.58 =
$$\begin{array}{r} 11 \\ \$1.46 \\ +4.58 \\ \hline \$6.04 \end{array}$$

Use **regrouping** when necessary to add the numbers. Draw circles around even sums to show the dog's path to the bone.

a	$8.45 + 1.17	$3.47 + 2.16	$4.03 + 9.44	$5.25 + .94	$1.00 + .01
b	$4.28 + 2.36	$5.42 + .67	$5.51 + 2.96	$8.36 + 2.93	$5.03 + 1.70
c	$5.75 + 2.49	$4.21 + 2.38	$ .46 + 2.82	$5.00 + 2.22	$8.48 + 2.96
d	$3.14 .25 + 1.43	$8.14 .25 + 2.03	$9.25 6.34 + 8.05	$5.23 4.42 + 6.52	$3.25 1.87 + 3.42

Milk Shake
$2.25

Sundae
$1.50

Soda Pop
$.69

Cone
$.75

Find the change from a $5 bill.

1. Milk Shake

$ 5.00
(4 9 10)
− 2.25
$ 2.75

2. Cone

$ 5.00
− .75
$ _.2_

3. Soda Pop

$ 5.00
− .69
$4.__

4. Sundae

$ 5.00
− 1.50
$ _.5_

Find the change from a $20 bill.

5. Milk Shake

$ 20.00
− 2.25
$ _7.__

6. Cone

$ 20.00
− .75
$ 1 _.__

7. Soda Pop

$ 20.00
− .69
$ _9.__

Even numbers have a 0, 2, 4, 6, or 8 in the ones place.
Odd numbers have a 1, 3, 5, 7, or 9 in the ones place.

The number of fingers on one hand is the odd number 5.
A dozen eggs is the even number 12.

Rules for odd and even numbers

odd + odd = even	odd × odd = odd
odd + even = odd	odd × even = even
even + odd = odd	even × odd = even
even + even = even	even × even = even

Write whether the number is *even* or *odd* for each of the following.

1. number of tires on a car _____
2. number of sides on a pentagon _____
3. number of hours in a day _____
4. minutes in one quarter of an hour _____
5. days in a week _____
6. letters in the alphabet _____
7. number of cents in a quarter _____
8. basketball score of 57 points _____
9. the number of inches in a foot _____

Find each answer and write *even* or *odd.*

a 14 + 17 = ___ _____   b 10 × 3 = ___ _____

c 12 + 12 = ___ _____   d 21 + 21 = ___ _____

e 9 × 9 = ___ _____   f 8 × 4 = ___ _____

g 5 × 50 = ___ _____   h 19 + 20 = ___ _____

i The number of cards in three decks of 52 cards = ___
_____

Customary Units

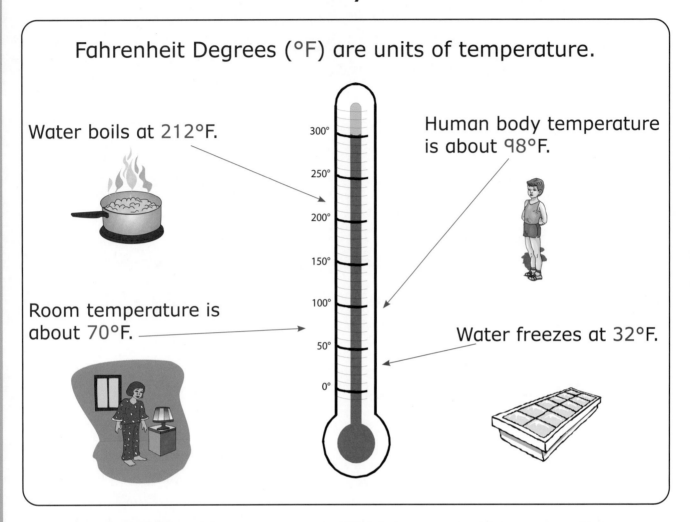

Fahrenheit Degrees (°F) are units of temperature.

Water boils at 212°F.

Human body temperature is about 98°F.

Room temperature is about 70°F.

Water freezes at 32°F.

300°
250°
200°
150°
100°
50°
0°

Circle the best estimated temperature for the activity.

1. Swimming   25°F   90°F

2. Playing in the snow   30°F   50°F

3. Flu season   50°F   101°F

4. Cooking in the oven   100°F   350°F

5. Refrigerator   40°F   25°F

Metric Units

Celsius Degrees (°C) are units of temperature.

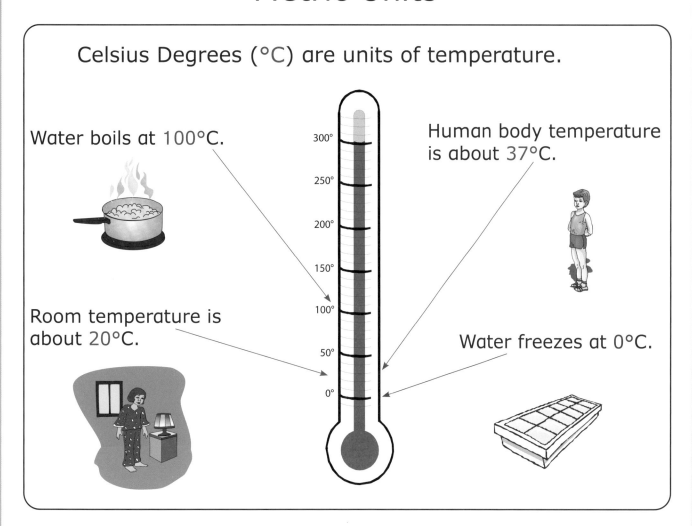

Water boils at 100°C.

Human body temperature is about 37°C.

Room temperature is about 20°C.

Water freezes at 0°C.

300°
250°
200°
150°
100°
50°
0°

Circle the best estimated temperature for the activity.

1.	Swimming	1°C	32°C
2.	Playing in the snow	1°C	35°C
3.	Flu season	10°C	38°C
4.	Cooking in the oven	38°C	180°C
5.	Refrigerator	3°C	27°C

Customary Units

Units of Capacity		
2 cups	=	1 pint
2 pints	=	1 quart
4 quarts	=	1 gallon

Fill in the blank.

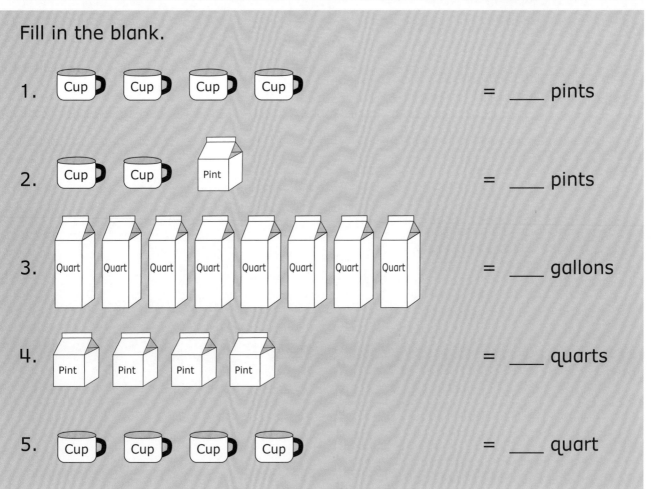

1. Cup Cup Cup Cup = ___ pints

2. Cup Cup Pint = ___ pints

3. Quart Quart Quart Quart Quart Quart Quart Quart = ___ gallons

4. Pint Pint Pint Pint = ___ quarts

5. Cup Cup Cup Cup = ___ quart

Metric Units

Units of Capacity
1,000 milliliters (mL) = 1 liter (L)

A water bottle holds about 1 liter (L).

An eye dropper holds about 1 milliliter (mL).

Circle the best estimate.

1. A glass of water   400 mL   400 L

2. A spoon full of water   10mL   10 L

3. Coffee thermos   500 mL   500 L

4. Pan   3 mL   3 L

5. Large container of soda pop   2 mL   2 L

6. Kiddy swimming pool   1,000 mL   1,000 L

7. Medicine dose   10 mL   10 L

8. Laundry detergent bottle   2 mL   2 L

| The most likely outcome is the one with the largest chance of happening. | The least likely outcome is the one with the smallest chance of happening. |

If you spin the spinner, what is most likely to happen?

Green is the most likely outcome (5 out of 8).
Purple is the least likely outcome (3 out of 8).

1. Finish coloring the area of the spinner with blue and red to make the following statements true.

   - most likely to land on a red area

   - least likely to land on a blue area

2. Color the area of the spinner with green and red to make the following statements true.

   - most likely to land on a red area

   - least likely to land on a green area

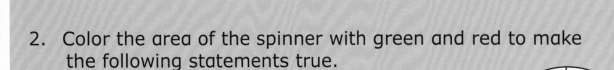

Theo put the marbles above in the empty black jar and shook them up.

1.   If Theo closed his eyes and picked one marble from the jar, what color is he most likely to get?

   _____

2.   If Theo put the marble back, shook the jar again and picked a marble, what color is he least likely to get?

   _____

3.   Is it possible to pick a black marble out of the jar?

   _____

1. List the possible outcomes when using the spinner.

    _____, _____, _____

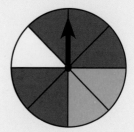

2. List the possible outcomes of tossing a coin.

    _____, _____

3. Which outcome is two in eight?

    _____

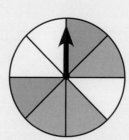

4. Write the likely outcomes from the spinner.

    Yellow _____ in ___8___

    Red _____ in _____

    Blue _____ in _____

An **array** shows objects in rows and columns.

3 × 5 means an amount equal to 3 rows of 5.

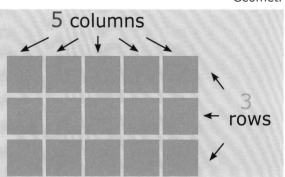

1. Draw and shade in an array for 2 × 4 (2 rows of 4).

2. Draw and shade in an array for 4 × 2.

3. Draw and shade in an array for 3 × 4.

4. Draw and shade in an array for 4 × 5.

5. Draw and shade in an array for 2 × 3.

6. Draw and shade in an array for 5 × 6.

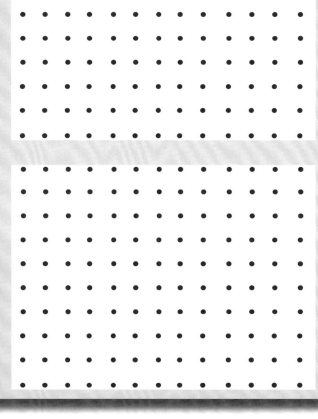

The Commutative Property of Multiplication

states that the <u>order</u> of the factors does not matter to the product. $5 \times 2 = 2 \times 5$

2 × 5 means 2 fives   OR   5 twos

$$5 + 5 = 2 + 2 + 2 + 2 + 2$$

2×5 can be represented by an **array**.

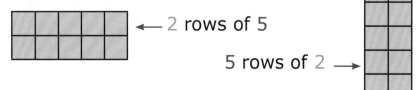 ← 2 rows of 5

5 rows of 2 →

The figures both represent $5 \times 2 = 10$

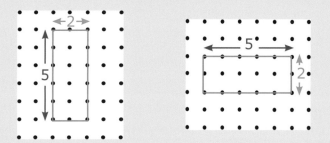

Draw and shade in two arrays that represent the multiplication problems.

$4 \times 2 = 8$

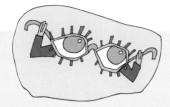

3 x 5 = 15

5 x 4 = 20

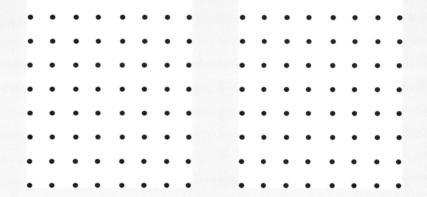

2 x 6 = 12

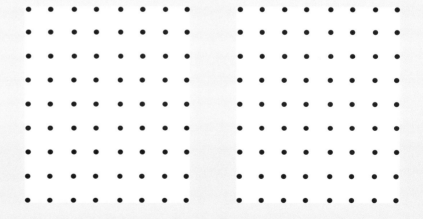

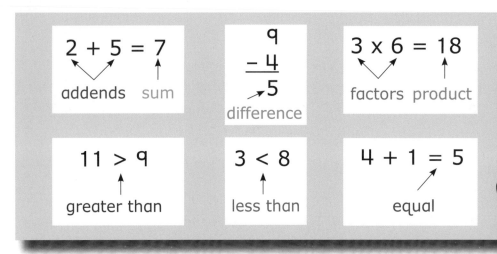

Use the words above to fill in the blanks.

1. In a multiplication problem, the numbers to be multiplied are

    called _____.

2. Four is smaller than five or four is _____ five.

3. In the problem 3 + 9 = 12, 3 and 9 are _____.

4. The answer to a subtraction problem is called the _____.

5. Amounts that are the same are called _____.

6. The answer to a multiplication problem is called the

    _____.

7. Nine is more than two or nine is _____ two.

8. The answer to an addition problem is called the _____.

Fill in the following multiplication chart.

← Columns →

×	0	1	2	3	4	5	6	7	8	9
0										
1										
2										
3										
4										
5										
6										
7										
8										
9										

↑
Rows
↓

What number am I?

1. I am found in both row 7 and row 5. _____

2. I am found in both row 4 and row 5. _____

3. I am found in both row 2 and row 3. ____ ____ ____

4. I am found in both row 4 and row 6. ____ ____ ____

5. I am found in row 3, row 4, and row 8. _____

A survey was taken in Miss Jenkin's 3rd grade class.

Favorite Hot Lunch

	Hamburger	6
	Hotdog	3
	Pizza	8
	Taco	5

1. How many selected a hotdog? _____

2. How many selected a taco? _____

3. How many students voted? _____

4. How many students did not vote for pizza? _____

5. How many students did not vote for tacos or hotdogs? _____

6. Make a bar graph of the results.

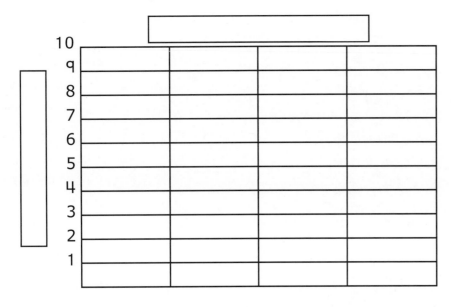

2 groups of 4 =

4 + 4 = 8

2 × 4 = 8

Write an addition and a multiplication sentence for each.

1.

3 groups of 6 = _____

_____ + _____ + _____ = __18__

_____ × _____ = _____

2.

4 groups of 3 = _____

_____ + _____ + _____ + _____ = _____

_____ × _____ = _____

3.

2 groups of _____ = _____

_____ + _____ = _____

_____ × _____ = _____

Separate the 10 bugs into 2 equal groups.

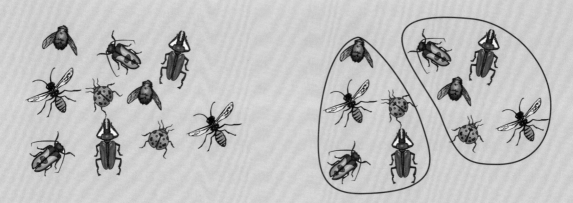

1. Separate the 12 people into 3 equal groups. How many people are in each group? _____

2. Separate the 15 flowers into 5 equal groups. How many flowers are in each group? _____

1. Separate the 12 guitars into 4 equal groups. How many guitars are in each group?

_____

2. Separate the 18 pieces of candy into 3 equal groups. How many pieces of candy are in each group?

_____

3. If $1.00 was equally shared among 4 students, how much would each student get?

_____ + _____ + _____ + _____ = $1.00

Multiplication puts equal groups together.

Division is used to separate into equal groups.

1. How many groups of 4 are in 8 balloons?

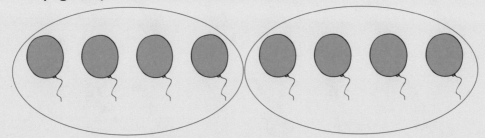

Complete the division number sentence to show your answer.
The ÷ sign means "divided by." $\underline{\quad 8 \quad} \div \underline{\quad 4 \quad} = \underline{\qquad}$

balloons   number   groups
            in each
            group

2. How many groups of 5 are in 15 dogs?

$\underline{\quad 15 \quad} \div \underline{\qquad} = \underline{\qquad}$

dogs   number   groups
            in each
            group

3. How many groups of 3 are in 12 doves?

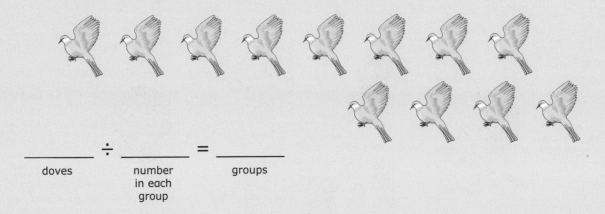

$\underline{\qquad} \div \underline{\qquad} = \underline{\qquad}$

doves   number   groups
            in each
            group

4. How many groups of 4 are in 12 CDs?

    $\underline{12} \div \underline{} = \underline{}$
    CDs   number   groups
         in each
         group

5. How many groups of 8 are in 16 cars?

    $\underline{} \div \underline{} = \underline{}$
    cars   number   groups
         in each
         group

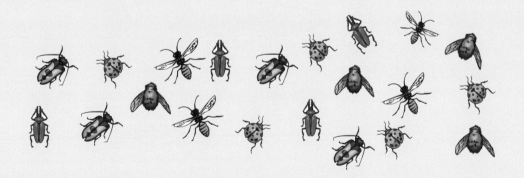

6. How many groups of 7 are in 21 bugs?

    $\underline{} \div \underline{} = \underline{}$
    bugs   number   groups
         in each
         group

Complete each division number sentence and the matching drawing.

a   8 ÷ 4 = <u>2</u>

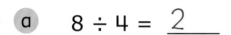

b   9 ÷ 3 = _____

c   10 ÷ 2 = _____

d   12 ÷ 3 = _____

e   12 ÷ 4 = _____

f   6 ÷ 1 = _____

g   18 ÷ 9 = _____

h   14 ÷ _____ = _____

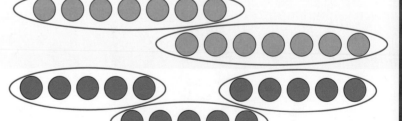

i   15 ÷ _____ = _____

j   _____ ÷ _____ = _____

k   _____ ÷ _____ = _____

The answer to a division problem is called the quotient.

Another way to write the division

sentence 6 ÷ 3 = 2 is

$$3\overline{)6}^{\,2}$$

Find the missing quotients and circle the matching groups.

a   8 ÷ 2 = _____ $2\overline{)8}$

b   9 ÷ 3 = _____ $3\overline{)9}$

c   16 ÷ 4 = _____ $4\overline{)16}$

d   25 ÷ 5 = _____ $5\overline{)25}$

e   24 ÷ 8 = _____ $8\overline{)24}$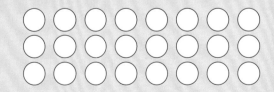

Subtract and use the answers to solve the riddle.

a   79
    − 18

b   83
    − 16

c   32
    − 13

d   48
    − 12

e   64
    − 38

f   92
    − 15

g   35
    − 17

h   80
    − 11

i   52
    − 14

j   85
    − 23

k   821
    − 417

l   300
    − 109

m   502
    − 146

n   312
    − 145

o   207
    − 148

p   524
    − 217

q   346
    − 178

r   236
    − 145

s   800
    − 623

t   913
    − 287

u   100
    −   1

v   138
    − 92

w   904
    − 705

x   456
    − 78

y   300
    −   3

What is an astronaut's favorite meal?

___ ___ ___ ___ ___ ___
191   61   99   167   19   69

Complete the number sentences.

9 ÷ 3 = _____   3)‾1‾2‾   4 ÷ 2 = _____

4)‾1‾2‾   15 ÷ 5 = _____   6)‾1‾8‾

14 ÷ 7 = _____   10)‾2‾0‾   25 ÷ 5 = _____

9)‾1‾8‾   16 ÷ 4 = _____   8)‾2‾4‾

14 ÷ 2 = _____   7)‾2‾1‾   15 ÷ 3 = _____

8)‾1‾6‾   20 ÷ 5 = _____   9)‾2‾7‾

> Multiplication puts equal groups together.
>
> Division is used to separate into equal groups.

1. How many groups of 2 are in 8 fish?

    _____ ÷ _____ = _____

    fish   number   groups
            in each
            group

    Complete the multiplication sentence to prove your answer.

    _____ x _____ = _____

2. How many groups of 8 are in 24 pigs?

    $$\underset{\substack{\text{number in}\\\text{each group}}}{\quad}\overline{)\underset{\text{pigs}}{\qquad}}\ \ = \text{groups}$$

Complete the multiplication sentence to prove your answer.

_____ x _____ = _____

number   groups   pigs
in each
group

3. How many groups of four are in 16 turtles?

    _____ ÷ _____ = _____

    Complete the multiplication sentence to prove your answer.

    _____ x _____ = __16__

4. How many groups of 5 are in 20 circles?

    __20__ ÷ _____ = _____

    Complete the multiplication sentence to prove your answer.

    _____ x _____ = __20__

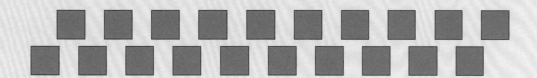

5. How many groups of 4 are in 20 squares?

    _____ ÷ _____ = _____

    Complete the multiplication sentence to prove your answer.

    _____ x _____ = _____

<u>Repeated subtraction</u> can be used to answer **division** problems.

How many groups of 4 are in 12 people?

```
  12        8        4
-  4      - 4      - 4
   8        4        0
```

4 can be subtracted from 12 a total of
3 times. There are 3 groups of 4 in 12.

Complete each number sentence.

a　　　$10 \div 2 =$ _____　or
```
  10      8      6      4      2
- 2    - 2    - 2    - 2    - 2
```

b　　　$\overline{)24}$　or
```
  24     16      8
-  8    - 8    - 8
```

c　$28 \div$ _____ $=$ _____　or
```
  28     21     14      7
-  7    - 7    - 7    - 7
```

d　$5\overline{)20}$　or　_____ / _____ / _____ / _____

Six people need to share 12 pieces of candy. Use division to find how many pieces each person should have.

$$\overline{\smash{)}12}$$

Write in the missing answers to make true number sentences. Then write the matching letter of each answer below to read the message.

3 x E = 6	8 x A = 24	3 x U = 12
6 ÷ 3 = E	24 ÷ 8 = A	12 ÷ 3 = U
E = ___	A = ___	U = ___

2 x W = 14	4 x Y = 20	10 x N = 10
14 ÷ 2 = W	20 ÷ 4 = Y	10 ÷ 10 = N
W = ___	Y = ___	N = ___

4 x O = 32	3 x I = 27	5 x R = 30
32 ÷ 4 = O	27 ÷ 3 = I	30 ÷ 5 = R
O = ___	I = ___	R = ___

Message:

___ ___ ___   ___ ___ ___   ___ ___ ___ ___ ___ ___ ___
 5   8   4   3   6   2   3   7   9   1   1   2   6

Thousands	Hundreds	Tens	Ones
2	1	3	4
Thousands	Hundreds	Tens	Ones
	5	8	1

```
 T H T O
    1
 2,1 3 4
+  5 8 1
 2,7 1 5
```

Find the sums, then circle the matching answer below.

a
34	829	9	925	9,528
18	5,183	37	482	324
+ 293	+ 492	+ 318	+ 917	+ 100

b
248	245	34	138	8,291
129	36	82	296	263
+ 63	+ 127	+ 9	+ 832	+ 1,294

c   82 + 57 + 6 + 192 =

d   129 + 64 + 5,000 + 23 =

e   7,000 + 800 + 70 + 8 =

f   696 + 29 + 34 + 5 =

 9,952
 408
 345
 1,266
 9,848
 364
 5,216

 6,504
 125
 440
 2,324
 7,878
 764
 337

Divide and use the letters of the answers to solve the riddle below.

r 18 ÷ 9 = _____   y 4)‾32‾ _____   l 8 ÷ 8 = _____

b 8)‾72‾ _____   a 36 ÷ 9 = _____   t 6)‾30‾ _____

e 49 ÷ 7 = _____   i 4)‾24‾ _____   h 15 ÷ 5 = _____

a 8)‾32‾ _____   b 81 ÷ 9 = _____   y 8)‾64‾ _____

What building has the most stories?

___ ___ ___   ___ ___ ___ ___ ___ ___ ___ ___
 5   3   7   1   6   9   2   4   2   8

A set of related multiplication and division number sentences is called a fact family.

2 × 5 = 10		3 × 4 = 12
5 × 2 = 10	or	4 × 3 = 12
10 ÷ 2 = 5		12 ÷ 3 = 4
10 ÷ 5 = 2		12 ÷ 4 = 3

Fill in the missing numbers in each fact family.

6 × 8 = 48

8 × ___ = 48

48 ÷ 8 = ___

48 ÷ ___ = 8

---

4 × 7 = 28

___ × 4 = 28

28 ÷ 7 = ___

28 ÷ ___ = 7

---

5 × 9 = ___

9 × ___ = 45

45 ÷ 9 = ___

45 ÷ 5 = ___

___ × 7 = 42

7 × 6 = ___

___ ÷ 7 = 6

42 ÷ ___ = 7

---

2 × 8 = 16

___ × 2 = 16

16 ÷ ___ = 2

___ ÷ 2 = 8

---

3 × 9 = ___

9 × 3 = ___

27 ÷ 9 = ___

___ ÷ 3 = 9

$3 \times 5 =$ ___

___ $\times 3 = 15$

$15 \div 3 =$ ___

$15 \div$ ___ $= 3$

$5 \times$ ___ $= 20$

$4 \times$ ___ $= 20$

$20 \div 5 =$ ___

$20 \div$ ___ $= 5$

$7 \times$ ___ $= 21$

$3 \times$ ___ $= 21$

$21 \div 7 =$ ___

___ $\div 3 = 7$

$4 \times$ ___ $= 12$

$3 \times 4 =$ ___

$12 \div$ ___ $= 4$

$12 \div$ ___ $= 3$

___ $\times 6 = 30$

$6 \times 5 =$ ___

$30 \div$ ___ $= 6$

___ $\div 6 = 5$

$8 \times 3 =$ ___

___ $\times 8 = 24$

$24 \div$ ___ $= 8$

$24 \div 8 =$ ___

$9 \times$ ___ $= 18$

$2 \times$ ___ $= 18$

$18 \div 2 =$ ___

___ $\div 9 = 2$

$7 \times 4 =$ ___

___ $\times 7 = 28$

___ $\div 4 = 7$

$28 \div 7 =$ ___

$5 \times$ ___ $= 40$

$8 \times$ ___ $= 40$

$40 \div$ ___ $= 8$

$40 \div$ ___ $= 5$

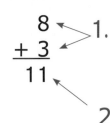

8
+ 3   1.
11

2.   5 − 4 = 1

3.   3 × 4 = 12

4.   5.

16 ÷ 2 = 8   2 < 3   8 > 1

6.   7.   8.

Use the diagram to match each number
with the correct word.

1. ____   a. difference

2. ____   b. product

3. ____   c. less than

4. ____   d. addends

5. ____   e. quotient

6. ____   f. factors

7. ____   g. sum

8. ____   h. greater than

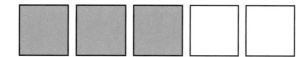

3 of 5 parts can be written as $\frac{3}{5}$, called a fraction.

Write a fraction showing the number of red parts.

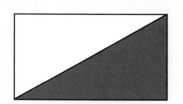 _____

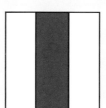 _____

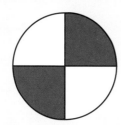 _____

 _____

 _____

 _____

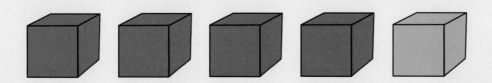

$= \dfrac{1}{2}$

The numerator tells parts considered.

The denominator tells total number of equal parts.

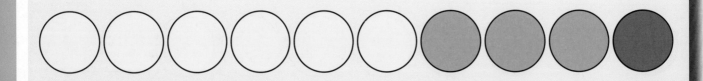

1. The blue box is what fraction of all the boxes? _____

2. The red boxes are what fraction of all the boxes? _____

3. The blue circles are what fraction of all the circles? _____

4. The red circle is what fraction of all the circles? _____

5. The yellow circles are what fraction of all the circles? _____

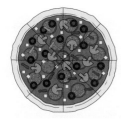 8 pieces out of 8 pieces = $\dfrac{8}{8}$ = the whole pizza

Fill in the blanks.

1.

There are _____ brown squares out of _____ squares =   ——— = 1

2.

There are _____ purple parts out of _____ parts =   ——— = 1

3.

There are _____ pink parts out of_____ parts =   ——— = 1

$$\dfrac{1}{1} = \dfrac{2}{2} = \dfrac{3}{3} = \dfrac{4}{4} = \dfrac{5}{5} = \dfrac{6}{6} = 1$$

4. Write 5 fractions (different from above) that equal 1.

$$\text{——} = \text{——} = \text{——} = \text{——} = \text{——} = 1$$

Fractions that name the <u>same</u> amount
are called equivalent fractions.

Shade and write an equivalent fraction for each pair.

$\dfrac{1}{4}$ 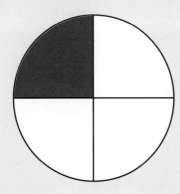 $\dfrac{2}{8}$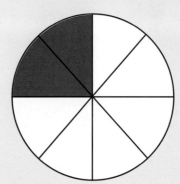

$\dfrac{2}{3}$ 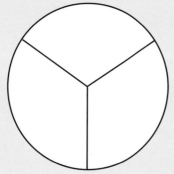 ——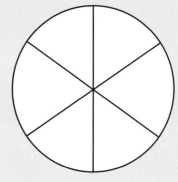

$\dfrac{3}{4}$ 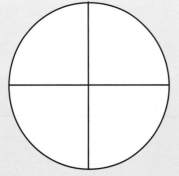 ——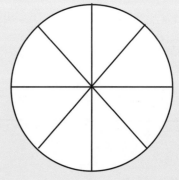

$\dfrac{2}{4}$ 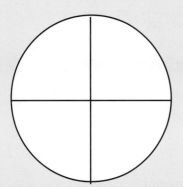 ——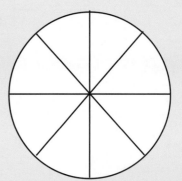

 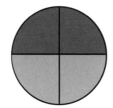  

$$\frac{1}{2} \times \frac{2}{2} = \frac{2}{4}$$

$$\frac{2}{5} \times \frac{3}{3} = \frac{6}{15}$$

Multiplying the numerator and denominator by the same whole number, except zero, makes an equivalent fraction.

 Fill in the blanks below to make equivalent fractions.

a $\frac{1}{4} \times \frac{2}{2} = $ ____ $\frac{1}{3} \times \frac{2}{2} = $ ____ $\frac{2}{3} \times \frac{3}{3} = $ ____

b $\frac{3}{4} \times \frac{2}{2} = $ ____ $\frac{5}{8} \times \frac{3}{3} = $ ____ $\frac{3}{8} \times \frac{1}{1} = $ ____

c $\frac{2}{5} \times \frac{4}{4} = $ ____ $\frac{3}{5} \times \frac{4}{4} = $ ____ $\frac{1}{6} \times \frac{5}{5} = $ ____

 $\dfrac{2}{3}$ = $\dfrac{\text{numerator (part of whole)}}{\text{denominator (whole in equal parts)}}$

Write a fraction that corresponds to the colored area.

1.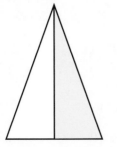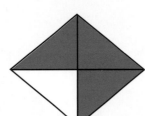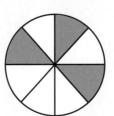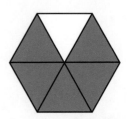

———   ———   ———   ———

2.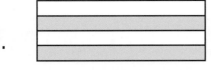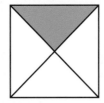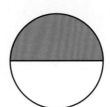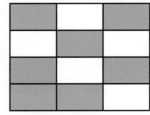

———   ———   ———   ———

3. Shade $\dfrac{3}{5}$

4. Shade $\dfrac{5}{8}$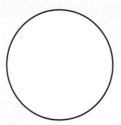

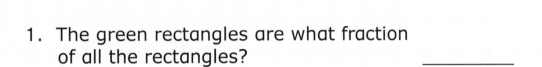

1. The green rectangles are what fraction
   of all the rectangles?   _____

2. The orange rectangle is what fraction
   of all the rectangles?   _____

3. What two colors are $\frac{6}{7}$ of all the rectangles?

   _____   _____

4. Color the pentagons so that $\frac{3}{8}$ are black,
   $\frac{2}{8}$ are white, and $\frac{3}{8}$ are striped.

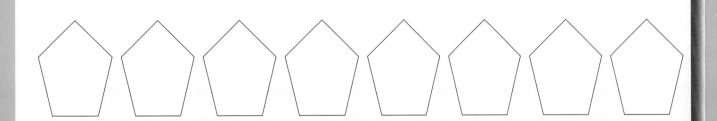

The distance between 0 and 1 has been cut into equally spaced intervals in each problem. Write the fraction represented by each point.

1 A

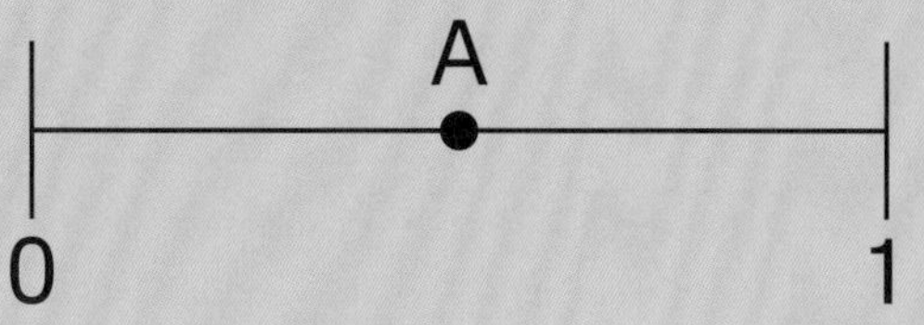

0   1

A is at $\frac{1}{2}$

1 out of 2 intervals

2 A   B

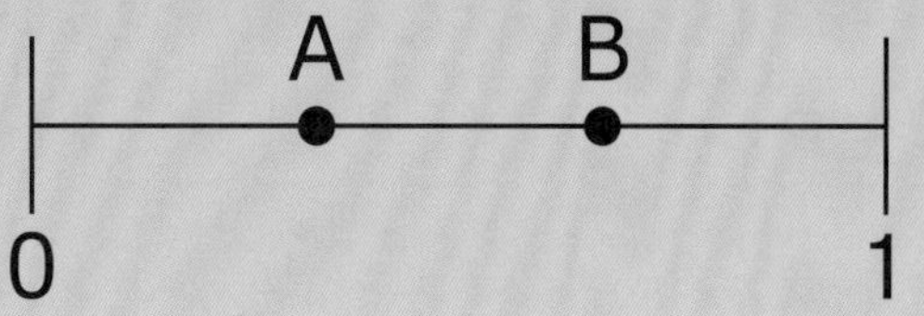

0   1

A is at _____

B is at _____

3 A   B   C

0   1

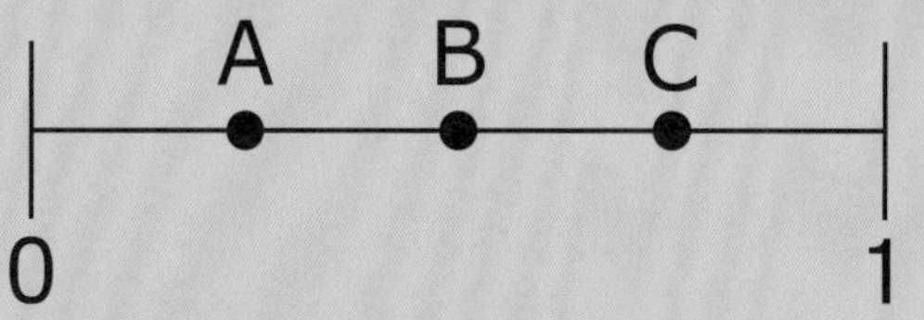

A is at _____

B is at _____

C is at _____

4 A B C D

0   1

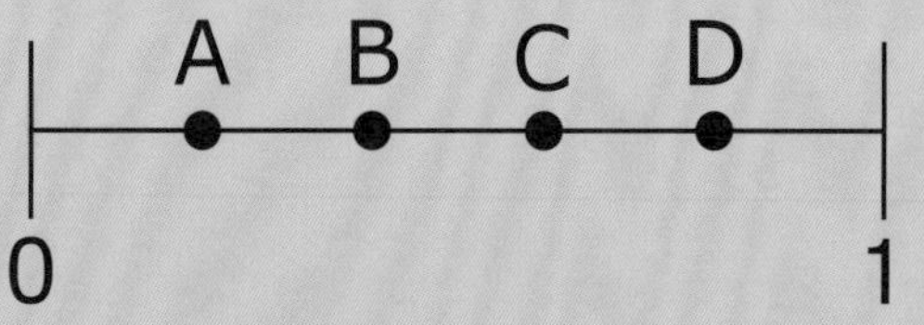

A is at _____

B is at _____

C is at _____

D is at _____

5 Put a mark on the line at $\frac{1}{8}, \frac{2}{8}, \frac{3}{8}, \frac{4}{8}, \frac{5}{8}, \frac{6}{8}, \frac{7}{8},$ and $\frac{8}{8}$.

0   1

102 – 41 =

$$\begin{array}{r} {}^{0}\cancel{1}^{1}02 \\ -\ \ 41 \\ \hline 61 \end{array}$$

Use a scrap piece of paper to find each difference. Regroup when necessary, then complete the puzzle below.

Across

1 102 – 41 = **61**
3 82 – 14 =
5 99 – 61 =
8 100 – 27 =
9 421 – 345 =
11 831 – 669 =
13 629 – 143 =
16 200 – 175 =
19 2,136 – 1,928 =
20 424 – 399 =
21 457 – 264 =

Down

1 1,000 – 325 =
2 68 – 55 =
4 141 – 54 =
6 954 – 138 =
7 100 – 8 =
10 90 – 26 =
12 81 – 29 =
14 495 – 406 =
15 100 – 50 =
17 401 – 349 =
18 63 – 24 =

1 **6**	2 **1**			3	4		5	6		7
8					9	10		11		
				12		13	14			
	15			16	17				18	
19					20			21		

Multiplication is commutative, which means the order of the factors does not matter.

$$8 \times 3 = 3 \times 8 = 24$$

factors   product

x	0	1	2	3	4	5	6	7	8	9
0	0	0	0	0	0	0	0	0	0	0
1	0	1	2	3	4	5	6	7	8	9
2	0	2	4	6	8	10	12	14	16	18
3	0	3	6	9	12	15	18	21	24	27
4	0	4	8	12	16	20	24	28	32	36
5	0	5	10	15	20	25	30	35	40	45
6	0	6	12	18	24	30	36	42	48	54
7	0	7	14	21	28	35	42	49	56	63
8	0	8	16	24	32	40	48	56	64	72
9	0	9	18	27	36	45	54	63	72	81

Multiply and use the chart above to check your answer.

a.

5	2	2	6	3	5
× 2	× 5	× 6	× 2	× 5	× 3

b.

2	4	5	7	8	5
× 4	× 2	× 7	× 5	× 5	× 8

c.

7	6	9	5	1	7
× 6	× 7	× 5	× 9	× 7	× 1

d.

4	7	8	3	3	7
× 7	× 4	× 3	× 8	× 7	× 3

BINGO

32	35	7	27	9
10	21	16	40	36
8	14	FREE	45	64
15	81	12	30	24
18	0	42	6	28

How many fives in forty?

$$40 \div 5 = ?$$

There are 8 fives in forty.

$$8 \times 5 = 40$$

x	0	1	2	3	4	5	6	7	8	9
0	0	0	0	0	0	0	0	0	0	0
1	0	1	2	3	4	5	6	7	8	9
2	0	2	4	6	8	10	12	14	16	18
3	0	3	6	9	12	15	18	21	24	27
4	0	4	8	12	16	20	24	28	32	36
5	0	5	10	15	20	25	30	35	40	45
6	0	6	12	18	24	30	36	42	48	54
7	0	7	14	21	28	35	42	49	56	63
8	0	8	16	24	32	40	48	56	64	72
9	0	9	18	27	36	45	54	63	72	81

Use the multiplication chart to find the missing quotients.

a $5\overline{)10}$ $4\overline{)4}$ $3\overline{)15}$ $7\overline{)28}$ $9\overline{)27}$

b $2\overline{)2}$ $6\overline{)24}$ $8\overline{)16}$ $2\overline{)6}$ $7\overline{)35}$

c $4\overline{)8}$ $2\overline{)2}$ $7\overline{)21}$ $6\overline{)30}$ $8\overline{)32}$

d $2\overline{)12}$ $7\overline{)63}$ $8\overline{)64}$ $6\overline{)42}$

e $5\overline{)45}$ $7\overline{)49}$ $6\overline{)48}$ $2\overline{)12}$

f $6\overline{)36}$ $4\overline{)36}$ $1\overline{)8}$ $4\overline{)28}$

Did you notice anything about the answers in rows a-c and rows d-f?

_____

A place-value chart can help you understand **whole numbers**. Each digit in a number has a value based on its placement.

MOVING UP

Write each number in the place-value chart.

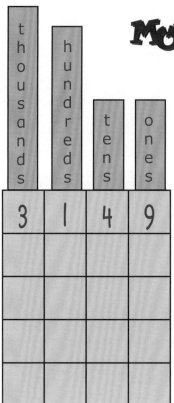

thousands	hundreds	tens	ones
3	1	4	9

a 3,149 ⟷

b 3,694

c 63

d 6,405

e 1,954

Write the place-value name for the 4 in each number.

f 4,659   _thousands_

g 5,428   _____

h 1,764   _____

i 8,046   _____

Write in expanded notation.

j 1,782   _1,000 + 700 + 80 + 2_____

k 4,876   _____

l 3,467   _____

m 8,703   _____

Write in words.

n 4,604   _four thousand, six hundred four_

o 7,213   _____

The symbol > means is greater than.	6 > 2
The symbol < means is less than.	5 < 8
The symbol = means is equal to.	4 = 4

Note: The arrow always points to the smaller number.

Write <, >, or = in the blank to make a true sentence.

a   16 __<__ 46

b   128 __>__ 124

c   4,871 _____ 5,000

d   408 _____ 409

e   31 _____ 60

f   297 _____ 290

g   101 _____ 93

h   98 _____ 90

i   45,259 _____ 50,000

j   567 _____ 509

k   411 _____ 411

l   60,108 _____ 59,899

Place the numbers in order from least to greatest (left to right).

m   24, 45, 18   18, 24, 45

n   39, 48, 41   _____

o   398, 300, 401   _____

p   76, 29, 52, 48   _____

Elapsed time is the amount of time that passes from the start of an activity to the end of an activity.

Flight Schedule from Kansas City, Missouri

Destination	Departs	Arrives
New Orleans, Louisiana	9:15 a.m.	11:00 a.m.
Tulsa, Oklahoma	7:30 a.m.	8:30 a.m.
Chicago, Illinois	1:10 p.m.	2:25 p.m.
Little Rock, Arkansas	3:00 p.m.	4:05 p.m.

Use the flight schedule to find the elapsed time.

1. How long is the flight from Kansas City to New Orleans?

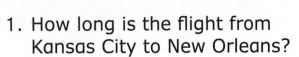

$$11:00$$
$$- \; 9:15$$

eleven hours = ten hours and 60 minutes
− nine hours and 15 minutes
one hour and 45 minutes

2. How long is the flight from Kansas City to Tulsa? _____

3. How long is the flight from Kansas City to Chicago? _____

4. How long is the flight from Kansas City to Little Rock? _____

5. Which is the longest flight on the schedule? _____

Calendar Units
7 days = 1 week
52 weeks = 1 year
12 months = 1 year

a   14 days = _____ weeks   b   24 months = _____ years

c   3 weeks = _____ days   d   28 days = _____ weeks

e   1 year = _____ months   f   4 weeks = _____ days

Write <, >, or = in the blank to make a true sentence.

g   12 days   2 weeks   h   1 month   27 days

i   25 months   2 years   j   20 days   2 weeks

k   104 weeks   2 years   l   12 months   1 year

m   5 weeks   28 days   n   5 weeks   36 days

o   36 months   3 years   p   8 weeks   60 days

July						
Sun.	Mon.	Tue.	Wed.	Thu.	Fri.	Sat.
	1	2	3	4	5	6
7	8	9	10	11	12	13
14	15	16	17	18	19	20
21	22	23	24	25	26	27
28	29	30	31			

August						
Sun.	Mon.	Tue.	Wed.	Thu.	Fri.	Sat.
				1	2	3
4	5	6	7	8	9	10
11	12	13	14	15	16	17
18	19	20	21	22	23	24
25	26	27	28	29	30	31

September						
Sun.	Mon.	Tue.	Wed.	Thu.	Fri.	Sat.
1	2	3	4	5	6	7
8	9	10	11	12	13	14
15	16	17	18	19	20	21
22	23	24	25	26	27	28
29	30					

October						
Sun.	Mon.	Tue.	Wed.	Thu.	Fri.	Sat.
		1	2	3	4	5
6	7	8	9	10	11	12
13	14	15	16	17	18	19
20	21	22	23	24	25	26
27	28	29	30	31		

November						
Sun.	Mon.	Tue.	Wed.	Thu.	Fri.	Sat.
					1	2
3	4	5	6	7	8	9
10	11	12	13	14	15	16
17	18	19	20	21	22	23
24	25	26	27	28	29	30

December						
Sun.	Mon.	Tue.	Wed.	Thu.	Fri.	Sat.
1	2	3	4	5	6	7
8	9	10	11	12	13	14
15	16	17	18	19	20	21
22	23	24	25	26	27	28
29	30	31				

1. Two days after October 20th is

_____ _____.
month   date

2. The second Tuesday in August is

_____ _____.
month   date

3. One week after November 29th is

_____ _____.
month   date

4. Three days after the last Monday in July is

_____ _____.
month   date

5. Twenty-one days after August 21st is

_____ _____.
month   date

6. If one week ago, it was July 14, then today is

_____ _____.
month   date

7. If yesterday was September 10, then in one week it will be

_____ _____.
month   date

8. If tomorrow is October 2, then a week ago, it was _____ _____.
month   date

Continue the pattern.

a   1, 2, 3, 4, 5, _____, _____, _____, _____, _____ (skip counting by one)

b   2, 4, 6, 8, 10, _____, _____, _____, _____, _____ (skip counting by two)

c   3, 6, 9, 12, 15, 18, _____, _____, _____, _____, _____

d   4, 8, 12, 16, 20, 24, _____, _____, _____, _____, _____

e   5, 10, 15, 20, 25, _____, _____, _____, _____, _____

f   6, 12, 18, 24, 30, _____, _____, _____, _____, _____

g   7, 14, 21, 28, 35, _____, _____, _____, _____, _____

h   8, 16, 24, 32, 40, _____, _____, _____, _____, _____

i   9, 18, 27, 36, 45, _____, _____, _____, _____, _____

j   10, 20, 30, 40, 50, _____, _____, _____, _____, _____

k   11, 22, 33, 44, 55, _____, _____, _____, _____, _____

l   12, 24, 36, 48, 60, _____, _____, _____, _____, _____

Fill in the blanks.

m   10, _____, 16, _____, _____, 25, _____

n   7, _____, _____, 22, 27, _____, _____

Skip count by 3 to find multiples of 3.
Circle the numbers that are multiples
of 3. Do you see a pattern?

_____

1	2	③	4	5	⑥	7	8	9	10
11	12	13	14	15	16	17	18	19	20
21	22	23	24	25	26	27	28	29	30
31	32	33	34	35	36	37	38	39	40
41	42	43	44	45	46	47	48	49	50
51	52	53	54	55	56	57	58	59	60
61	62	63	64	65	66	67	68	69	70
71	72	73	74	75	76	77	78	79	80
81	82	83	84	85	86	87	88	89	90
91	92	93	94	95	96	97	98	99	100

Skip count by 4 to find multiples of 4.
Circle the numbers with multiples of 4.
Do you see a pattern?

_____

1	2	3	4	5	6	7	8	9	10
11	12	13	14	15	16	17	18	19	20
21	22	23	24	25	26	27	28	29	30
31	32	33	34	35	36	37	38	39	40
41	42	43	44	45	46	47	48	49	50
51	52	53	54	55	56	57	58	59	60
61	62	63	64	65	66	67	68	69	70
71	72	73	74	75	76	77	78	79	80
81	82	83	84	85	86	87	88	89	90
91	92	93	94	95	96	97	98	99	100

Circle each number to show the path from 25 to 500, counting by 25s. You can only move up, down, left, or right.

Start

25	25	25	25	25	25	25	25
50	50	325	300	50	50	50	50
75	350	350	275	100	125	100	75
100	375	375	250	225	300	125	400
125	400	400	425	200	175	150	425
450	425	425	300	225	425	175	450
475	475	450	475	475	475	475	475
500	500	500	500	500	500	500	500

Finish

> means greater than
< means less than
= means equal to

$$3 + 4 \underline{\quad > \quad} 5 - 1$$
7   4

Note: The arrow always points to the smaller number.

Place either <, >, or = in the blanks to make the sentences true.

a   9 + 5 _____ 8 + 3

b   80 − 20 _____ 40 + 30

c   8 + 2 + 4 + 6 _____ 5 + 5 + 5 + 5

d   20 − 1 _____ 17 + 1

e   46 + 3 + 4 + 7 _____ 55 + 15 − 10

f   45 + 8 + 13 _____ 100 − 35

g   5 × 6 _____ 6 + 6 + 6 + 6 + 6

h   3 × 8 _____ 3 + 3 + 3 + 3 + 3 + 3 + 3 + 3

i   35 + 19 + 27 _____ 90 − 26

j   122 − 46 _____ 50 + 90

k   8 × 0 _____ 0 × 8

l   56 + 39 + 27 _____ 5 × 5 × 5

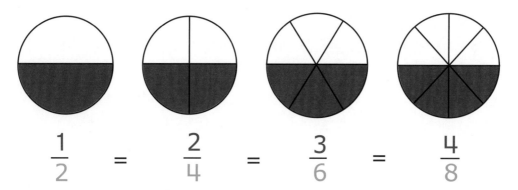

$$\frac{1}{2} = \frac{2}{4} = \frac{3}{6} = \frac{4}{8}$$

Fractions that show the same amount are called equivalent fractions.

Draw a line to connect the equivalent fractions, then write the fractions.

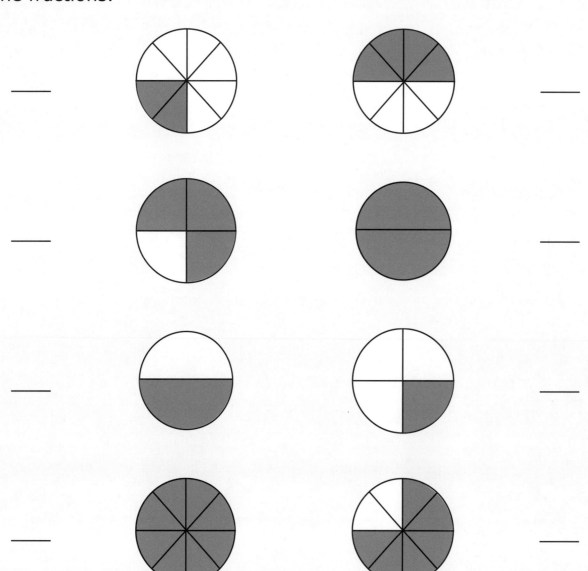

Finish the drawing and fraction to make the number sentence true.

$\frac{1}{4}$ 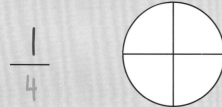 = $\frac{}{8}$

___ 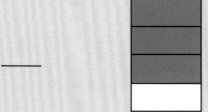 = 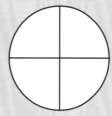 ___

___ 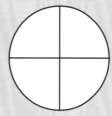 =  ___

___ 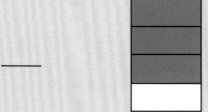 = ___

___ 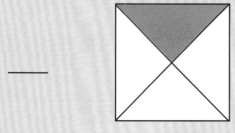 = 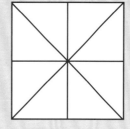 ___

___ 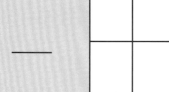 = ___

Make equivalent fractions.

1. Fold a sheet of notebook paper in half.

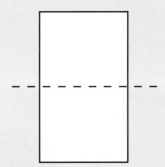

2. Shade the top half.

    $\frac{1}{2}$ is shaded

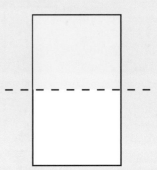

3. Fold the paper in half again.

    $\frac{2}{4}$ is shaded

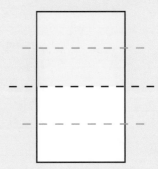

4. Fold the paper in half a third time.

    What part is shaded? _____

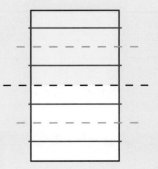

$\frac{1}{2}$, $\frac{2}{4}$, and $\frac{4}{8}$ all show the same amount of the page shaded yellow. They are equivalent fractions.

Fill in **Y** for yes and **N** for no as you solve the puzzle. Be sure to fill in all your no answers to help you solve the puzzle.

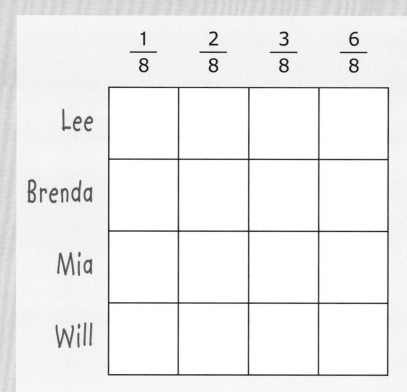

Lee, Brenda, Mia, and Will have a pie and a half to share. Use the chart and the clues to find how many pieces each person ate.

1. Lee had less than half a pie, but didn't have the least pie.

2. Brenda had less than Lee, but didn't have the least pie.

3. Mia had more pie than Will.

Fractions that name the same amount are called equivalent fractions.

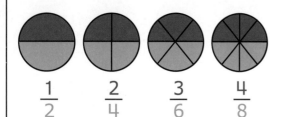

$$\frac{1}{2} \qquad \frac{2}{4} \qquad \frac{3}{6} \qquad \frac{4}{8}$$

Multiplying the numerator and denominator by the same whole number, except zero, makes an equivalent fraction.

$$\frac{1}{2} \times \frac{2}{2} = \frac{2}{4}$$

$$\frac{1}{2} \times \frac{3}{3} = \frac{3}{6}$$

Complete the drawing and fractions to make each number sentence true.

1. $$\frac{1}{2} \times \frac{2}{2} = \frac{2}{4}$$

2. 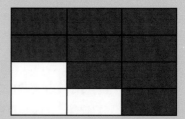 $$\frac{3}{4} \times \frac{3}{3} = \underline{\quad\quad}$$

3. 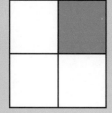 $$\frac{1}{4} \times \frac{4}{4} = \underline{\quad\quad}$$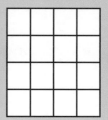

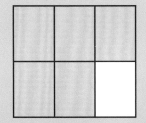 4. _____ x $\dfrac{2}{2}$ = _____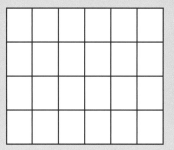

5. 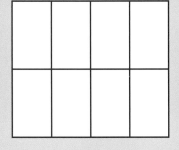 _____ x $\dfrac{3}{3}$ = _____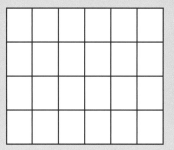

6. 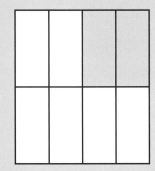 _____ x $\dfrac{2}{2}$ = _____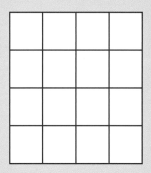

7. 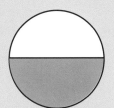 _____ x $\dfrac{4}{4}$ = _____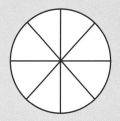

8. 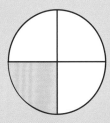 _____ x $\dfrac{5}{5}$ = _____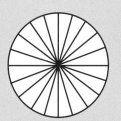

Complete the drawing and place either <, >, or = in the blanks to make the sentences true.

1.

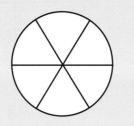

$\frac{1}{6}$ ___ $\frac{2}{6}$

2.

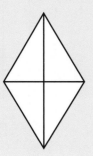

$\frac{1}{4}$ ___ $\frac{2}{4}$

3.

$\frac{3}{5}$ ___ $\frac{2}{5}$

4.

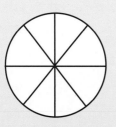 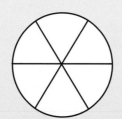

$\frac{4}{8}$ ___ $\frac{3}{6}$

5. Write the fractions $\frac{3}{8}$, $\frac{1}{8}$, and $\frac{2}{8}$ in order

from least to greatest (left to right). _____ _____ _____

6. Write $\frac{1}{2}$, 0 , and 1 in order from least

to greatest (left to right). _____ _____ _____

Tom, Jim, and Jason shared an apple pie and a raspberry pie. The apple pie was cut into quarters and the raspberry pie was cut into eighths.

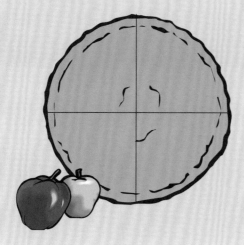 

Tom ate $\frac{2}{4}$ of the apple pie and $\frac{3}{8}$ of the raspberry.

Jim ate $\frac{1}{4}$ of the apple pie and $\frac{1}{8}$ of the raspberry pie.

Jason ate the rest of the apple and raspberry pies.

1. Who ate the least of the pies Tom, Jim, or Jason? _____

2. Who ate the 2nd most pieces of the raspberry pie? _____

3. What two boys ate most of the raspberry pie?

    _____ _____

4. What two boys together ate half an apple pie?

_____ _____

If in a fraction the numerator matches its denominator, then the fraction equals 1.

$$\frac{2}{2} = 1$$

$$\frac{6}{6} = 1$$

$$\frac{8}{8} = 1$$

A mixed number is a whole number and a fraction.

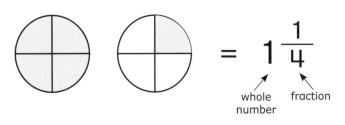

$$= 1\frac{1}{4}$$

whole number   fraction

Write a mixed number for each drawing.

1         $1\frac{1}{2}$

2   _____

3

_____

4

_____

5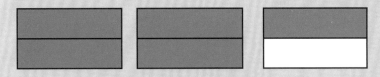

_____

6

_____

7

_____

8

_____

9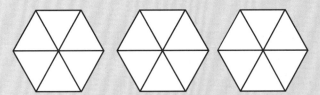

_____

10 Jenna needs $\frac{1}{2}$ apple for each apple muffin she makes. How many apples will she need for 6 muffins?

_____

Draw a line segment connecting each mixed fraction with the matching picture.

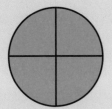
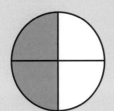

$2\frac{1}{5}$

$2\frac{1}{2}$

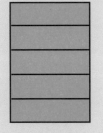
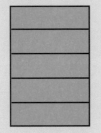
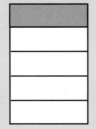

$1\frac{3}{4}$

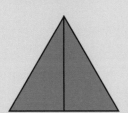

$1\frac{1}{2}$

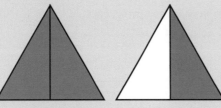

$1\frac{7}{8}$

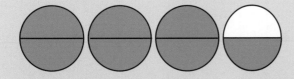

$3\frac{1}{2}$

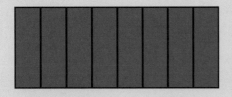

$3\frac{1}{4}$

When you add
like fractions
(same denominators), you
only add the numerators.

The denominators stay
the same.

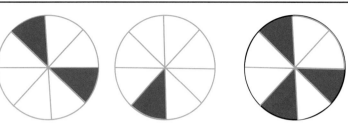

$$\frac{2}{8} \quad + \quad \frac{1}{8} \quad = \quad \frac{3}{8}$$

Add the like fractions, then write and shade the solutions.

1.

$$\frac{1}{3} \quad + \quad \frac{1}{3} \quad = \quad \frac{2}{3}$$

2.

$$\frac{3}{5} \quad + \quad \frac{1}{5} \quad = \quad \frac{}{5}$$

3.

$$\frac{3}{10} \quad + \quad \frac{4}{10} \quad = \quad \underline{\qquad}$$

Write a fraction number sentence for each drawing.

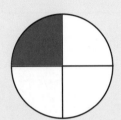 +    __ + __ =

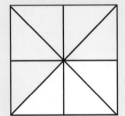 + 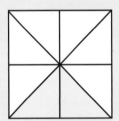   __ + __ =

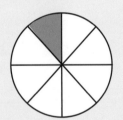 + 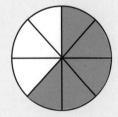   __ + __ =

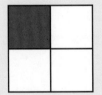 + 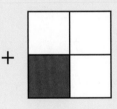   __ + __ =

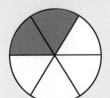 + + +   __ + __ + __ =

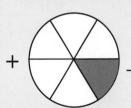 + + +   __ + __ + __ =

Like fractions are fractions with the same denominators.

$\dfrac{1}{4}$ and $\dfrac{3}{4}$ are like fractions

$\dfrac{2}{3}$ and $\dfrac{1}{3}$ are like fractions

$\dfrac{1}{4}$ and $\dfrac{1}{3}$ are not like fractions

They have different denominators.

To add like fractions, just add the numerators. You do not add the denominators.

$\dfrac{1}{4}$ + $\dfrac{2}{4}$ = $\dfrac{3}{4}$

Draw a line to connect the like fractions.

$\dfrac{2}{3}$　　　　　　　　　　　　　　$\dfrac{3}{4}$

$\dfrac{1}{5}$　　　　　　　　　　　　　　$\dfrac{2}{5}$

$\dfrac{1}{4}$　　　　　　　　　　　　　　$\dfrac{3}{6}$

$\dfrac{2}{6}$　　　　　　　　　　　　　　$\dfrac{1}{3}$

Subtract these like fractions.
Shade in the solutions.

1.

$$\frac{2}{3} - \frac{1}{3} = \frac{1}{3}$$

2.

   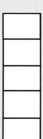

$$\frac{3}{5} - \frac{1}{5} = \frac{}{5}$$

3.

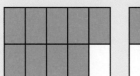   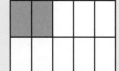   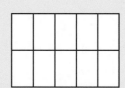

$$\frac{9}{10} - \frac{2}{10} = \underline{\quad}$$

Draw a line segment from each difference to the matching figure.

$\dfrac{5}{8} - \dfrac{2}{8} = $ _____

$\dfrac{4}{4} - \dfrac{1}{4} = $ _____

$\dfrac{7}{8} - \dfrac{2}{8} = $ _____

$\dfrac{5}{8} - \dfrac{1}{8} = $ _____

$\dfrac{5}{16} - \dfrac{2}{16} = $ _____

$\dfrac{3}{4} - \dfrac{2}{4} = $ _____

$\dfrac{2}{3} - \dfrac{1}{3} = $ _____

$\dfrac{13}{16} - \dfrac{8}{16} = $ _____

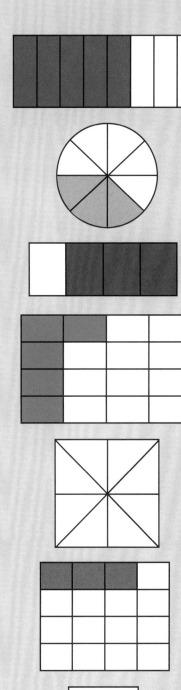

St. Louis to Orlando	996 miles
St. Louis to New York	982 miles
New York to Orlando	1,080 miles
St. Louis to Los Angeles	1,842 miles
St. Louis to Seattle	2,118 miles
Los Angeles to Seattle	1,151 miles

Miles Between Cities

1. How many miles are there from St. Louis to Los Angeles and back?

   _____

2. How many miles are there from St. Louis to Orlando and back?

   _____

3. How many miles are there from New York to Orlando and back?

   _____

4. How many miles are there from St. Louis to Seattle and back?

_____

5. How many miles is the trip from St. Louis to New York to Orlando and then St. Louis?

_____

6. How many miles is the trip from St. Louis to Los Angeles to Seattle and then St. Louis?

_____

7. If a family traveled about 500 miles a day, how many days would the trip in #6 take?

_____

BOB'S CAFE

Garden Salad	90 calories
French Fries	400 calories
Onion Rings	310 calories
Hamburger	400 calories
Cheeseburger	540 calories
Turkey Sandwich	276 calories
Taco	180 calories
Cheese Pizza (1 slice)	213 calories

Subtraction can be used for comparisons and finding the difference.

1. How many more calories does a cheeseburger have than a hamburger?

   _____

2. What is the difference in calories between french fries and onion rings?

   _____

3. How many more calories does a hamburger have than a garden salad?

   _____

BOB'S CAFE

4. What is the difference in calories between
   a turkey sandwich and a taco?

   _____

5. What two menu items have no difference
   in calories?

   _____ _____

6. What is the difference in calories of
   the 2 meal totals?

   _____

Meal 1: Hamburger   **Meal 2:** Garden Salad

       Onion Rings   Slice of Cheese Pizza

_____   _____

Subtraction is the inverse operation of addition. You can use subtraction to check your addition and addition to check your subtraction.

$$12 + \underline{\quad\quad} = 20 \qquad \begin{array}{r} 20 \\ - \ 12 \\ \hline \end{array}$$

Make each sentence true. Be sure to read the sentence when you are finished.

1 If $\underline{\ 19\ }$ + 14 = 33   then   33 − $\underline{\ 14\ }$ = $\underline{\ 19\ }$

2 If $\underline{\quad\quad}$ + 18 = 35   then   35 − 18 = $\underline{\quad\quad}$

3 If 29 + $\underline{\quad\quad}$ = 41   then   41 − 29 = $\underline{\quad\quad}$

4 If 32 = $\underline{\quad\quad}$ + 17   then $\underline{\quad\quad}$ − 17 = 15

5 If 15 + $\underline{\quad\quad}$ = 51   then   51 − $\underline{\quad\quad}$ = $\underline{\quad\quad}$

6 If 17 + $\underline{\quad\quad}$ = 69   then $\underline{\quad\quad}$ − 17 = 52

7 If 14 + $\underline{\quad\quad}$ = 83   then $\underline{\quad\quad}$ − $\underline{\quad\quad}$ = $\underline{\quad\quad}$

8 If $\underline{\quad\quad}$ + 35 = 76   then $\underline{\quad\quad}$ − $\underline{\quad\quad}$ = $\underline{\quad\quad}$

9 If Robbie has saved $21, how much more does he need to buy a $50 electronic game? $\underline{\quad\quad\quad\quad}$
Write a number sentence and solve.

$\underline{\quad\quad\quad\quad\quad\quad\quad\quad\quad\quad\quad\quad\quad\quad\quad\quad}$

10   If 11 – _____ = 6   then _____ + _____ = 11

11   If 21 – _____ = 11   then _____ + _____ = 21

12   If 39 – _____ = 17   then _____ + _____ = 39

13   If 23 – _____ = 14   then _____ + _____ = 23

14   If 42 – _____ = 23   then _____ + 23   = 42

15   If 100 – _____ = 25   then   75   + _____ = 100

16   If 28 – _____ = 16   then   16   + _____ = 28

17   If 50 – _____ = 25   then _____ + _____ = 50

18   If 72 – _____ = 43   then _____ + _____ = _____

19   If 63 – _____ = 45   then _____ + _____ = _____

20   John took $45 to the store. He left the store with only $10.
     How much money did John spend at the store. Write a
     number sentence and solve.

     _____

Subtracting more than one number in a series is done left to right.

$9 - 6 - 2 =$ _____

$3 - 2 = 1$

$9 - 6 - 2 =$ _____

$9 - 4 = \cancel{5}$

Series subtraction is done left to right. Subtract and write the letter that matches the answer to solve the riddle below.

a $30 - 10 - 9$ = _____   E

b $43 - 24 - 15$ = _____   T

c $142 - 59 - 44$ = _____   B

d $201 - 150 - 34$ = _____   N

e $94 - 68 - 14$ = _____   C

f $126 - 79 - 38$ = _____   L

g $240 - 96 - 97$ = _____   I

What did the zero say to the eight?

____ ____ ____ ____   ____ ____ ____ ____
17   47   12   11   39   11   9   4

Division **asks how many of one number are in another number.**

4 ÷ 2 means how many 2s are in 4.

Draw a line segment from each division problem to the matching description. Then write the quotient.

6 ÷ 3   How many twos in six? _____

8 ÷ 4   How many threes in nine? _____

6 ÷ 2   How many fours in twelve? _____

9 ÷ 3   How many threes in six? _____

10 ÷ 5   How many fours in eight? _____

12 ÷ 4   How many fives in ten? _____

14 ÷ 7   How many threes in fifteen? _____

15 ÷ 3   How many sevens in fourteen? _____

Division asks how many of one number is in another number.

6 ÷ 3 means how many 3s are in 6.

Draw a line segment to connect each
number sentence to the matching picture.

8 ÷ 4

9 ÷ 3

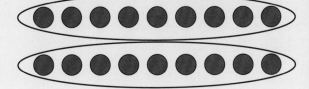

16 ÷ 4

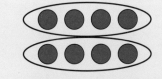

12 ÷ 6

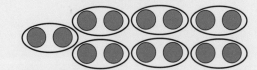

15 ÷ 5

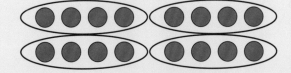

10 ÷ 2

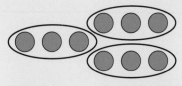

18 ÷ 9

21 ÷ 7

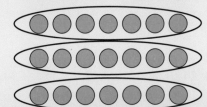

14 ÷ 2

$6 \div 3$ Means how many 3s are in 6. It can also be written like this → $3\overline{)6}$

Fill in the missing information.

$8 \div 2$ Means how many twos are in 8. It can also be written →

$15 \div 5$ Means how many fives are in 15. It can also be written →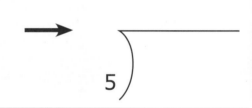

$12 \div 6$ Means how many ____ sixes are in ____ . It can also be written →

$16 \div 4$ Means how many ____ ____ are in ____ . It can also be written →

$18 \div 3$ Means how many ____ ____ are in ____ . It can also be written →

Complete each number sentence, then draw a line from each number sentence to a matching picture.

3 × 5 = _____

5)‾20‾

3 × 7 = _____

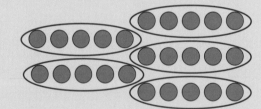

32 ÷ 8 = _____

5 × _____ = 25

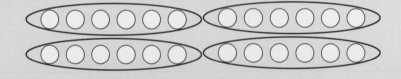

6)‾24‾

9)‾27‾

18 ÷ 6 = _____

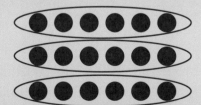

Fill in **Y** for yes and **N** for no as you solve the puzzle. Be sure to fill in all your no answers to help you solve the puzzle.

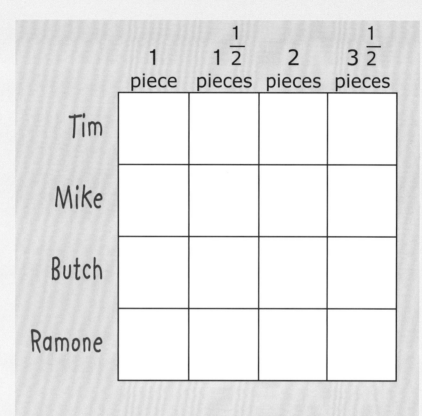

	1 piece	$1\frac{1}{2}$ pieces	2 pieces	$3\frac{1}{2}$ pieces
Tim				
Mike				
Butch				
Ramone				

Use the chart and the clues to find out how much of the candy bar each boy ate.

1. Tim had more than Butch, but less than Ramone and Mike.

2. Ramone had $\frac{1}{4}$ of the candy bar.

Division is the inverse operation of multiplication.

You can use division to prove your multiplication
or use multiplication to prove your division.

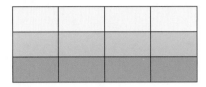

If **three** 4s equal **12**   then   **12** divided by 4 equals **3**.

Make each sentence true. Be sure to read
the sentence when you are finished.

1   If 10   × _____   = 50   then   10) 50

2   If _____ × 7   = 56   then   7) 56

3   If 4   × _____   = 36   then   4) 36

4   If _____ × 3   = 18   then   ____) 18

Complete the multiplication and division number sentences.

5   If 3 × ____ = 27   then   3) 27

6   If ____ × 6 = 24   then    4)

7   If 6 × ____ = 30   then   ) 30

8   If 9 × ____ = 54   then   )

9   Write a number sentence that would solve how many people have to give $5 each to collect $45.

_____

$12 \div 6 = 2$ so $2 \times 6 = 12$

Multiplication is the inverse operation of division.
A division problem can be rewritten as a multiplication sentence.

Complete each number sentence.

a $8 \div 2$ = _____   so $2 \times$ _____ $= 8$

b $15 \div$ _____ $= 3$ so   _____ $\times 3$ $= 15$

c $24 \div$ _____ $= 4$ so   _____ $\times 6$ $= 24$

d $32 \div 8$ = _____   so $8 \times$ _____ $= 32$

e   _____ $\div 3 = 7$ so 3×7 = _____

f $42 \div 7$ = _____   so $7 \times$ _____ $= 42$

g   Write a number sentence that would solve how
many groups of 3 people there are in 27 people?

_____

Complete each number sentence, then draw a line segment to connect each number sentence with an equivalent number sentence.

4 + 4 + 4 = _____

3 + 3 + 3 + 3 + 3 = _____

9 + 9 = _____

3 × 6 = _____

5 x 3 = _____

3 × 4 = _____

6 + 6 + 6 = _____

2 × 9 = _____

5 × 4 = _____

4 × 8 = _____

7 + 7 + 7 = _____

5 × 5 = _____

8 + 8 + 8 + 8 = _____

4 × 5 = _____

5 + 5 + 5 + 5 + 5 = _____

3 × 7 = _____

A line is straight and continues in both directions without ending. The black line is a line.

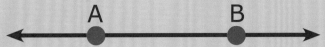

A point (denoted by capitol letter) is a location. Both A ● and B ● are points on the line.

A line segment is part of a line. It has two endpoints. There is a line segment between points A ● and B ●.   ───────────

Lines that never cross are called parallel lines. They stay an equal distance apart.

1. Draw two parallel lines.

2. Draw two points on one of the lines and label one point C and the other point D.

3. Circle the line segment.

4. Name the two end points of the line segment _____ _____.

Connect two red points to make a line segment parallel to the one given.

1

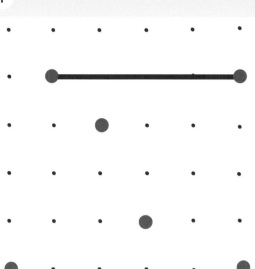

2

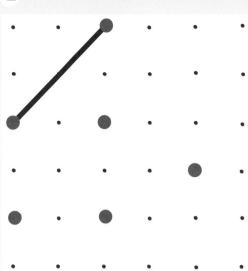

3

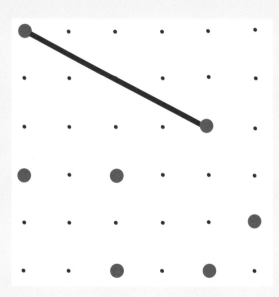

4 Draw at least 4 pairs of parallel line segments.

5 Circle each polygon with parallel lines segments.

   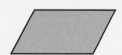

A ray is a part of a line. It has one endpoint and continues in one direction. In this example "A" is the endpoint of this ray.

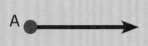

An angle is formed by two rays with the same endpoint.

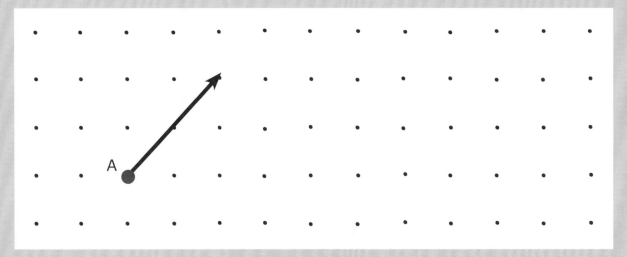

1. Complete the angle with endpoint A.

2. Draw a new endpoint B, then use the endpoint to draw an angle.

3. Draw an angle with an endpoint C.

4. Draw an angle with an endpoint D.

right angle

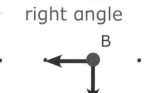

A right angle is a special angle that can be used to form a square.

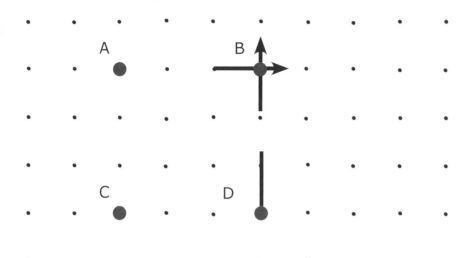

1. Connect points A, B, C, and D to form a square.

2. Circle each object with a right angle and put an X over each object without a right angle.

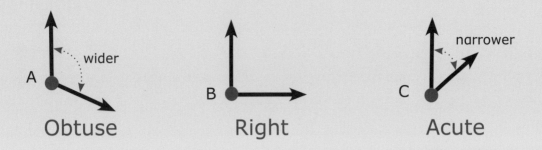

Obtuse   Right   Acute

Angle "A" is an obtuse angle. It is wider than a right angle. It **cannot** be used to form a square.

Angle "B" is a right angle. It **can** be used to form a square.

Angle "C" is an acute angle. It is narrower than a right angle. It **cannot** be used to form a square.

Write obtuse, right, or acute to describe each angle.

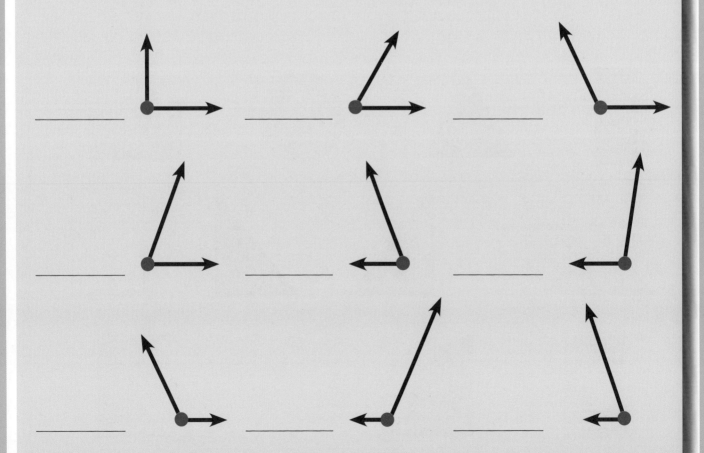

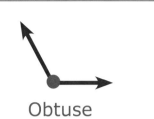 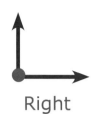 

Obtuse　　Right　　Acute

Draw each description.

An obtuse angle
with endpoint A

An acute angle
with endpoint B

A right angle
with endpoint C

Two obtuse angles with
the same endpoint D

Three acute angles with
the same endpoint E

Four right angles with
the same endpoint F

1. Draw a triangle with an obtuse angle and a triangle with three acute angles.

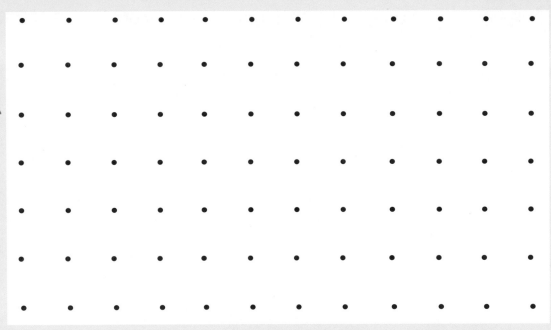

2. Draw a right angle and a triangle with a right angle.

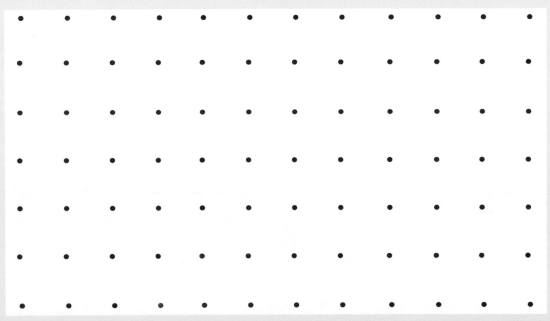

3. List at least 4 objects in the room you are in that contain a right angle.

_____   _____

_____   _____

The sides of this pentagon are made up of
5 line segments and the corners form 5 angles.
One of the angles is a right angle (use corner of
paper to tell). The other 4 angles are obtuse.

right angle

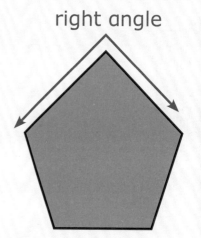

- **Hexagon**: A 6-sided polygon
- **Pentagon**: A 5-sided polygon
- **Square**: A rectangle with 4 equal sides
- **Right Triangle**: A triangle that has a right angle
- **Equilateral Triangle**: A triangle with 3 equal sides

Complete the description of each object in the chart below.

	Number of Sides	Number of Angles	Number of Right Angles	Name the polygons in problem 1 – 8.
1.	4	4	4	Rectangle
2.				
3.				
4.				
5.				Parallelogram
6.				
7.				Trapezoid
8.				

To estimate 3 × 28, round 28 to the nearest ten and multiply.

$$\begin{array}{r} 28 \\ \times\ \ 3 \\ \hline \end{array} \longrightarrow \begin{array}{r} 30 \\ \times\ \ 3 \\ \hline 90 \end{array}$$ is the **estimated product**

To estimate 2 × 183, round 183 to the nearest hundred and multiply.

$$\begin{array}{r} 183 \\ \times\ \ \ 2 \\ \hline \end{array} \longrightarrow \begin{array}{r} 200 \\ \times\ \ \ 2 \\ \hline 400 \end{array}$$ is the **estimated product**

Round the larger number to the nearest ten to estimate each product, then circle your answer below.

a
59	41	36	74	89	57
× 4	× 7	× 5	× 3	× 6	× 2

b
17	37	32	29	84
× 8	× 9	× 5	× 6	× 4

Round the larger number to the nearest 100 to estimate each product.

c
826	469	137	253	692
× 7	× 8	× 9	× 2	× 3

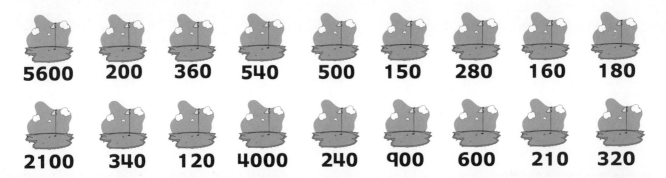

5600   200   360   540   500   150   280   160   180

2100   340   120   4000   240   900   600   210   320

Fill in **Y** for yes and **N** for no as you solve the puzzle. Be sure to fill in all your no answers to help you solve the puzzle.

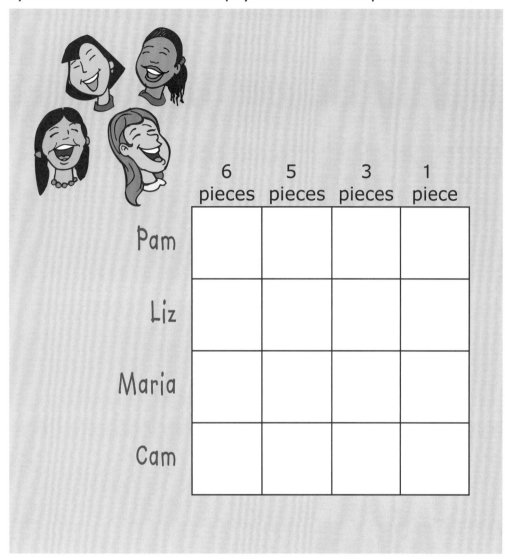

	6 pieces	5 pieces	3 pieces	1 piece
Pam				
Liz				
Maria				
Cam				

Pam, Liz, Maria, and Cam split a square of chocolate into 15 congruent pieces. Use the chart and clues to find out how many pieces each girl ate.

1. Liz had one third of all the pieces.

2. Maria ate less than Liz, but more than Cam.

The Muffin Shop sells muffins in containers of 4. How many containers would they need to sell 24 muffins?

Think   24 ÷ 4 = [____]   or   →

Use a related multiplication fact to check your answer.

4 × [____] = 24

The Muffin Shop

Find the missing factor or quotient.

1

20 ÷ 4 = [____]   How many   4 × [____] = 20
                        4s in 20?

2

21 ÷ 7 = [____]   How many   7 × [____] = 21
                      _____ in 21?

3

32 ÷ 8 = [____]   How many 8s   8 × [____] = 32
                      in _____?

4

45 ÷ 9 = [____]   How many   9 × [____] = 45
                    _____ in _____?

5

18 ÷ 6 = [____]   How many   6 × [____] = 18
                    _____ in _____?

6

$72 \div 8 = $ ☐

How many _____ in _____?

$8 \times$ ☐ $= 72$

7

$3 \div 1 = $ ☐

How many _____ in _____?

$1 \times$ ☐ $= 3$

8

$40 \div 5 = $ ☐

How many _____ in _____?

$5 \times$ ☐ $= 40$

q

$27 \div 3 = $ ☐

How many _____ in _____?

$3 \times$ ☐ $= 27$

Write a division sentence for each.

10

$=$ $\overline{}$

11

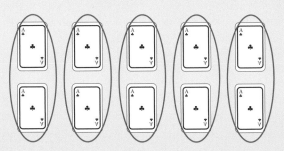

$=$ _____ $\div$ _____

12

$=$ $\overline{}$

x	0	1	2	3	4	5	6	7	8	9
0	0	0	0	0	0	0	0	0	0	0
1	0	1	2	3	4	5	6	7	8	9
2	0	2	4	6	8	10	12	14	16	18
3	0	3	6	9	12	15	18	21	24	27
4	0	4	8	12	16	20	24	28	32	36
5	0	5	10	15	20	25	30	35	40	45
6	0	6	12	18	24	30	36	42	48	54
7	0	7	14	21	28	35	42	49	56	63
→ 8	0	8	16	24	32	40	48	56	64	72
9	0	9	18	27	36	45	54	63	72	81

Use the multiplication chart to find each quotient.

a

$$8\overline{)24}^{\;3} \qquad 16 \div 2 = \qquad 35 \div 7 = \qquad 6\overline{)42} \qquad 4 \div 4 =$$

b

$$3\overline{)12} \qquad 6\overline{)24} \qquad 16 \div 4 = \qquad 9\overline{)54} \qquad 20 \div 5 =$$

c

$$7\overline{)7} \qquad 2\overline{)18} \qquad 5\overline{)35} \qquad 4\overline{)20} \qquad 54 \div 9 =$$

d

$$8\overline{)32} \qquad 5\overline{)5} \qquad 1\overline{)6} \qquad 9\overline{)72} \qquad 49 \div 7 =$$

e

$$9\overline{)36} \qquad 8\overline{)72} \qquad 6\overline{)42} \qquad 4\overline{)8}$$

Write a number sentence to solve each problem, then draw a line to the matching drawing.

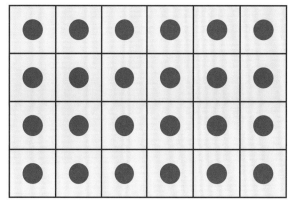

1. Maria has a photo album that holds 6 pictures per page. If she has 24 pictures to put in her album, how many pages will she need?

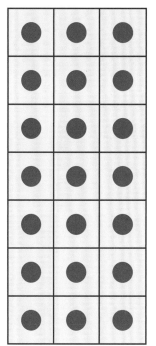

2. Tom shared 21 cookies with his two friends. He divided the cookies up so that all three of them had the same number of cookies. Write a number sentence to show how many each boy received.

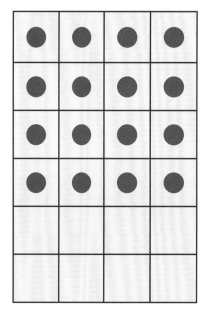

The distance around a figure is called its perimeter. Unit squares have a length of 1 unit on each side of the square. When the figure is made up of unit squares, count around the outside of the figure to find the perimeter.

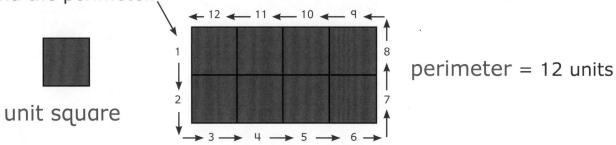

unit square

perimeter = 12 units

1.   Write the perimeter of each figure.

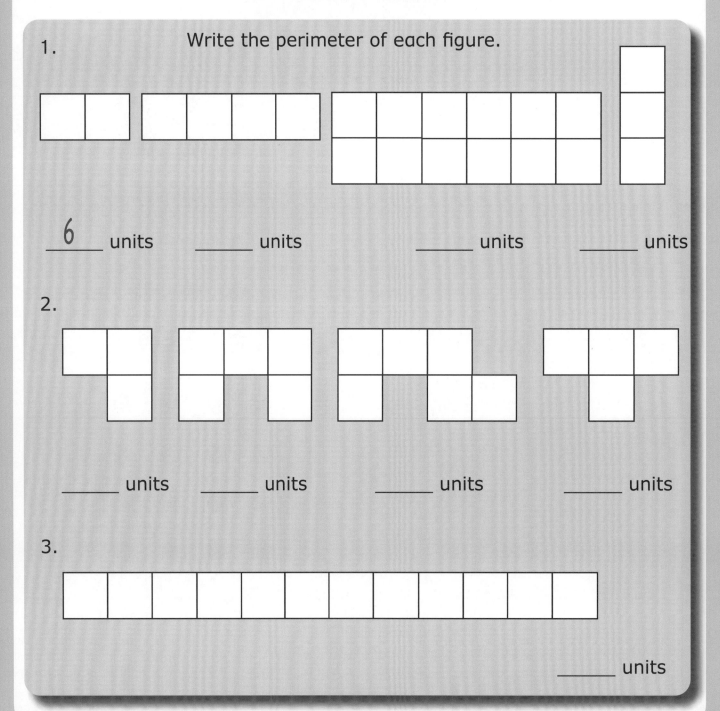

____6____ units   _____ units   _____ units   _____ units

2.

_____ units   _____ units   _____ units   _____ units

3.

_____ units

1. Draw a square with a perimeter of 12 units.

2. Draw a square with a perimeter of 4 units.

3. Draw a square with a perimeter of 8 units.

4. Draw a square with a perimeter of 4 units inside a rectangle of 18 units. The two figures should not have any common sides.

Perimeter is the distance around a figure. Measure the sides of the polygon to the nearest centimeter (cm) and find the perimeter.

perimeter = 2 + 3 + 2 + 3 = 10 cm

Find each perimeter. Measure to the nearest centimeter.

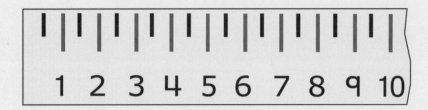

1.

_____ cm

2.

_____ cm

4.

_____ cm

3.

_____ cm

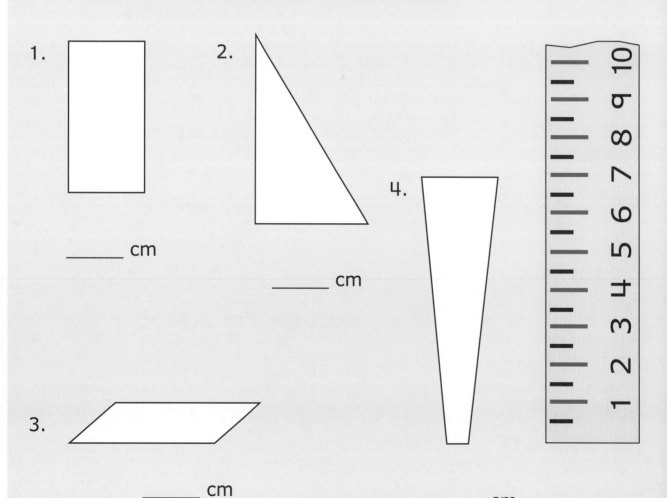

1. Draw a rectangle with two 4 cm sides and two 2 cm sides.

   perimeter = _____ centimeters

   centimeter dots

2. Draw a square with 3 cm sides. Find the perimeter.

   perimeter = _____ centimeters

   centimeter dots

3. Draw a rectangle with a perimeter of 10 centimeters.

   centimeter dots

Area is the number of square units needed to cover a flat surface.

When the figure is made from square units, count the number of squares to find the area.

Area is always in terms of square units.

unit square

| 1 | 2 | 3 | 4 |
| 5 | 6 | 7 | 8 |

Area = 8 square units

1. Find the area of each figure.

_____
square units

_____
square units

_____
square units

2.

_____
square units

_____
square units

_____
square units

_____
square units

Find the area of each figure.

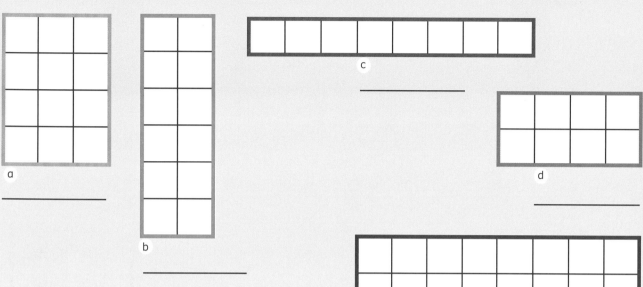

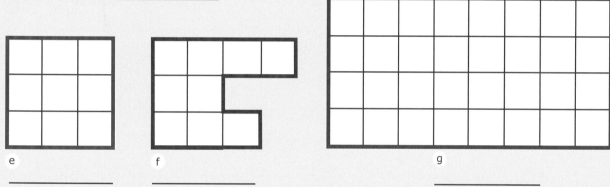

Find the area and perimeter of each figure on the centimeter grid.

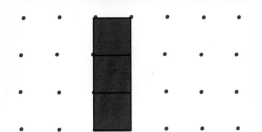

Perimeter = ___ centimeters

Area = ___ square centimeters

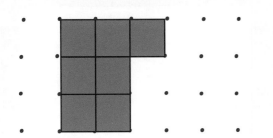

Perimeter = ___ centimeters

Area = ___ square centimeters

Perimeter = ___ centimeters

Area = ___ square centimeters

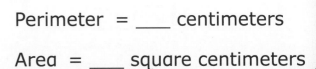

Perimeter = ___ centimeters

Area = ___ square centimeters

Draw this figure.

Perimeter = _8_ centimeters

Area = _4_ square centimeters

Draw this figure.

Perimeter = _10_ centimeters

Area = _6_ square centimeters

Can you figure a way of finding the area of a rectangle without counting each unit square?

_____

Make a congruent copy of each design.

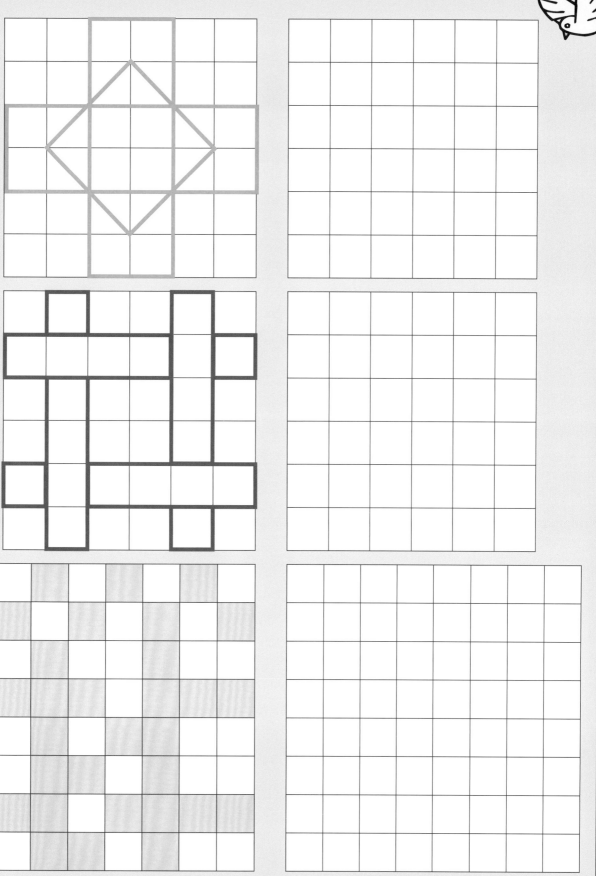

An ounce (oz) and a pound (lb) are customary units for measuring weight.

1 ounce is about the weight of a serving of dry cereal.

1 pound is about the weight of a loaf of bread.

16 ounces = 1 pound

Complete the following sentences by putting in the units. Write ounce(s) or pound(s) in the blank.

1. A pair of dress shoes weighs about 1 _____.

2. A slice of bread weighs about 1 _____.

3. A baby weighs about 8 _____.

4. An adult woman weighs about 130 _____.

5. A hamburger weighs about 5 _____.

6. A car weighs about 4,000 _____.

7. A bag of potatoes weighs about 5 _____.

8. 20 pennies weigh about 2 _____.

9. A slice of cheese weighs about 1 _____.

10. A math textbook weighs about 4 _____.

The gram (g) and the kilogram (kg) are metric units for measuring weight.

1 gram is about the weight of a paper clip.

1 kilogram is about the weight of a large book.

1,000 grams = 1 kilogram

Complete the following sentences by putting in the units. Write gram(s) or kilogram(s) in the blank.

1. A strawberry weighs about 2 _____.

2. A pair of dress shoes weighs about 1 _____.

3. A nickel weighs about 5 _____.

4. An adult man weighs about 82 _____.

5. A bike weighs about 8 _____.

6. A car weighs about 1,800 _____.

7. A cell phone weighs about 100 _____.

8. A cat weighs about 2 _____.

9. A candy bar weighs about 45 _____.

10. A textbook weighs about $1\frac{1}{2}$ _____.

11. A baby weighs about 3 _____.

12. An aspirin weighs about $\frac{1}{2}$ _____.

Magic Trick 1,089!

Try this.

1. Pick 3 different digits from 1, 2, 3, 4, 5, 6, 7, 8, or 9.

   8, 1, 5

2. Arrange them to make the largest possible number.

   851

3. Arrange them to make the smallest possible number.

   158

```
    851
  - 158
  -----
    693
  + 396
  -----
  1,089
```

4. Subtract the smallest number from the largest number.

5. Reverse the digits in the difference and add.

6. The sum is always 1,089. Try it with someone.

 1 2 3 4 5 6 7 8 9

Pick 3 different digits from above.   ___, ___, ___

Make the largest possible number.   __ __ __

Make the smallest possible number.   - __ __ __

Subtract.   __ __ __

Add the reversed digits.   + __ __ __

___ ___ ___

Find all the possible numbers made using 2 and 3. Place them in order smallest to largest (left to right).

23, 32

Find all the possible numbers made using 2, 7, and 4. Place them in order smallest to largest (left to right).

247, 274, 427, 472, 724, 742

1. Find all the possible numbers made using 1 and 8. Place them in order from smallest to largest (left to right).

    _____, _____

2. Find all the possible numbers made using 3 and 6. Place them in order from smallest to largest (left to right).

    _____, _____

3. Find all the possible numbers made using 9, 1, and 5. Place them in order from smallest to largest (left to right).

    _____, _____, _____, _____, _____, _____

4. Find all the possible numbers made using 8, 3, and 4. Place them in order from smallest to largest (left to right).

    _____, _____, _____, _____, _____, _____

5. Find all the possible numbers made using 2, 1, and 1. Place them in order from smallest to largest (left to right).

    _____, _____, _____

Time Trial #1
Time how long it will take you to complete this page.

Start time _____ _____ _____   Finish time _____ _____ _____
             hour minutes seconds   hour minutes seconds

a
    4   7   8   1   2   6   5
  × 3   × 2   × 4   × 7   × 9   × 6   × 2

b
    1   8   3   9   8   6   4
  × 4   × 8   × 8   × 3   × 5   × 3   × 6

c
    5   8   3   5   7   9   5
  × 7   × 2   × 5   × 4   × 7   × 9   × 0

d
    3   6   8   9   7   1   6
  × 3   × 4   × 6   × 6   × 8   × 3   × 3

e
    5   4   9   9   0   1   8
  × 5   × 4   × 7   × 4   × 2   × 3   × 8

f
    6   5   7   7   5   7   9
  × 2   × 4   × 2   × 8   × 9   × 6   × 6

Your time _____ _____
           minutes seconds

Time Trial #2

Time how long it will take you to complete this page.

Start time _____ _____ _____   Finish time _____ _____ _____
hour   minutes   seconds   hour   minutes   seconds

a

$$5 \times 1 \qquad 8 \times 2 \qquad 6 \times 3 \qquad 4 \times 7 \qquad 6 \times 6 \qquad 3 \times 8 \qquad 4 \times 3$$

b

$$5 \times 5 \qquad 6 \times 9 \qquad 7 \times 8 \qquad 1 \times 2 \qquad 6 \times 4 \qquad 8 \times 4 \qquad 2 \times 6$$

c

$$7 \times 7 \qquad 8 \times 8 \qquad 3 \times 3 \qquad 5 \times 2 \qquad 6 \times 7 \qquad 5 \times 9 \qquad 4 \times 0$$

d

$$2 \times 2 \qquad 4 \times 4 \qquad 5 \times 7 \qquad 7 \times 4 \qquad 6 \times 5 \qquad 1 \times 9 \qquad 5 \times 5$$

e

$$7 \times 9 \qquad 4 \times 0 \qquad 5 \times 1 \qquad 8 \times 8 \qquad 9 \times 8 \qquad 6 \times 2 \qquad 4 \times 8$$

f

$$1 \times 1 \qquad 2 \times 4 \qquad 6 \times 8 \qquad 7 \times 6 \qquad 2 \times 9 \qquad 7 \times 6 \qquad 3 \times 8$$

Your time _____ _____
minutes   seconds

Information collected is called data.
A survey is the data recorded after asking a question.

Favorite Color	
Color	**Number**
blue	13
green	5
orange	7
red	7
yellow	3

A 3rd grade class was asked, "What is your favorite color?" The results are listed in the table.

1. What is the title of the table?

   _____

2. How many students answered the survey?

   _____

3. List the colors in order from fewest to most votes.

   _____ _____ _____ _____ _____

4. How many more students chose blue than chose red?

   _____

What is the total price
of three chairs?

An easy way to find the
total price is to multiply.

3 × $21

First multiply the ones.

3 × 1 = 3

Next, multiply the tens.

3 × 20 = 60

Finally add.

3 + 60

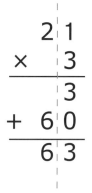

```
    2 1
  ×   3
 ─────
    3
 + 6 0
 ─────
  6 3
```

Fish
$12 each

$ 12
×   4
─────
+

How much are all four fish?
1. Multiply the ones.
2. Multiply the tens.
3. Add.

$
×   5
─────
+

Cats
$17 each

How much are all
five cats?

Find the product, then circle your answer below.

1
$$
\begin{array}{r}
53 \\
\times\ 7 \\
\hline
\\
+ \\
\hline
\end{array}
$$

2
$$
\begin{array}{r}
45 \\
\times\ 5 \\
\hline
\\
+ \\
\hline
\end{array}
$$

3
$$
\begin{array}{r}
92 \\
\times\ 4 \\
\hline
\\
+ \\
\hline
\end{array}
$$

4
$$
\begin{array}{r}
56 \\
\times\ 8 \\
\hline
\\
+ \\
\hline
\end{array}
$$

5
$$
\begin{array}{r}
45 \\
\times\ 3 \\
\hline
\\
+ \\
\hline
\end{array}
$$

6
$$
\begin{array}{r}
83 \\
\times\ 2 \\
\hline
\\
+ \\
\hline
\end{array}
$$

225   448   135   371   221   298   166   368

7   83
      ×   9
    _____

    +
    _____

8   56
      ×   5
    _____

9   37
      ×   7
    _____

10   71
      ×   4
    _____

11   97
      ×   8
    _____

12   38
      ×   6
    _____

280   727   380   776   228   747   284   259

Make a table grouping the figures below by number of sides.
Title and complete the table.

Polygon	**Number of this Shape**	**Number of Sides**	**Number of Angles**
triangle			
quadrilateral			4
pentagon			5
hexagon			

A tally table uses tally marks to record data. After placing four marks, a diagonal mark shows a group of five.

Below is a tally table of class members surveyed. They were asked "What is your favorite ice cream flavor?"

Favorite Ice Cream

Flavor	Number
chocolate	||||
chocolate chip	|||
strawberry	⫫
vanilla	⫫ ||

1. What is the title of the tally table? _____

2. How many students chose strawberry ice cream? _____

3. How many students chose vanilla ice cream? _____

4. How many students were asked? Write a number sentence and solve.

   _____

5. How many more students chose vanilla than chocolate. Write a number sentence and solve.

   _____

Ray has eight cards. Three are black and five are red. He shuffles the cards and turns them over.

1. A card is selected from the eight cards, what is the most likely

   color? _____

2. A card is selected from the eight cards, what is the least likely

   color? _____

3. You have a **3** out of **8** chance of choosing a _____ card.

   You have a **5** out of **8** chance of choosing a _____ card.

A die has six sides with 1, 2, 3, 4, 5, or 6 dots on a side.

4. If a die is tossed, what is the chance the number one will be selected? _____

5. If a die is tossed, what is the chance the number six will be selected? _____

6. If a die is tossed, what is the chance either 1, 2, 3, 4, or 5 will be selected? _____

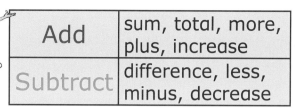

Ben is seven years old.

Jennifer is eight years old.

Add	sum, total, more, plus, increase
Subtract	difference, less, minus, decrease

Circle the keyword to help you decide to add or subtract, then write a number sentence and solve.

1.   Find the sum of Ben and Jennifer's age.

_____

2.   Decrease Jennifer's age three years.

_____

3.   What is the total of their ages?

_____

4.   Find the difference of their ages in years.

_____

5.   What is the difference between an 11-year-old's age and Jennifer's?

_____

6.   How much less is Ben's age from his 16-year-old brother's age?

_____

7.   What is twenty-one minus Jennifer's age?

_____

8.   What would Ben's age have to decrease by for him to be one year old?

_____

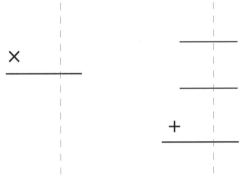		
cap $17	baseball $8	bat $15

Complete an addition and multiplication problem for each cost.

1 Three bats

$$
\begin{array}{r}
\$\ 15 \\
\times\ \ 3 \\
\hline
15 \\
+\ 30 \\
\hline
\$\ 45
\end{array}
$$

$$
\begin{array}{r}
\$\ 15 \\
15 \\
+\ 15 \\
\hline
\$\ 45
\end{array}
$$

2 Three basells

× _____

+ _____

3 Three caps

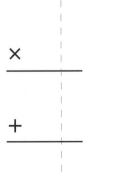

× _____

+ _____

4 Five bats

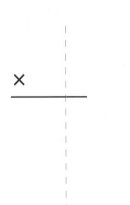

× _____

+ _____

5   Six bats

6   Six caps

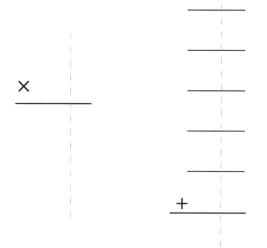

7   Six baseballs

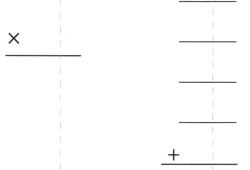

8   Eight baseballs

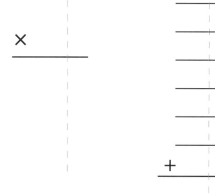

9   Nine caps

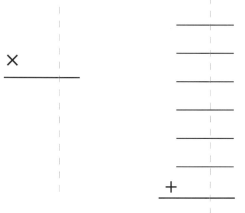

10   Nine bats

Find the number of people in each group and
write a division equation for the problem.

1. How many groups of 5 each can be formed from 30 people?

    $\underline{30} \div \underline{5} = \underline{6}$ groups

2. How many groups of 4 each can be formed from 24 people?

    $\underline{} \div \underline{} = \underline{}$

3. How many groups of 9 each can be formed from 72 people?

    $\underline{} \div \underline{} = \underline{}$

4. How many groups of 6 each can be formed from 36 people?

    $\underline{} \div \underline{} = \underline{}$

Write a division equation for each problem.

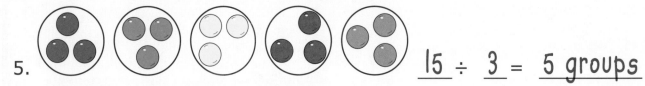

5. $\underline{15} \div \underline{3} = \underline{5}$ groups

6. $\underline{} \div \underline{} = \underline{}$ groups

7. $\underline{} \div \underline{} = \underline{}$ groups

Find the sums. Regroup when needed. Then write the letter that matches each answer to solve the riddle below.

e	t	c	y	i	r	l
56	15	83	64	49	34	67
29	23	74	89	50	92	92
+ 83	+ 46	+ 92	+ 76	+ 35	+ 46	+89

What kind of city has no people?

‾‾‾‾ ‾‾‾‾ ‾‾‾‾ ‾‾‾‾ ‾‾‾ ‾‾‾ ‾‾‾ ‾‾‾ ‾‾‾ ‾‾ ‾‾‾
168 248 168 249 84 172 134 249 134 84 229

Find the differences. Regroup when needed. Then write the letter that matches each answer to solve the riddle below.

t	e	d	y	a	r	s
822	713	565	904	529	832	400
− 470	− 139	− 317	− 618	− 413	− 496	− 124

What is something everyone has seen but will never see again?

‾‾‾‾ ‾‾‾‾ ‾‾‾‾ ‾‾‾‾ ‾‾‾‾ ‾‾‾ ‾‾‾ ‾‾‾ ‾‾‾
286 574 276 352 574 336 248 116 286

👽 = 5	⚡ = 6	👄 = 3	✈ = 9	🎧 = 8
🎵 = 2	💰 = 7	🍎 = 1	♣ = 0	

Draw a line segment to connect the matching number sentences.

👽 + 👽 + 👽 = _15_	$6 \times 3 =$ _____

⚡ + ⚡ + ⚡ + ⚡ + ⚡ = _____	$8 \times 8 =$ _____

👄 + 👄 + 👄 + 👄 + 👄 + 👄 = _____	$9 \times 4 =$ _____

✈ + ✈ + ✈ + ✈ = _____	$7 \times 5 =$ _____

🎧 + 🎧 + 🎧 + 🎧 + 🎧 + 🎧 + 🎧 + 🎧 = _____	$3 \times 5 =$ _____

🎵 + 🎵 + 🎵 + 🎵 + 🎵 + 🎵 = _____	$2 \times 6 =$ _____

💰 + 💰 + 💰 + 💰 + 💰 = _____	$4 \times 0 =$ _____

🍎 + 🍎 + 🍎 + 🍎 + 🍎 + 🍎 = _____	$6 \times 1 =$ _____

♣ + ♣ + ♣ + ♣ = _____	$5 \times 6 =$ _____

Marge's Chart

Marge works at the football stadium. Each admission ticket costs $6.

Complete her chart.

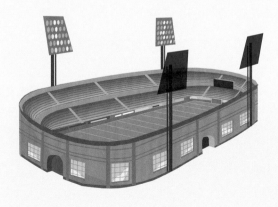

Number of Tickets	Ticket Cost
1	$6
2	$12
3	$18
4	
5	
6	
7	
8	
9	
10	
11	$66
12	
13	
14	
15	
16	
17	$102
18	
19	
20	
21	
22	
23	
24	$144
25	
26	
27	
28	
29	
30	

Add	total or sum
Subtract	take away or comparison
Multiplication	join equal groups
Division	separate into equal groups

David saw 5 deer, 3 ducks, and 6 squirrels in the woods on Monday. He collected 12 wildflowers and 16 pine cones as he walked in the woods.

Write a number sentence and solve.

1. How many more deer than ducks did he see?

    5 – 3 = 2 more deer than ducks

2. How many animals did he see in the woods?

    _____

3. The squirrels he saw were equally divided among 2 trees. How many squirrels were in each tree?

    _____

4. David went into the woods four days in a row. Each day he saw 5 deer. How many deer did he see in all?

    _____

5. Together, how many wildflowers and pine cones did David collect?

    _____

6. How many more pine cones than wildflowers did David collect?

    _____

7. David put the same number of wildflowers in each of 3 vases. How many wildflowers were in each vase?

    _____

Write a number sentence and solve.

1. Carol baked 4 batches of cookies. She had a total of 24 cookies. How many cookies were in each batch?

   $24 \div 4 = 6$ cookies in each batch

2. Madison had 40 pictures from a trip. Her photo album holds 8 pictures on a page. How many pages will her pictures fill?

   _____

3. Katy collects pencils. She has boxes that hold 8 pencils each. How many pencils does she have in 6 boxes?

   _____

4. Stan has 7 sheets of stickers. Each sheet has 8 stickers on it. How many stickers does Stan have?

   _____

5. Kim buys 4 pizzas each costing $8. How much does she spend?

   _____

6. Create a word problem for multiplication.

   _____

   _____

7. Create a word problem for division.

   _____

   _____

A line graph is a graph that uses a line to show how something changes over time.

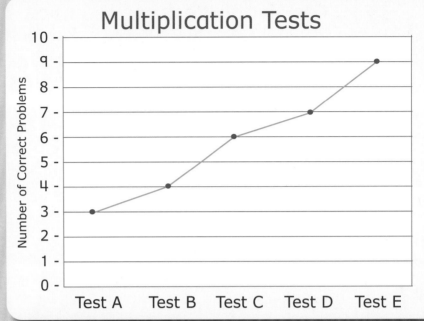

Nathan made a line graph to show his progress on a multiplication test he was given five times.

1. On which test did Nathan get the most problems correct?

    _____

2. On which test did Nathan get the least problems correct?

    _____

3. List the number of problems Nathan got correct in each of the five tests in order from least to greatest (left to right).

    _____   _____   _____   _____   _____

4. What is the difference in the number of questions he got correct from Test A to Test E?

    _____

5. What was the total number of problems Nathan answered correctly after completing 5 tests?

    _____

Everyone in the 3rd grade class was asked how they got to school. The tally table shows the results.

HOW THE 3rd GRADERS GOT TO SCHOOL

🚲	Bike	‖‖‖ ‖ ‖
🚌	Bus	‖‖‖ ‖‖‖ ‖‖‖ ‖‖‖ ‖‖‖ ‖‖‖
🚗	Car	‖‖‖ ‖ ‖ ‖
🚶	Walk	‖ ‖ ‖ ‖

1. How many children rode their bike to school? _____

2. How many children rode the bus to school? _____

3. How many children answered the survey? _____

4. How many more rode the bus than walked? _____

When twenty 4th graders answered the question how they got to school, they said

bike, bus, walk, bus, bus, walk, bus, car, bus, bus, bike, bike, walk, walk, bus, car, walk, bike, bus, bus

Finish the tally table for the 4th grade.

HOW THE 4th GRADERS GOT TO SCHOOL

🚲	Bike	
🚌	Bus	
🚗	Car	
🚶	Walk	

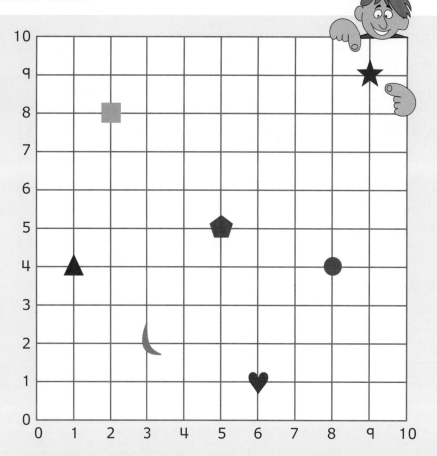

Points on a grid are located by ordered pairs within parentheses. The first number tells how many spaces to move to the right. The second number tells how many spaces to move up. Answer the questions below.

1. Which shape is found at (6,1)?   _heart_

2. Which shape is found at (2,8)?   _____

3. Which shape is found at (8,4)?   _____

4. Which shape is found at (3,2)?   _____

5. What is the ordered pair for the star?   _____

6. What is the ordered pair for the triangle?   _____

7. What is the ordered pair for the pentagon?   _____

A translation (slide) moves the entire figure in some direction.

Slide the red square three units to the right and color it blue. Then slide the red square two units down and color it green.

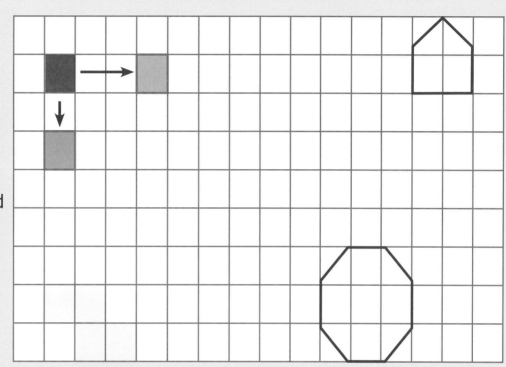

1. Slide the yellow figure five units to the right and color it red.

2. Slide the yellow figure three units up and color it blue.

3. Slide the yellow figure six units to the right and then 4 units up and color it green.

4. Slide the pentagon three units to the left and two units down and shade it in.

5. Slide the octagon three units to the right and shade it in.

A reflection (flip) moves the entire figure over the dotted line, and creates a mirror image.

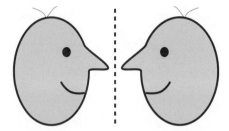

Reflect (flip) each shape over the dotted line, color it, then write its letter from the list below.

a Equilateral Triangle   c Pentagon

b Parallelogram   d Right Triangle

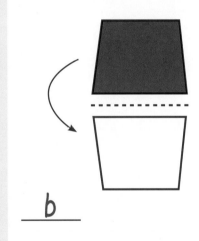

b

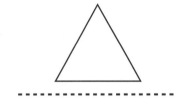

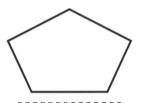

Find the sum. Regroup when needed. Then write the letter that matches each answer to solve the riddle below.

e	82	w	34	r	42	c	214	a	389
	56		50		73		523		216
	+ 11		+ 126		+16		+ 105		+ 324

u	53	s	52	o	829	b	142	p	403
	42		91		103		23		296
	+ 23		+ 68		+ 204		+ 6		+147

i	318	g	426	l	58	t	153	h	82
	24		107		23		298		546
	+ 123		+ 300		+ 14		+ 123		+ 29

How does a cow add?

___ ___ ___ ___   ___
210 465 574 657   929

___ ___ ___ ___ ___ ___ ___ ___ ___ ___
842 1,136 210 842 118 95 929 574 1,136 131

Find the difference, then cross out the answer below. Remember to regroup when necessary.

a
83
− 12

b
281
− 146

c
529
− 143

d
256
−140

e
285
−149

f
100
− 22

g
505
− 203

h
200
− 1

i
305
− 129

j
934
− 727

k
429
− 281

l
210
− 198

m
430
− 219

n
503
− 104

o
725
− 104

p
623
− 128

q
521
− 419

r
400
− 310

s
217
− 136

t
420
− 129

u
349
− 126

v
527
− 298

w
777
− 666

x
929
− 289

399	71	90	12	386
116	102	176	291	199
148	111	91	78	621
495	136	223	640	207
302	229	211	135	81

Complete the multiplication chart.

72

×	0	1	2	3	4	5	6	7	8	9
0	0	0	0	0	0	0	0	0	0	0
1	0	1	2	3	4	5	6	7	8	9
2	0	2	4	6	8		12	14	16	18
3	0	3	6	9	12	15	18	21	24	
4	0	4	8		16	20	24		32	36
5	0	5	10	15		25	30	35		45
6	0	6		18	24	30			48	54
7	0	7	14		28	35	42	49	56	
8	0	8	16	24		40	48		64	72
9	0	9		27	36		54	63	72	

Find the product.

a

$$\begin{array}{r} 8 \\ \times\, 2 \\ \hline \end{array} \qquad \begin{array}{r} 3 \\ \times 7 \\ \hline \end{array} \qquad \begin{array}{r} 6 \\ \times\, 4 \\ \hline \end{array} \qquad \begin{array}{r} 9 \\ \times\, 5 \\ \hline \end{array} \qquad \begin{array}{r} 3 \\ \times\, 2 \\ \hline \end{array} \qquad \begin{array}{r} 9 \\ \times\, 1 \\ \hline \end{array}$$

b

$$\begin{array}{r} 5 \\ \times\, 8 \\ \hline \end{array} \qquad \begin{array}{r} 7 \\ \times\, 7 \\ \hline \end{array} \qquad \begin{array}{r} 5 \\ \times\, 6 \\ \hline \end{array} \qquad \begin{array}{r} 3 \\ \times\, 4 \\ \hline \end{array} \qquad \begin{array}{r} 9 \\ \times\, 2 \\ \hline \end{array} \qquad \begin{array}{r} 8 \\ \times\, 3 \\ \hline \end{array}$$

c

$$\begin{array}{r} 42 \\ \times\, 3 \\ \hline \end{array} \qquad \begin{array}{r} 56 \\ \times\, 4 \\ \hline \end{array} \qquad \begin{array}{r} 63 \\ \times\, 5 \\ \hline \end{array} \qquad \begin{array}{r} 49 \\ \times\, 7 \\ \hline \end{array} \qquad \begin{array}{r} 83 \\ \times\, 9 \\ \hline \end{array} \qquad \begin{array}{r} 43 \\ \times\, 8 \\ \hline \end{array}$$

d

$$\begin{array}{r} 216 \\ \times\, 5 \\ \hline \end{array} \qquad \begin{array}{r} 429 \\ \times\, 8 \\ \hline \end{array} \qquad \begin{array}{r} 725 \\ \times\, 6 \\ \hline \end{array} \qquad \begin{array}{r} 807 \\ \times\, 7 \\ \hline \end{array} \qquad \begin{array}{r} 901 \\ \times\, 4 \\ \hline \end{array} \qquad \begin{array}{r} 623 \\ \times\, 9 \\ \hline \end{array}$$

The fact family
for 2, 4, and 8 is

$$2 \times 4 = 8$$
$$4 \times 2 = 8$$
$$8 \div 2 = 4$$
$$8 \div 4 = 2$$

A fact family is a set of
related multiplication and
division number sentences.

1. Write the fact family for 4, 6, and 24.

    ____ × ____ = ____   ____ ÷ ____ = ____

    ____ × ____ = ____   ____ ÷ ____ = ____

2. Write the fact family for 3, 6, and 18.

    ____ × ____ = ____   ____ ÷ ____ = ____

    ____ × ____ = ____   ____ ÷ ____ = ____

3. Write the fact family for 5, 8, and 40.

    ____ × ____ = ____   ____ ÷ ____ = ____

    ____ × ____ = ____   ____ ÷ ____ = ____

4. Write the other three sentences in the fact family.

    __9__ × __2__ = __18__   ____ ÷ ____ = ____

    ____ × ____ = ____   ____ ÷ ____ = ____

The **Least Common Multiple (LCM)** of two numbers is the smallest whole number, other than 1, that both numbers divide evenly into.

The least common multiple for **3** and **4** is **12**. Look at all the multiples of each number until you find one in common.

X	0	1	2	3	4	5	6	7	8	9
0	0	0	0	0	0	0	0	0	0	0
1	0	1	2	3	4	5	6	7	8	9
2	0	2	4	6	8	10	12	14	16	18
3	0	3	6	9	12	15	18	21	24	27
4	0	4	8	12	16	20	24	28	32	36
5	0	5	10	15	20	25	30	35	40	45
6	0	6	12	18	24	30	36	42	48	54
7	0	7	14	21	28	35	42	49	56	63
8	0	8	16	24	32	40	48	56	64	72
9	0	9	18	27	36	45	54	63	72	81

Find the least common multiple for each group.

a   2 and 3   _____   b   3 and 5   _____

c   4 and 5   _____   d   4 and 8   _____

e   3 and 9   _____   f   3 and 6   _____

g   5 and 8   _____   h   8 and 9   _____

i   4 and 6   _____   j   4 and 10   _____

k   6 and 9   _____   l   2, 3, and 4   _____

Congruent

Two figures are congruent if they have the same size and shape.

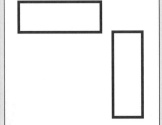

Right Angle

Angle "A" is a right angle. It **can** be used to form a square.

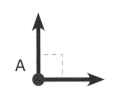

Acute Angle

Angle "B" is an acute angle. It is narrower than a right angle. It **cannot** be used to form a square.

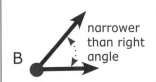

Obtuse Angle

Angle "C" is an obtuse angle. It is wider than a right angle. It **cannot** be used to form a square.

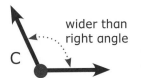

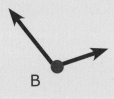

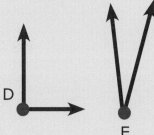
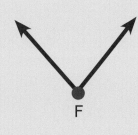

Name the right angles.   _____   _____

Name the acute angles.   _____   _____   _____

Name the obtuse angle.   _____

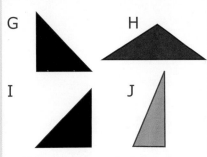

What two triangles are congruent?

_____ _____

How many congruent sides in this square?

_____

A Right Triangle has a right angle.

A Scalene Triangle has no congruent sides.

An Equilateral Triangle has 3 congruent sides.

An Isosceles Triangle has 2 congruent sides.

Connect each description with the matching set of lines and triangle.

Scalene Triangle

has 2 congruent sides

Isosceles Triangle

has 3 congruent sides

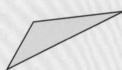

Equilateral Triangle

has no congruent sides

Right Scalene Triangle

has a right angle with no congruent sides

Right Isosceles Triangle

has a right angle with 2 congruent sides

Polygons are closed figures made up of line segments.
Quadrilaterals are polygons with 4 sides.

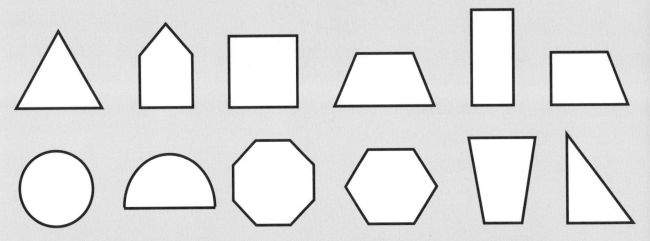

1. Shade all the polygons, then circle all the quadrilaterals.

2. Draw a figure that is a polygon,
   but not a quadrilateral.

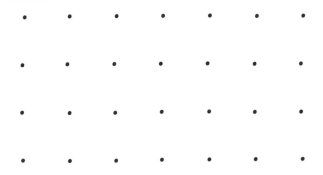

3. Draw a figure that is a polygon
   and a quadrilateral.

4. Are all polygons quadrilaterals? _____
   yes/no

5. Are all quadrilaterals polygons? _____
   yes/no

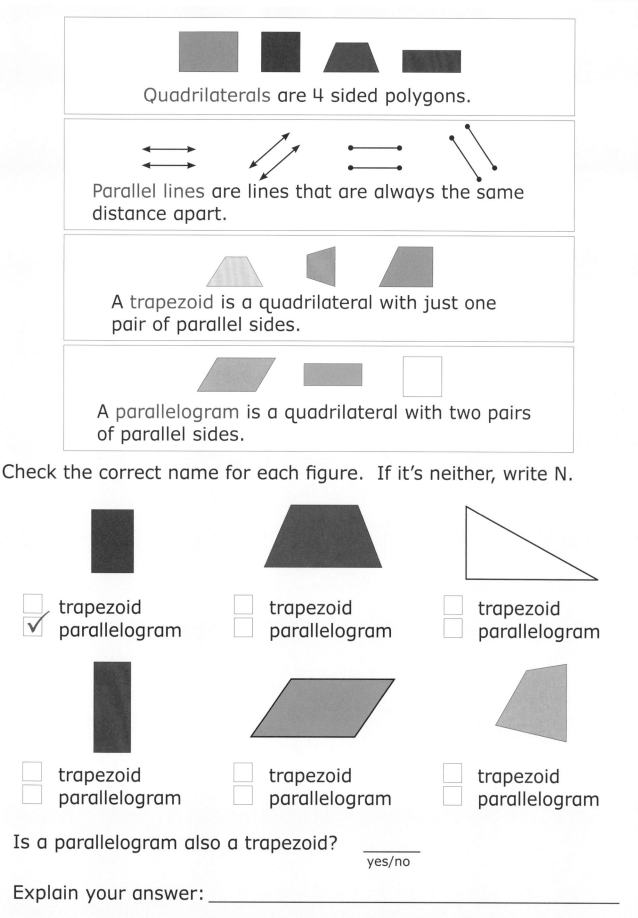

Quadrilaterals are 4 sided polygons.

Parallel lines are lines that are always the same distance apart.

A trapezoid is a quadrilateral with just one pair of parallel sides.

A parallelogram is a quadrilateral with two pairs of parallel sides.

Check the correct name for each figure. If it's neither, write N.

☐ trapezoid
✓ parallelogram

☐ trapezoid
☐ parallelogram

☐ trapezoid
☐ parallelogram

☐ trapezoid
☐ parallelogram

☐ trapezoid
☐ parallelogram

☐ trapezoid
☐ parallelogram

Is a parallelogram also a trapezoid? _____
yes/no

Explain your answer: _____

_____

Find and color each shape in the figure to the right of it.

1. Quadrilateral

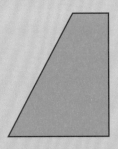 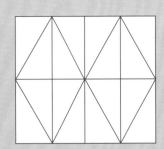

2. Square

 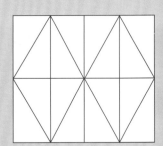

3. Trapezoid

 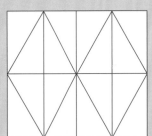

4. Pentagon

 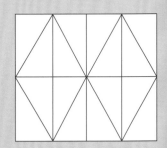

5. Rectangle

 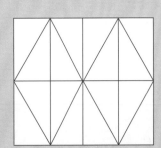

6. Hexagon

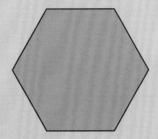 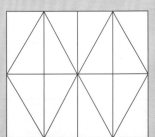

7. Rhombus

 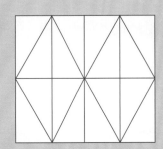

8. Right Triangle

 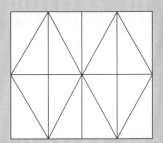

Kim has 7 gift boxes.

1. How many gift boxes are red?

    _____3_____ out of _____7_____ are red.

    $\dfrac{3}{7}$ of the gift boxes are red.

2. How many gift boxes are blue?

    _____ out of _____ are blue.

    ____ of the gift boxes are blue.

3. How many gift boxes are yellow?

    _____ out of _____ are yellow.

    ____ of the gift boxes are yellow.

4. How many gift boxes are green?

    _____ out of _____ are green.

    ____ of the gift boxes are green.

5. Kim finds another gift box colored pink.

    _____ out of _____ are colored pink.

    ____ of the gift boxes are pink.

$$\frac{1}{2} = \frac{3}{6}$$

Equivalent Fractions are fractions that equal the same amount.

Make an equivalent fraction. Shade in the figure to match.

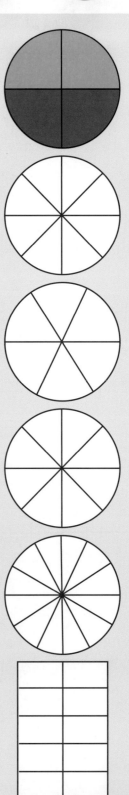

a $\frac{1}{2} = \frac{2}{4}$

b $\frac{1}{2} = \frac{}{8}$

c $\frac{2}{3} = \frac{}{6}$

d $\frac{3}{4} = \frac{}{8}$

e $\frac{1}{4} = \frac{}{12}$

f $\frac{3}{5} = \frac{}{10}$

All the fractions below have the same denominator, called the common denominator. When fractions have common denominators, compare the numerators for size.

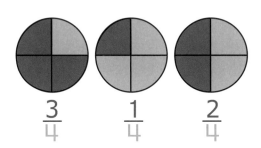

$$\frac{3}{4} \qquad \frac{1}{4} \qquad \frac{2}{4}$$

Write <, >, or = to make the sentence true.

a $\frac{1}{4}$ < $\frac{3}{4}$ b $\frac{8}{11}$ ☐ $\frac{4}{11}$

c $\frac{3}{8}$ ☐ $\frac{2}{8}$ d $\frac{12}{15}$ ☐ $\frac{14}{15}$

e $\frac{2}{3}$ ☐ $\frac{1}{3}$ f $\frac{3}{10}$ ☐ $\frac{7}{10}$

g $\frac{2}{4}$ ☐ $\frac{1}{4}$ h $\frac{1}{100}$ ☐ $\frac{1}{100}$

i $\frac{5}{8}$ ☐ $\frac{7}{8}$ j ⊘ ☐ ⊘

k $\frac{2}{9}$ ☐ $\frac{8}{9}$ l $\frac{1}{2}$ ☐ $\frac{2}{2}$

m $\frac{3}{5}$ ☐ $\frac{1}{5}$ n ▦ ☐ ▦

o $\frac{1}{2}$ ☐ $\frac{1}{2}$

The smallest number divisible by two or more numbers is the
Least Common Multiple (LCM).

The smallest
number that
both 2 and 3
divide into is

6.

Six is the
least common multiple
of 2 and 3.

X	0	1	2	3	4	5	6	7	8	9
0	0	0	0	0	0	0	0	0	0	0
1	0	1	2	3	4	5	6	7	8	9
2	0	2	4	6	8	10	12	14	16	18
3	0	3	6	9	12	15	18	21	24	27
4	0	4	8	12	16	20	24	28	32	36
5	0	5	10	15	20	25	30	35	40	45
6	0	6	12	18	24	30	36	42	48	54
7	0	7	14	21	28	35	42	49	56	63
8	0	8	16	24	32	40	48	56	64	72
9	0	9	18	27	36	45	54	63	72	81

1. What is the least common multiple for 4 and 6?

$4\overline{)?}$ and $6\overline{)?}$?= ____

2. What is the least common multiple for 6 and 9?

$6\overline{)?}$ and $9\overline{)?}$? = ____

3. What is the least common multiple for 3 and 4?

$3\overline{)?}$ and $4\overline{)?}$? = ____

4. What is the least common multiple for 4 and 8?

$4\overline{)?}$ and $8\overline{)?}$? = ____

5. What is the least common multiple for 8 and 9?

? = ____

$8\overline{)?}$ and $9\overline{)?}$

Inches

Estimate the length to the nearest half-inch. Then measure to the nearest half-inch. Label your answers.

1.   estimated = _____   actual = _____

2.   estimated = _____   actual = _____

3.   estimated = _____   actual = _____

4.   estimated = _____   actual = _____

5.   estimated = _____   actual = _____

Figure out what measurement length each letter represents. Then write the letter that matches each answer to solve the riddle below.

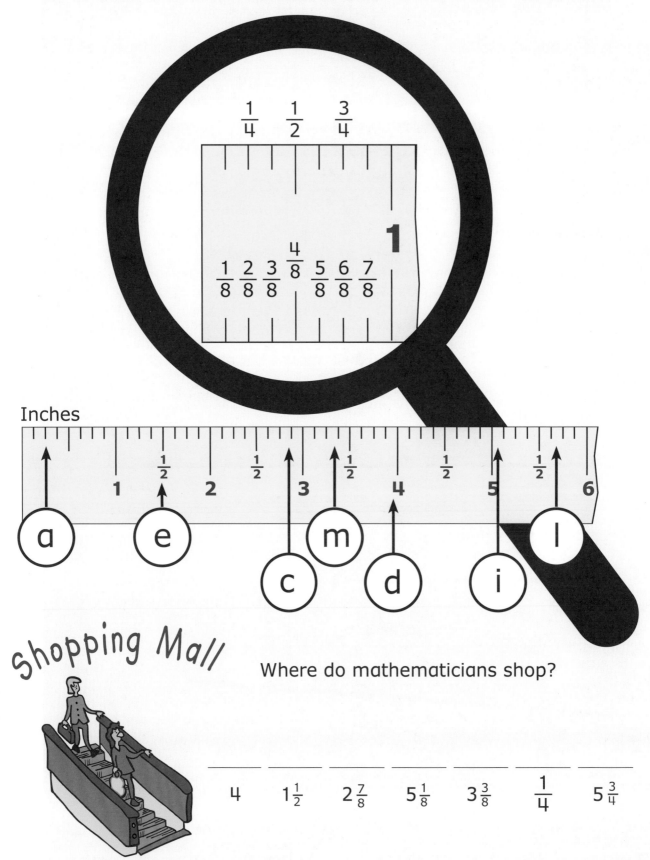

Shopping Mall

Where do mathematicians shop?

| 4 | $1\frac{1}{2}$ | $2\frac{7}{8}$ | $5\frac{1}{8}$ | $3\frac{3}{8}$ | $\frac{1}{4}$ | $5\frac{3}{4}$ |

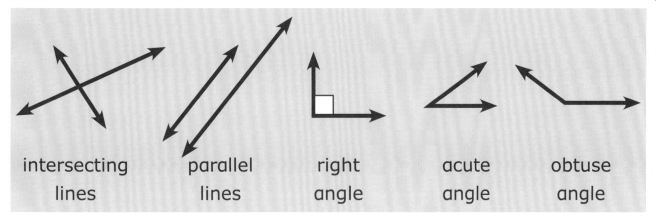

intersecting lines   parallel lines   right angle   acute angle   obtuse angle

1. Draw a line segment from point A to point B.
   Draw a line segment from point C to point D.
   Are these two line segments parallel or intersecting? _____

2. Draw a line segment from point E to point F.
   Draw a line segment from point G to point C.
   Are these two line segments parallel or intersecting? _____

3. Draw a ray from point H to point A.
   Draw a ray from point H to point D.
   Is this angle a right, acute, or obtuse angle? _____

4. Draw a ray from point E to point A.
   Draw a ray from point E to point G.
   Is this angle a right, acute, or obtuse angle? _____

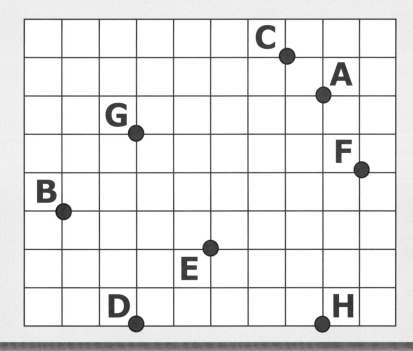

A line of symmetry divides a figure into halves. If you fold a figure along a line of symmetry, both sides match. Some figures have one or more lines of symmetry while others have no lines of symmetry.

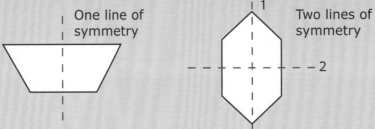

One line of symmetry

Two lines of symmetry

Draw a line of symmetry (when possible) for the following shapes.

Complete the pictures. Make the right side the same as the left.

Select the correct sums from the choice box.

| $3.35 | $1.75 | $2.22 |
| $3.92 | $1.70 | $3.82 |

1.  _____

2.  _____

3. _____

4.  _____

5.  _____

6.  _____

The Sweet Shop

Cookies
50 cents
each

Apple
$1.00
each

Gum
25 cents
each

Lollipop
75 cents
each

Candy
5 cents
each

Find each total cost, then complete the answer below.

a   1 gum, 1 apple, 2 lollipops $ ___ . ___ _5_

b   3 candies, 3 cookies $ ___ . _6_ ___

c   4 lollipops, 4 candies $ _3_ . ___ ___

d   2 apples, 5 cookies $ ___ . _5_ ___

e   3 gums, 4 cookies, 7 candies $ _____ . _____ <u>0</u>

f   3 lollipops, 1 apple $ _____ . <u>2</u> _____

g   5 apples, 5 cookies $ <u>7</u> . _____ _____

h   4 lollipops, 8 candies $ _____ . <u>4</u> _____

i   3 gums, 2 cookies $ _____ . _____ <u>5</u>

j   10 cookies $ _____ . <u>0</u> _____

k   2 of each item $ <u>5</u> . _____ _____

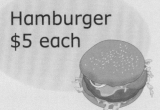

Hamburger
$5 each

Sandwich
$7 each

Taco
$2 each

Soup
$3 each

Pizza
$11 each

Figure out what was purchased given the sum.

1. Two different items were purchased for a total of $12. What were they?

_____   _____

2. Three different items were purchased for a total of $20. What were they?

_____   _____   _____

3. Three different items were purchased for a total of $15. What were they?

    _____   _____   _____

4. Two hamburgers and three different items were purchased for a total of $22. What were they?

    2 hamburgers   _____   _____

    _____

5. Three sandwiches and another item were purchased for a total of $32. What was the other item?

    3 sandwiches   _____

6. Five different items were purchased for a total of $28. What were they?

    _____   _____   _____

    _____   _____

$$\$4.00 - \$1.25 = \overset{3\ \ 9\ \ 1}{\cancel{\$4.00}}$$
$$\underline{-\ \ 1.25}$$
$$\$2.75$$

Find each difference, then cross out the matching answer below.

a

$5.18	$4.28	$3.95	$6.20	$2.92
− 2.43	− 1.36	− .03	− 1.45	− 1.40

b

$2.00	$1.25	$8.29	$4.53	$2.05
− .45	− .92	− .99	− .89	− .96

c

$9.22	$4.00	$6.28	$9.29	$3.21
− 6.75	− 1.05	− 1.69	− 5.08	− 1.46

$10 − $6.75 = _____ $5 − $2.10 = _____

$9 − $ .69 = _____ $ .91 − 5¢ = _____

$9.23 − $1.67 = _____ $1 − 50¢ = _____

$1.09	$3.25	$4.75	$2.95	$1.55	$8.31	$3.92
$2.92	$3.64	$7.56	$ .33	$2.90	$2.47	$ .86
$1.52	$4.59	$2.75	$1.75	$7.30	$ .50	$4.21

Like fractions are fractions with the same denominators. To add like fractions, add only the numerators and use the same denominator for the sum.

$$\frac{1}{3} + \frac{1}{3} = \frac{1+1}{3} = \frac{2}{3}$$

Find the sum. Color the figures to show the problem.

a $\frac{4}{6} + \frac{1}{6}$ = ———

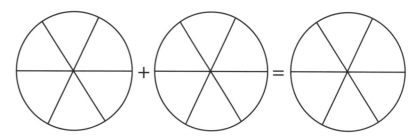

b $\frac{4}{8} + \frac{3}{8}$ = ———

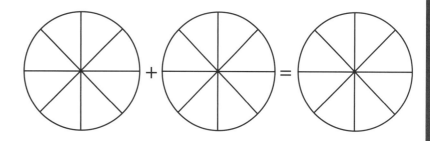

c $\frac{2}{4} + \frac{1}{4}$ = ———

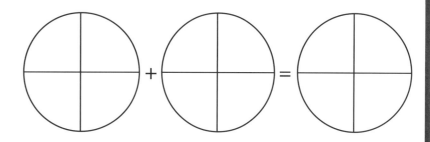

d $\frac{5}{10} + \frac{2}{10}$ = ———

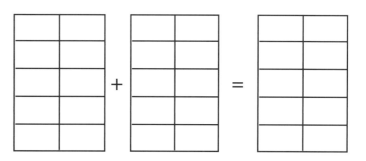

Like fractions are fractions with the same denominators. To subtract like fractions, subtract only the numerators and use the same denominator for the difference.

$$\frac{4}{5} - \frac{2}{5} = \frac{4-2}{5} = \frac{2}{5}$$

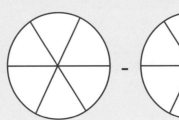 =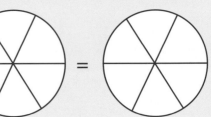

Find the difference. Color the figures (as above) to show the problem.

a $\frac{4}{6} - \frac{1}{6} =$ _____

b $\frac{4}{8} - \frac{3}{8} =$ _____

c $\frac{2}{4} - \frac{1}{4} =$ _____

d $\frac{5}{10} - \frac{2}{10} =$ _____

THE QUICK WAY!

$$\begin{array}{r} 40 \\ \times\ 3 \\ \hline 120 \end{array}$$ or $3 \times 40 = 120$ Write a zero in the answer, then multiply the number of tens.

Write two zeros in the answer, then multiply the number of hundreds.

$$\begin{array}{r} 700 \\ \times\ 5 \\ \hline 3,500 \end{array}$$ or $5 \times 700 = 3,500$

Multiply the quick way.

a
$$\begin{array}{r} 40 \\ \times\ 8 \\ \hline \end{array}$$
$$\begin{array}{r} 30 \\ \times\ 9 \\ \hline \end{array}$$
$$\begin{array}{r} 70 \\ \times\ 6 \\ \hline \end{array}$$

b
$$\begin{array}{r} 90 \\ \times\ 5 \\ \hline \end{array}$$
$$\begin{array}{r} 20 \\ \times\ 7 \\ \hline \end{array}$$
$$\begin{array}{r} 40 \\ \times\ 3 \\ \hline \end{array}$$

c
$$\begin{array}{r} 80 \\ \times\ 6 \\ \hline \end{array}$$
$$\begin{array}{r} 50 \\ \times\ 8 \\ \hline \end{array}$$
$$\begin{array}{r} 70 \\ \times\ 1 \\ \hline \end{array}$$

d
$$\begin{array}{r} 60 \\ \times\ 4 \\ \hline \end{array}$$
$$\begin{array}{r} 90 \\ \times\ 7 \\ \hline \end{array}$$
$$\begin{array}{r} 80 \\ \times\ 9 \\ \hline \end{array}$$

e
$$\begin{array}{r} 20 \\ \times\ 8 \\ \hline \end{array}$$
$$\begin{array}{r} 40 \\ \times\ 9 \\ \hline \end{array}$$
$$\begin{array}{r} 30 \\ \times\ 6 \\ \hline \end{array}$$

Multiply the quick way.

a)
$$100 \times 6 \qquad 200 \times 5 \qquad 300 \times 6$$

b)
$$800 \times 8 \qquad 700 \times 7 \qquad 800 \times 3$$

c)
$$600 \times 4 \qquad 900 \times 9 \qquad 200 \times 1$$

d)
$$900 \times 8 \qquad 900 \times 5 \qquad 700 \times 6$$

e)
$$90 \times 8 \qquad 800 \times 6 \qquad 500 \times 7$$

f)
$$40 \times 5 \qquad 700 \times 8 \qquad 600 \times 9$$

Multiply to find each product, then cross out the answer below.

$$
\begin{array}{r}
56 \\
\times\ 4 \\
\hline
24 \\
+200 \\
\hline
224
\end{array}
$$

a

56	42	25	72	83	63
× 3	× 8	× 4	× 3	× 9	× 6

b

71	83	76	39	62	29
× 2	× 1	× 8	× 7	× 5	× 6

c

66	38	56	32	44	58
× 7	× 4	× 9	× 8	× 4	× 7

d

32	29	40	83	19	26
× 7	× 8	× 5	× 3	× 7	× 6

152	336	200	310	504	747
133	83	256	168	608	242
406	273	232	100	462	156
378	142	249	174	216	176

Customary Units

Measure Length

12 inches (in.)   = 1 foot (ft)
3 feet   = 1 yard (yd)
5,280 feet   = 1 mile (mi)

Measure Weight

16 ounces (oz)   = 1 pound (lb)

Measure Capacity

2 cups (c)   = 1 pint (pt)
2 pints   = 1 quart (qt)
4 quarts   = 1 gallon (gal)

1 inch (in.)

A small bowl of cereal weights about 1 ounce (oz).

A small school milk carton holds 1 cup (c).

Milk

Complete the following sentences by putting in the units. Write one of the units listed above in the blank.

1. The length of an ink pen is about 6 _____.

2. The height of a male teacher is about 6 _____.

3. The distance between New Orleans and Los Angeles is about 1,700 _____.

4. The length of a sheet of notebook paper is about 1 _____.

5. The weight of a carrot is about 3 _____.

6. The weight of a lion is about 495 _____.

7. A car holds about 15 _____ of gasoline.

8. A small mug of coffee holds 1 _____ of coffee.

20 squares of 4 different colors.

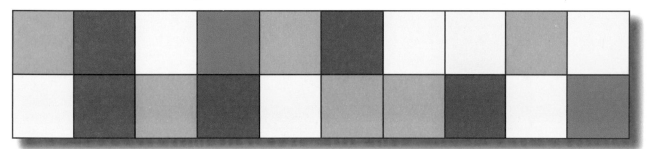

Use the data above to complete the table.

Square Colors

Color	Number of Squares
blue	
purple	
red	
yellow	

Use the data to make a bar graph.

Colors

	blue	purple	red	yellow
8				
7				
6				
5				
4				
3				
2				
1				
0				

Number of Squares

Close your eyes, then point to a square on the previous page. Record the color your finger landed on. Do this twenty times, then make a table and bar graph with the data. Put titles on the bar graph.

Choice 1 = _____   Choice 2 = _____   Choice 3 = _____

Choice 4 = _____   Choice 5 = _____   Choice 6 = _____

Choice 7 = _____   Choice 8 = _____   Choice 9 = _____

Choice 10 = _____   Choice 11 = _____   Choice 12 = _____

Choice 13 = _____   Choice 14 = _____   Choice 15 = _____

Choice 16 = _____   Choice 17 = _____   Choice 18 = _____

Choice 19 = _____   Choice 20 = _____

Square Colors

Color	Number of Squares
blue	
purple	
red	
yellow	

blue   purple   red   yellow

Metric Units

Measure Length

100 centimeters (cm) = 1 meter (m)

1,000 meters   = 1 kilometer (km)

Measure Weight

1,000 grams (g)   = 1 kilogram (kg)

Measure Capacity

1,000 milliliters (mL)   = 1 liter (L)

1 centimeter (cm)

A paper clip weighs about 1 gram (g).

A eyedropper holds about 1 milliliter (mL).

Complete the following sentences by putting in the units. Write one of the units listed above in the blank.

1. The distance between San Francisco and Los Angeles is about 800 _____.

2. The height of a door is about 2 _____.

3. The length of a pencil is about 17 _____.

4. The weight of a small truck is about 2,000 _____.

5. A dollar bill weighs about 1 _____.

6. A glass of orange juice holds about 250 _____.

7. A pail holds about 10 _____ of water.

8. The width of this sheet of paper is about 22 _____.

Degrees Fahrenheit (°F) **are customary units of temperature, and degrees** Celsius (°C) **are metric units of temperature.**

		°Fahrenheit	°Celsius
	Boiling point of water	212°	100°
	Freezing point of water	32°	0°

°C	°F
100°	212°
	194°
85°	
	167°
70°	
	140°
45°	113°
25°	
	68°
	59°
10°	50°
5°	41°
0°	32°

As the Celsius temperature increases five degrees, the Fahrenheit temperature increases nine degrees. Complete the chart, then answer the questions below.

1. Room temperature of 20° Celsius is what in Fahrenheit?   _____°F

2. Swimming at 95° Fahrenheit is what in Celsius?   _____°C

3. Snowing at 0°C is what in Fahrenheit?   _____°F

4. What is the difference in degrees between the boiling point of water and the freezing point of water in Celsius?   _____°

5. What is the difference in degrees between the boiling point of water and the freezing point of water in Fahrenheit?   _____°

A square unit is a square with 1 unit long sides.

Area is the number of square units needed to cover a flat surface.

1 square unit

4 square units

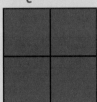

Find the area. Label in square units.

1.   Area = _____

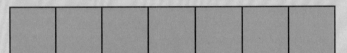

2.   Area = _____

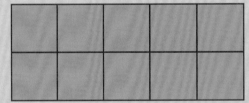

3.

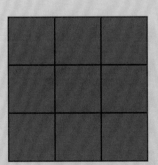

Area = _____

4.

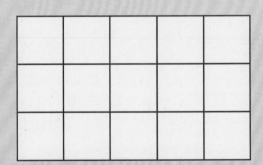

Area = _____

5.   How can multiplication be used to find the area of a rectangle?

_____

6.   Draw each rectangle.

Area = 6 square units

Area = 8 square units

Area = 12 square units

Area = 24 square units

Perimeter is the distance around a figure.

Perimeter = 4 units

Using a unit square, count units around the figure to find the perimeter.

Perimeter = 10 units

Find the perimeter.

1. Perimeter = _____

2. Perimeter = _____

3.

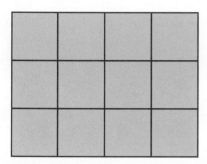

4.

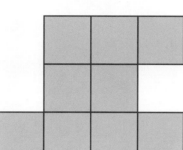

5.

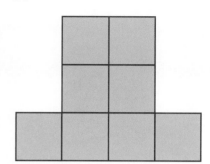

Perimeter = _____   Perimeter = _____   Perimeter = _____

6. Kim said the perimeter to #5 is 14 square units. What is wrong
   with her answer?

   _____

7. Draw three different shapes with perimeter of 10 units.

January						
Sun.	Mon.	Tue.	Wed.	Thu.	Fri.	Sat.
				1	2	3
4	5	6	7	8	9	10
11	12	13	14	15	16	17
18	19	20	21	22	23	24
25	26	27	28	29	30	31

March						
Sun.	Mon.	Tue.	Wed.	Thu.	Fri.	Sat.
1	2	3	4	5	6	7
8	9	10	11	12	13	14
15	16	17	18	19	20	21
22	23	24	25	26	27	28
29	30	31				

February						
Sun.	Mon.	Tue.	Wed.	Thu.	Fri.	Sat.
1	2	3	4	5	6	7
8	9	10	11	12	13	14
15	16	17	18	19	20	21
22	23	24	25	26	27	28

April						
Sun.	Mon.	Tue.	Wed.	Thu.	Fri.	Sat.
			1	2	3	4
5	6	7	8	9	10	11
12	13	14	15	16	17	18
19	20	21	22	23	24	25
26	27	28	29	30		

Student of the Month

7 days = 1 week

1. What date is 5 days after January 1? _____ _____
   Month   Date

2. The first Monday in April is what date? _____ _____

3. Three weeks from March 3rd is what date? _____ _____

4. On February 10th, Maria was invited to a party on February 22nd. How many days till the party? _____ days

5. Which month above has the least number of days? _____

6. What date is four weeks after March 28th? _____ _____

7. From January 1st to March 1st is how many days? _____ days

8. Estimate how many days there are from January 1st to April 1st. How many actual days are there?

   estimated = _____   actual = _____

9. Estimate how many days there are from January 15th to March 4th. How many actual days are there?

   estimated = _____   actual = _____

Match each name with the correct picture. Then use the letters of each answer to solve the riddle below.

_____ 1. Triangle

_____ 2. Parallelogram

_____ 3. Rectangle

_____ 4. Trapezoid

_____ 5. Rhombus

_____ 6. Pentagon

_____ 7. Hexagon

_____ 8. Octagon

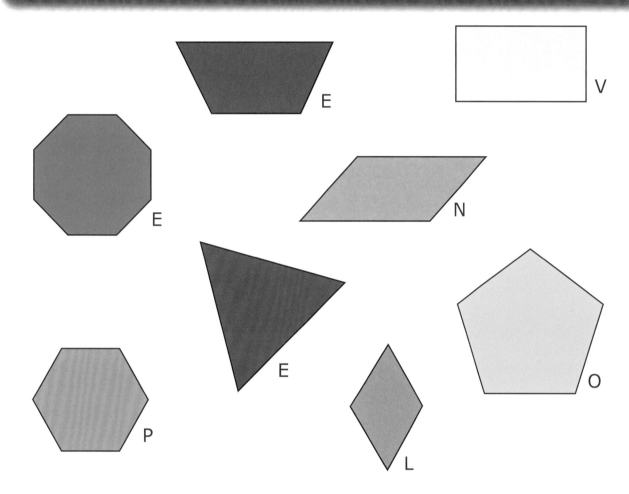

What word starts with an "E", but usually contains only one letter?

$\overline{}$ $\overline{}$ $\overline{}$ $\overline{}$ $\overline{}$ $\overline{}$ $\overline{}$ $\overline{}$
1   2   3   4   5   6   7   8

Solid Figures

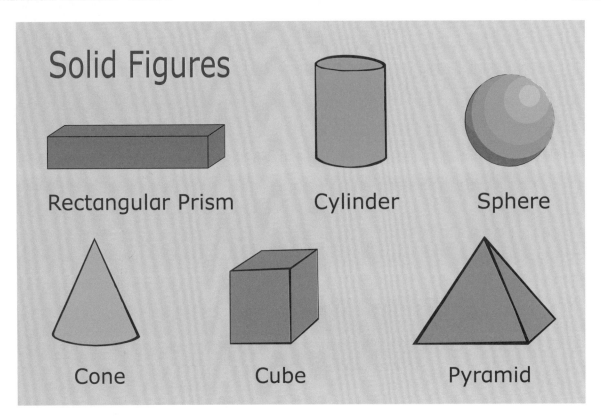

Rectangular Prism   Cylinder   Sphere

Cone   Cube   Pyramid

Write the name of each solid figure.

1.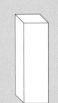

_____   _____   _____

2. What object have you seen that has the
   shape of a rectangular prism?   _____

3. What object have you seen that has the
   shape of a cylinder?   _____

4. What object have you seen that has the
   shape of a sphere?   _____

Solid Figures

5. What object have you seen that has the shape of a cone?

   _____

6. What object have you seen that has the shape of a cube?

   _____

7. What object have you seen that has the shape of a pyramid?

   _____

8. A basketball is an example of what solid figure?

   _____

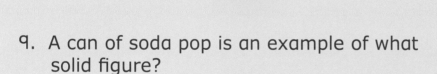

9. A can of soda pop is an example of what solid figure?

   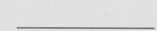

10. Ice in a glass of water is an example of what solid figure?

    _____

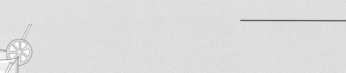

1

$$\begin{array}{r} 5 \\ + \ \triangle \\ \hline 12 \end{array}$$ $\triangle = \underline{\ 7\ }$,

$$\begin{array}{r} 21 \\ - \ \square \\ \hline 13 \end{array}$$ $\square = \underline{\ \ \ }$

2

$$\begin{array}{r} \square \\ + \ 34 \\ \hline 50 \end{array}$$ $\square = \underline{\ \ \ }$,

$$\begin{array}{r} \bigcirc \\ - \ 19 \\ \hline 32 \end{array}$$ $\bigcirc = \underline{\ \ \ }$

3

$$\begin{array}{r} 15 \\ + \ \bigcirc \\ \hline 50 \end{array}$$ $\bigcirc = \underline{\ \ \ }$,

$$\begin{array}{r} 42 \\ - \ \square \\ \hline 19 \end{array}$$ $\square = \underline{\ \ \ }$

4

$$\begin{array}{r} \square \\ + \ 27 \\ \hline 36 \end{array}$$ $\square = \underline{\ \ \ }$,

$$\begin{array}{r} \triangle \\ - \ 25 \\ \hline 40 \end{array}$$ $\triangle = \underline{\ \ \ }$

5

$$\begin{array}{r} 9 \\ \times \ \square \\ \hline 72 \end{array}$$ $\square = \underline{\ \ \ }$,

$32 \div \square = 8$ $\square = \underline{\ \ \ }$

6

$$\begin{array}{r} \triangle \\ \times \ 7 \\ \hline 42 \end{array}$$ $\triangle = \underline{\ \ \ }$,

$\bigcirc \div 4 = 9$ $\bigcirc = \underline{\ \ \ }$

7

$4 + 5 + 1 + 5 + 9 + \square = 50$ $\square = \underline{\ \ \ }$

Write each number in
the place-value chart.

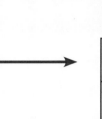

t h o u s a n d s	h u n d r e d s	t e n s	o n e s
5	2	4	7

a   5,247   ⟷

b   179

c   82

d   8,427

e   1,605

Write the place-value name for
the 5 in each number.

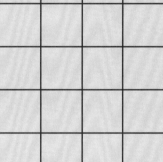

f   8,569   <u>hundreds</u>

g   5,187   _____

h   750   _____

i   8,245   _____

Write in expanded notation.

j   6,148   <u>6,000 + 100 + 40 + 8</u>

k   7,269   _____

l   693   _____

m   8,017   _____

Use the numbers in the choice box to make each number sentence true. Work from left to right.

→

Choice Box
3, 4, 5, or 7

a   4 + 5 + 7 = 16

b   ☐ + ☐ − ☐ = 6

c   ☐ + ☐ − ☐ = 9

d   ☐ + ☐ + ☐ + ☐ = 19

e   ☐ + ☐ − ☐ + ☐ = 9

f   ☐ + ☐ − ☐ − ☐ = 1

g   ☐ + ☐ + ☐ − ☐ = 13

h   ☐ + ☐ − ☐ − ☐ = 5

i   ☐ − ☐ + ☐ − ☐ = 3

Use the choice box to find the missing names of each number. Complete the name, then cross out the number.

8,060	9,350	2,174	7,666
4,501	6,423	3,212	1,839

two thousands , one hundreds   seven tens   four ones

six thousands , _____   _____   _____

_____ , _____   five tens   _____

eight thousands , _____   _____   _____

_____ , _____   six tens   _____

_____ , _____   _____   one ones

_____ , two hundreds   _____   _____

_____ , _____   _____   nine ones

Decimal places are to the right of the decimal point.

50.50

Write each decimal number in the place-value chart.

.1 ⟶

.9 ⟶

1.8 ⟶

ones	decimal	tenths
	.	1

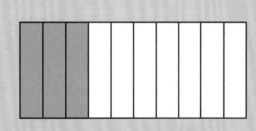

Area Shaded

Read: three tenths

Write: .3 or $\frac{3}{10}$

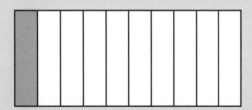

1 _____ or _____

2 _____ or _____

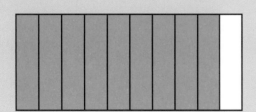

3 _____ or _____

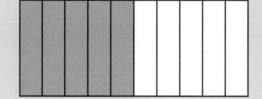

4 _____ or _____

Continue the pattern.

a   1, 3, 5, 7, 9, 11, 13, 15, _____, _____, _____

b   100, 98, 96, 94, 92, 90, _____, _____, _____

c   5, 10, 15, 20, 25, 30, 35, _____, _____, _____

d   11, 21, 31, 41, 51, 61, _____, _____, _____

e   3, 6, 9, 12, 15, 18, 21, _____, _____, _____

f   1, 2, 2, 3, 3, 3, 4, 4, 4, 4, _____, _____, _____

g   1, 4, 9, 16, 25, 36, 49, _____, _____, _____

h   1, 1, 2, 3, 5, 8, 13, 21, _____, _____, _____

i   5, 14, 23, 32, 41, 50, 59, _____, _____, _____

j   2, 4, 8, 16, 32, 64, 128, _____, _____, _____

k   5, 6, 8, 9, 11, 12, 14, 15, 17, _____, _____, _____

l   50, 45, 40, 35, 30, 25, _____, _____, _____

m   9, 18, 27, 36, 45, 54, _____, _____, _____

n   4, 4, 8, 8, 12, 12, 16, _____, _____, _____

Continue the pattern.

1.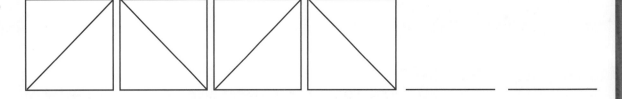

2.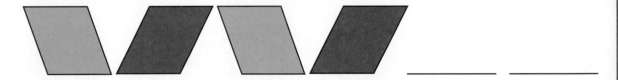

3.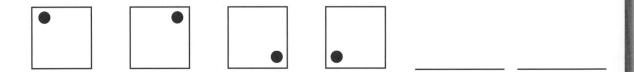

4.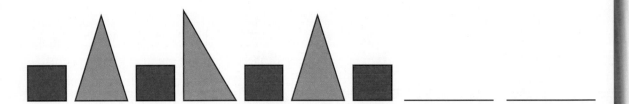

5.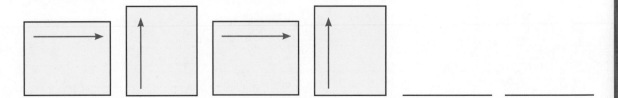

6.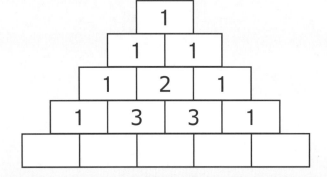

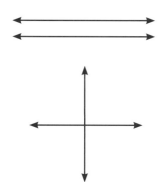 Parallel lines are always the same distance apart.

Perpendicular lines form right angles when they intersect.

Follow the directions below to complete a cereal box.

1. Draw a line segment connecting **C** and **F** that is parallel to the line connecting **A** and **E**.

2. Draw a line segment connecting **C** and **D** that is parallel to the line connecting **A** and **B**.

3. Draw a line segment connecting **F** and **G** that is parallel to the line connecting **C** and **D**.

4. Draw a line segment connecting **A** and **C** that is perpendicular to the line connecting **A** and **E**.

5. Draw a line segment connecting **E** and **F** that is perpendicular to the line connecting **A** and **E**.

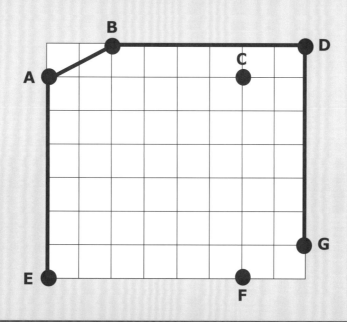

A right angle is a special angle that forms a square corner (sometimes denoted by ☐). Use a corner of a piece of paper to tell whether an angle is a right angle.	
An acute angle is less than a right angle.	
An obtuse angle is greater than a right angle.	

Write if the angle is a right, an acute, or an obtuse angle.

1.

2.

3.

4.

_____

5.

6.

7.

8.

_____

9. Draw a triangle with a right angle.

10. Draw a triangle with all acute angles.

11. Draw a triangle with an obtuse angle.

$\frac{2}{5}$ of the glasses are shaded.

1. Shade in $\frac{1}{2}$ of the signs.

2. Shade in $\frac{2}{3}$ of the balls.

3. Shade in $\frac{3}{4}$ of the ducks.

4. Shade in $\frac{5}{6}$ of the balloons.

5. Shade in $\frac{3}{7}$ of the sidewalk.

To multiply   147
              ×   6

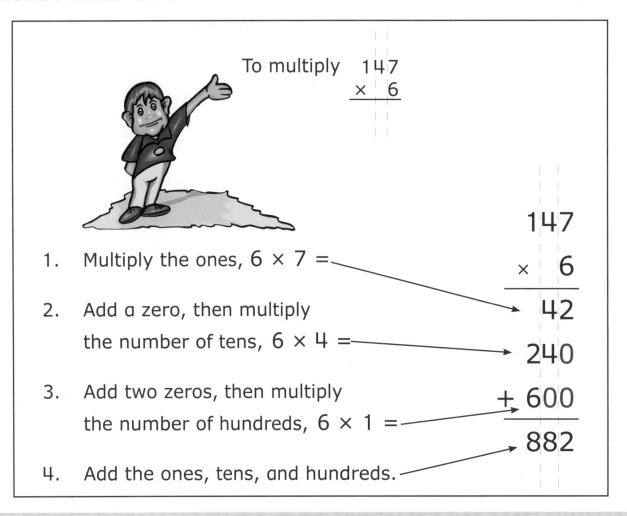

1. Multiply the ones, 6 × 7 =

2. Add a zero, then multiply
    the number of tens, 6 × 4 =

3. Add two zeros, then multiply
    the number of hundreds, 6 × 1 =

4. Add the ones, tens, and hundreds.

147
×   6
──────
  42
 240
+ 600
──────
 882

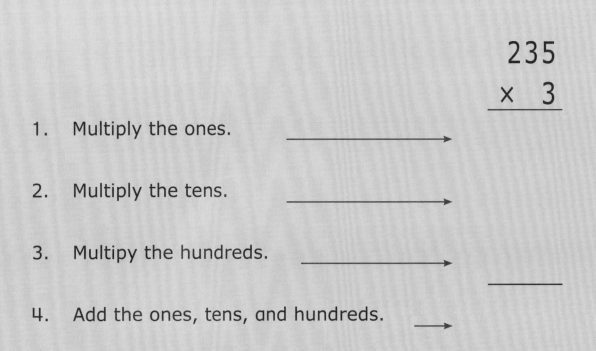

235
×   3
──────

1. Multiply the ones.

2. Multiply the tens.

3. Multipy the hundreds.

4. Add the ones, tens, and hundreds.

Find the product, then cross out the answer below.

a
$$\begin{array}{r} 165 \\ \times\ 4 \\ \hline \end{array}$$
$$\begin{array}{r} 721 \\ \times\ 8 \\ \hline \end{array}$$
$$\begin{array}{r} 283 \\ \times\ 4 \\ \hline \end{array}$$
$$\begin{array}{r} 904 \\ \times\ 3 \\ \hline \end{array}$$

b
$$\begin{array}{r} 120 \\ \times\ 9 \\ \hline \end{array}$$
$$\begin{array}{r} 222 \\ \times\ 6 \\ \hline \end{array}$$
$$\begin{array}{r} 236 \\ \times\ 2 \\ \hline \end{array}$$
$$\begin{array}{r} 816 \\ \times\ 1 \\ \hline \end{array}$$

c
$$\begin{array}{r} 592 \\ \times\ 8 \\ \hline \end{array}$$
$$\begin{array}{r} 924 \\ \times\ 7 \\ \hline \end{array}$$
$$\begin{array}{r} 128 \\ \times\ 5 \\ \hline \end{array}$$
$$\begin{array}{r} 341 \\ \times\ 6 \\ \hline \end{array}$$

2,712	6,468	472	1,132	816	2,086	1,080
2,046	6,428	5,768	4,736	660	1,332	640

Find the product, then cross out the answer below.

a
502
× 7

533
× 4

846
× 9

784
× 8

b
229
× 4

604
× 7

327
× 7

129
× 8

c
401
× 5

263
× 3

644
× 7

119
× 6

4,228	2,289	7,614	2,132	1,032	714	2,005
916	789	4,468	4,508	7,514	3,514	6,272

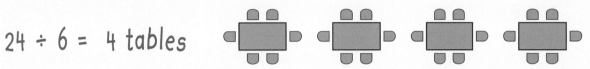

Solve the problem, then draw a picture to show the answer.

1. If each table has 6 chairs, how many tables are needed for 24 first graders?

   24 ÷ 6 = 4 tables

2. If each table has 4 chairs, how many tables are needed for 20 third graders?

   20 ÷ 4 = _____

3. If each table has 5 chairs, how many tables are needed for 25 fourth graders?

   25 ÷ 5 = _____

4. If each table has 6 chairs, how many tables are needed for 30 fifth graders?

   30 ÷ 6 = _____

Count by 25
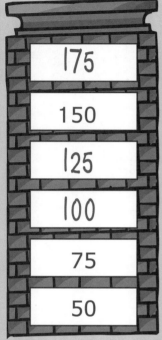
175
150
125
100
75
50

Count by 50
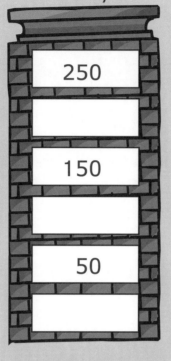
250
_____
150
_____
50
_____

Count by 15
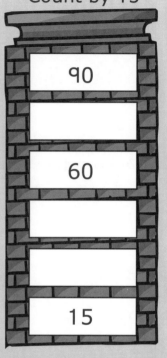
90
_____
60
_____
_____
15

Count by 20
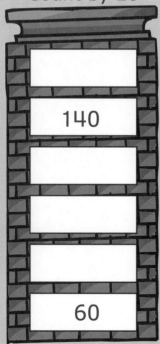
_____
140
_____
_____
60

Count by 100
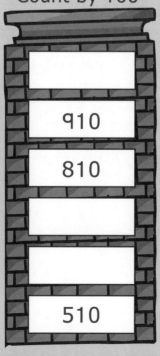
_____
910
810
_____
_____
510

Count by 250
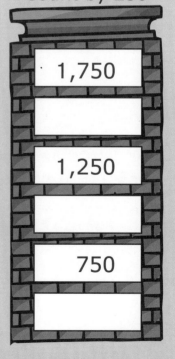
1,750
_____
1,250
_____
750
_____

Place the numbers in order from smallest to largest.

1

51, 37, 8, 29, 34

51
37
34
29
8

Smallest ↑

2

11, 9, 26, 89, 32

3

102, 121, 91, 131, 129

4

102, 24, 164, 43, 132

5

1,001, 1,011, 111, 1,100, 1,010

6

21, 32, 11, 33, 29

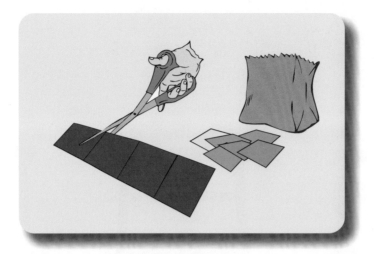

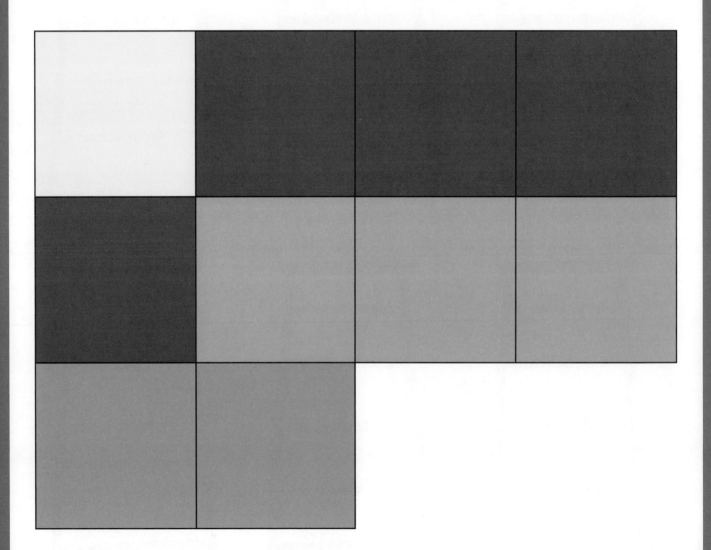

Cut out the ten squares on the previous page and place them in a bag. Draw out one at a time and record the color, then put the square back in the bag.

Estimate how many red squares will be drawn in all. _____

Draw # 1 color = _____   Draw #11 color = _____

Draw # 2 color = _____   Draw #12 color = _____

Draw # 3 color = _____   Draw #13 color = _____

Draw # 4 color = _____   Draw #14 color = _____

Draw # 5 color = _____   Draw #15 color = _____

Draw # 6 color = _____   Draw #16 color = _____

Draw # 7 color = _____   Draw #17 color = _____

Draw # 8 color = _____   Draw #18 color = _____

Draw # 9 color = _____   Draw #19 color = _____

Draw #10 color = _____   Draw #20 color = _____

1. _____   How many blue squares were selected in all?

2. _____   How many green squares were selected in all?

3. _____   How many yellow squares were selected in all?

4. _____   How many red squares were selected in all?

5. _____   What is the difference in the number of red squares estimated to be selected and actually selected?

6. _____   What color was selected the least?

7. _____   What color was selected the most?

8. _____   What is the difference between the color selected the most and the color selected the least?

A line graph uses a line to show how something changes over time.

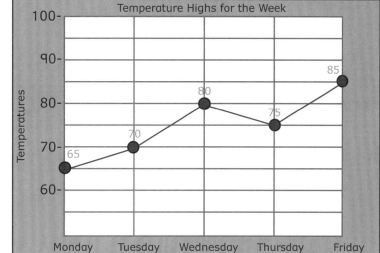

1. On what day was the temperature the highest? _____

2. The high temperature Wednesday was how much higher than Monday? _____

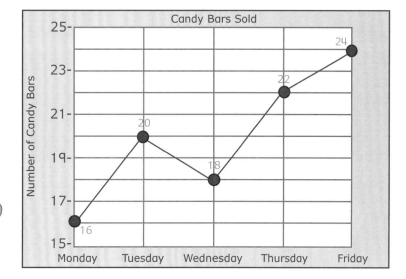

3. On what day were the most candy bars sold? _____

4. On what day were the fewest candy bars sold? _____

5. On which days were less than 20 candy bars sold?

_____

6. How many candy bars were sold Monday through Friday?_____

1   2,743 =

$$2,000 + 700 + 40 + 3$$

2   6,059 =

_____

3   5,720 =

_____

4   8,173 =

_____

5   Three thousand, two hundred sixteen =

_____

6   Five thousand, one hundred forty-three =

_____

Write each number in standard form in the puzzle.

1. → nine hundred seventy-one

2. ↓ seven thousand, three hundred forty-five

3. → six thousand, five hundred three

4. ↓ eight thousand, three hundred fifty

5. → seven hundred twenty

6. ↓ two thousand, four hundred sixty-one

7. → eight thousand, four hundred eleven

8. ↓ 1000 + 400 + 20 + 6

9. → 4000 + 300 + 6

10. ↓ 300 + 70 + 9

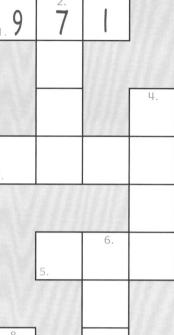

Write in word form.

a   701   = _____

b   5,243 = _____

c   1,600 = _____

d   9,147 = _____

e   6,018 = _____

Find the missing numbers.

1.   If   9 + ■   = 17   then,   ■ = __8__

2.   If   20 – ⬡   = 11   then,   ⬡ = _____

3.   If   ◆ × 9   = 63   then,   ◆ = _____

4.   If   32 ÷ ▲   = 8   then,   ▲ = _____

5.   If   ⬭ + 37   = 50   then,   ⬭ = _____

6.   If   ◣ – 16   = 19   then,   ◣ = _____

7.   If   ♥ × 7   = 42   then,   ♥ = _____

8.   If   ⬓ ÷ 9   = 2   then,   ⬓ = _____

Complete the equation, then circle the correct answer.

9.   ■ + ⬡ + ◆ + ▲ + ⬭ + ◣ + ♥ + ⬓ = _____

        100   92   101   87

10.   ⬡ + ▲ + ⬭ + ♥ + ⬓ - ■ - ◆ - ◣ = _____

        43   12   0   4

Solve each problem, then write <, >, or = to make the number sentence true.

a   12 + 4 = _____   20 – 3 = _____

b   32 – 16 = _____   4 × 6 = _____

c   11 + 19 = _____   3 × 7 = _____

d   35 – 18 = _____   18 + 7 = _____

e   81 ÷ 9 = _____   20 – 12 = _____

f   24 + 47 = _____   7 × 7 = _____

g   8 × 4 = _____   20 + 5 = _____

h   30 ÷ 5 = _____   15 - 9 = _____

i   10 × 5 = _____   14 + 46 = _____

j   20 + 14 = _____   6 × 6 = _____

Find the sum. Regroup when needed. Then write the letter of each matching answer to solve the riddle below.

g	i	b	e	r
53	82	92	64	82
62	13	63	28	49
+ 32	+ 42	+ 28	+ 63	+ 67

a	o	v	l	t
12	38	92	47	83
47	29	18	29	29
+ 26	+ 37	+ 36	+ 46	+ 49

h	m	w	s	p
60	29	429	823	218
39	83	128	149	328
+ 43	+ 92	+ 760	+ 298	+ 614

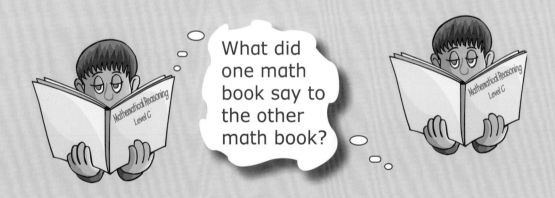

What did one math book say to the other math book?

___ ___ ___ ___ ___ ___ ___ ___
1,317 104 1,317   142   85 146 155   137

___ ___ ___ ___ ___ ___ ___ ___ ___ ___ ___.
147 104 161   1,160 198 104 183 122 155 204 1,270

Find the difference, then cross out the answer below.

a
512
− 123

b
246
− 183

c
563
− 351

d
210
− 126

e
426
− 219

f
129
− 46

g
205
− 62

h
400
− 215

i
123
− 45

j
623
− 143

k
523
− 149

l
627
− 126

m
519
− 419

n
207
− 149

o
409
− 203

p
248
− 176

q
818
− 627

r
329
− 137

s
231
− 144

t
308
− 290

u
713
− 429

v
881
− 699

w
237
− 146

x
246
− 178

207	84	58	374	191
206	480	384	63	192
501	389	72	91	185
212	182	143	100	87
68	78	18	83	284

Find the product.

a	b	c	d	e
34	87	62	18	57
× 5	× 4	× 9	× 3	× 3
20				
+ 150				
170				

f	g	h	i	j
51	46	98	56	94
× 6	× 7	× 1	× 8	× 4

k	l	m	n	o
83	71	99	78	87
× 6	× 2	× 9	× 6	× 9

p	q	r	s	t
33	22	92	77	80
× 2	× 5	× 7	× 7	× 8

$$30 \div 5 = 6$$
$$300 \div 5 = 60$$
$$3{,}000 \div 5 = 600$$

Use basic division facts and patterns to help you divide by multiples of 10 and 100.

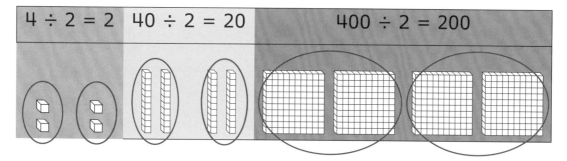

$4 \div 2 = 2$	$40 \div 2 = 20$	$400 \div 2 = 200$

a $25 \div 5 =$ _____   b $21 \div 7 =$ _____   c $12 \div 3 =$ _____

   $250 \div 5 =$ _____ $210 \div 7 =$ _____ $120 \div 3 =$ _____

   $2{,}500 \div 5 =$ _____ $2{,}100 \div 7 =$ _____ $1{,}200 \div 3 =$ _____

d $8 \div 4 =$ _____   e $24 \div 6 =$ _____   f $18 \div 9 =$ _____

   $80 \div 4 =$ _____ $240 \div 6 =$ _____ $180 \div 9 =$ _____

   $800 \div 4 =$ _____ $2{,}400 \div 6 =$ _____ $1{,}800 \div 9 =$ _____

Find the quotient.

g $800 \div 2 =$ _____   h $70 \div 7 =$ _____   i $28 \div 4 =$ _____

j $5 \overline{)50}$ k $4 \overline{)320}$ l $3 \overline{)900}$

Cut out or copy the figure at the bottom of the page. Fold the paper strip only on the marked dotted lines. Make the polygons listed.

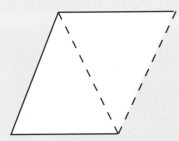

1.   small parallelogram

2.   small trapezoid

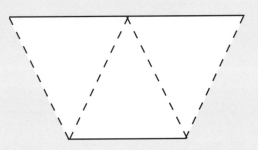

3.   hexagon (challenge)

translation 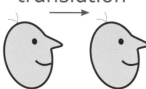   reflection 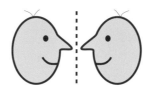   rotation

Tell what kind of motion was used to move each plane figure.
Write translation, reflection, or rotation.

1.

_____

2.

_____

3.

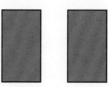

_____

4.

_____

5.

_____

6.

_____

7. Draw the reflection of the figure.

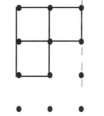

8. Draw the figure after a rotation.

Ordered pairs locate points on a grid. The first number inside the parentheses tells how many spaces to move to the right. The second number tells how many spaces to move up.

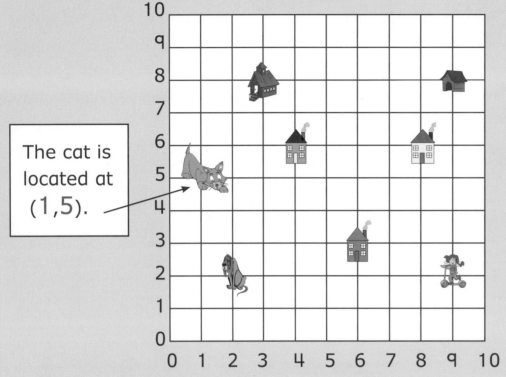

The cat is located at (1,5).

1. What is the ordered pair for the dog? (_____, _____)

2. What is the ordered pair for the doghouse? (_____, _____)

3. What is the ordered pair for the girl on a scooter? (_____, _____)

4. What is the ordered pair for the school? (_____, _____)

5. What is the color of the house at (8,6)? (_____)

6. What is the color of the house at (4,6)? (_____)

7. The line connecting the items at (4,6) and (8,6) is parallel

   to the line connecting the items at (_____, _____) and (_____, _____).

8. The line connecting the items at (9, 2) and (2, 2) is perpendicular

   to the line connecting the items at (_____, _____) and (_____, _____).

Make a congruent copy of each colored shape.

1.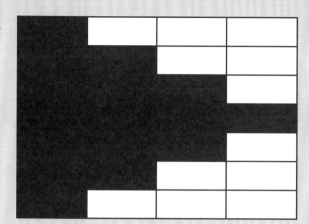

2.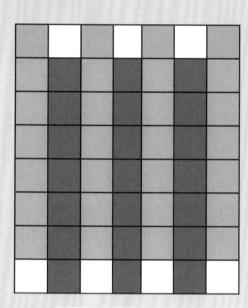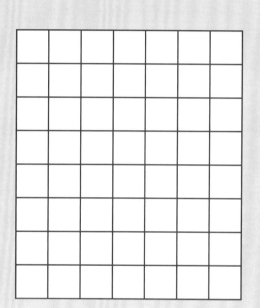

A line of symmetry divides a figure into two congruent halves. Complete the pictures. Make the right side the same as the left.

3.    4.

Estimate, then measure the length of the lines to the nearest centimeter. Label your measurements.

1.   estimated = __7 cm__   measured = __6 cm__

2.   estimated = _____   measured = _____

3.   estimated = _____   measured = _____

4.   estimated = _____   measured = _____

5.   estimated = _____   measured = _____

_____

6.   estimated = _____   measured = _____

_____

7.   estimated = _____   measured = _____

_____

8.   estimated = _____   measured = _____

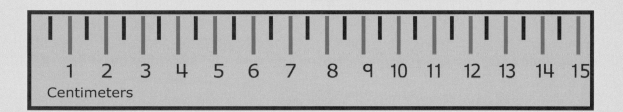

9. Draw a line 5 centimeters long.

10. Draw a line 2 centimeters long.

Measure the length of the line to the nearest half-inch. Then write the letter of each matching answer to solve the riddle below.

Inches

_____ o

_____ g

_____ m

_____ t

_____ e

_____ s

_____ p

_____ a

What goes around the world but stays in a corner?

5	4	$4\frac{1}{2}$	$3\frac{1}{2}$	1	$2\frac{1}{2}$	6
___	___	___	___	___	___	___

$4\frac{1}{2}$	$3\frac{1}{2}$	1	2	5
___	___	___	___	___

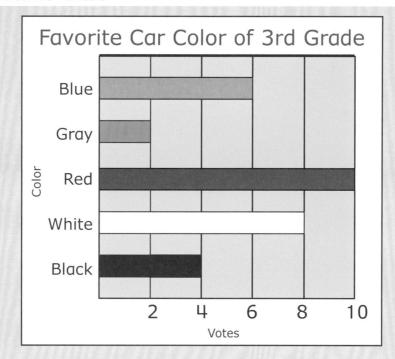

Favorite Car Color of 3rd Grade

1. Which color received the most votes? _____

2. Which color received the fewest votes? _____

3. Which color received 4 votes? _____

4. How many 3rd graders voted? _____

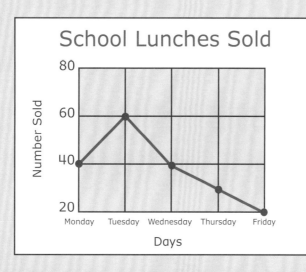

School Lunches Sold

5. Which day were the most school lunches sold? _____

6. Which day were the least school lunches sold? _____

7. What two days sold the same amount
   of lunches?   _____ _____

Roll two dice. Add the numbers rolled and record the sum.

Toss #1 sum = _____   Toss #11 sum = _____

Toss #2 sum = _____   Toss #12 sum = _____

Toss #3 sum = _____   Toss #13 sum = _____

Toss #4 sum = _____   Toss #14 sum = _____

Toss #5 sum = _____   Toss #15 sum = _____

Toss #6 sum = _____   Toss #16 sum = _____

Toss #7 sum = _____   Toss #17 sum = _____

Toss #8 sum = _____   Toss #18 sum = _____

Toss #9 sum = _____   Toss #19 sum = _____

Toss #10 sum = _____   Toss #20 sum = _____

1.   What sum occured the most? _____

2.   What sum occured the least? _____

3.   List all the possible sums.

____ ____ ____ ____ ____ ____ ____ ____ ____ ____ ____

4.   Complete the bar graph using the data above.

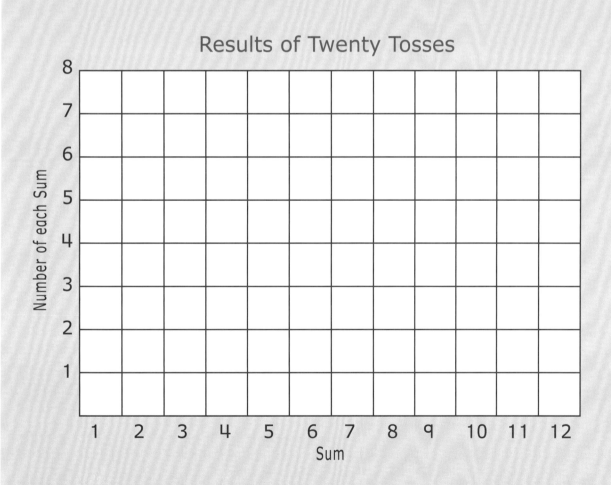

Results of Twenty Tosses

To find the perimeter of a polygon, add the lengths of its sides.

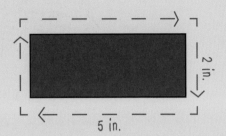

5 in.
2 in.
5 in.
+ 2 in.
_____
perimeter = 14 in.

1.
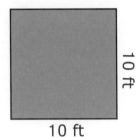

10 ft

10 ft

_____ ft

2.
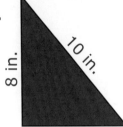

8 in.   10 in.

6 in.

_____   in.

3.
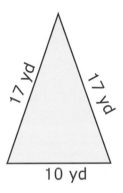

17 yd   17 yd

10 yd

_____ yd

4.
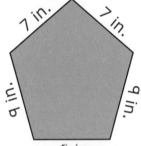

7 in.   7 in.

9 in.   9 in.

6 in.

_____   _____

5.

12 ft

18 ft

_____   _____

6.
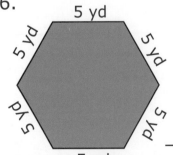

5 yd

5 yd   5 yd

5 yd   5 yd

5 yd

_____   _____

7. On Little League baseball diamonds, there are 60 feet
    between the bases. How far does a player run when
    a home run is hit? _____

The Area of a figure is the number of square units that cover its surface.

   Area = 6 square units

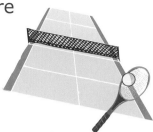

Find the area of each figure. Label the answers in square units.

1.
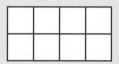

_____

2.
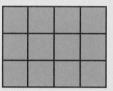

_____

3.

_____

4.

_____

5.

_____

6.
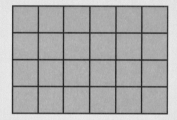

_____

7.

_____

8.
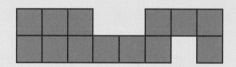

_____

Draw 4 different figures, each having an area of 6 square units.

Some Equivalent Sets

(5 pennies)	5 pennies = 1 nickel	(nickel)
(2 nickels)	2 nickels = 1 dime	(dime)
(5 nickels)	5 nickels = 1 quarter	(quarter)
(4 quarters)	4 quarters = 1 dollar	(dollar)
(10 dimes)	10 dimes = 1 dollar	(dollar)

1. Complete the table to show how many pennies could be traded for a different numbers of nickels.

nickels	1	2	3	4	5	6	7
pennies	5						

2. Complete the table to show how many nickels could be traded for a different numbers of dimes.

dimes	1	2	3	4	5	6	7
nickels	2						

3. Complete the table to show how many pennies, nickels, dimes, and quarters make a dollar.

 _____ pennies = 1 dollar

 _____ nickels = 1 dollar

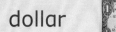 _____ dimes = 1 dollar

 _____ quarters = 1 dollar

4. List the fewest bills and coins you can use to make $1.47.

____ pennies ____ nickels ____ dimes ____ quarters ____ dollar

5. List the fewest bills and coins you can use to make $2.99.

____ pennies ____ nickels ____ dimes ____ quarters ____ dollar

Find the sum or difference.

a
$8.24
+ 3.15

b
$5.00
− 1.25

c
$4.59
+ 4.01

d
$9.50
− 2.25

e
$7.25
+ 6.75

f
$9.10
− 8.50

g
$4.99
+ 5.99

h
$8.35
− 5.49

i
$3.25 − $.75 = _____

j
$5.00 + $.50 = _____

Write either <, >, or = to make the number sentence true.

k $2.15 + $2.95 = _____ $5.00

l $10.50 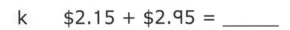 $12.00 − $2.50 = _____

m $25.00 + $5.75 = _____ $6.10

n $3.00 − $.50 = _____ $1.25 + $1.25= _____

Write a number sentence for each problem and solve.

1. Sue bought a notebook for $3.99 and pencil for $1.49. How much money did Sue spend?

2. Sue paid for the notebook and pencil with a $20 bill. How much change should she get?

3. Paul has $8.08. Jane has $5.75. How much more money does Paul have than Jane?

Place the numbers 1, 2, 3, 4, and 5 in the five circles making each row and column sum to 9.

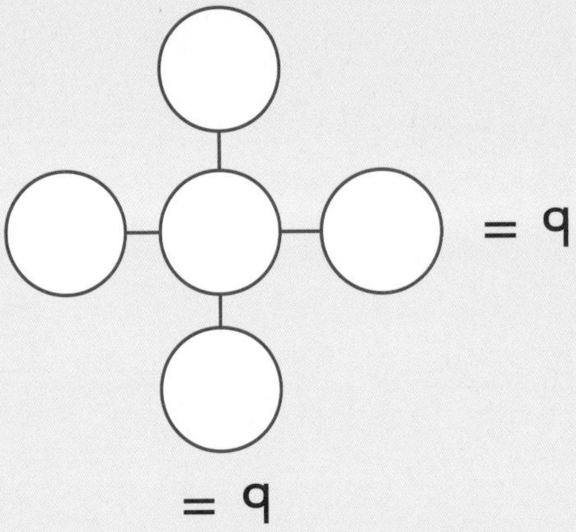

= 9

= 9

Place the numbers 1, 2, 3, 4, 5, and 6 in the six circles making each row and column sum to 12.

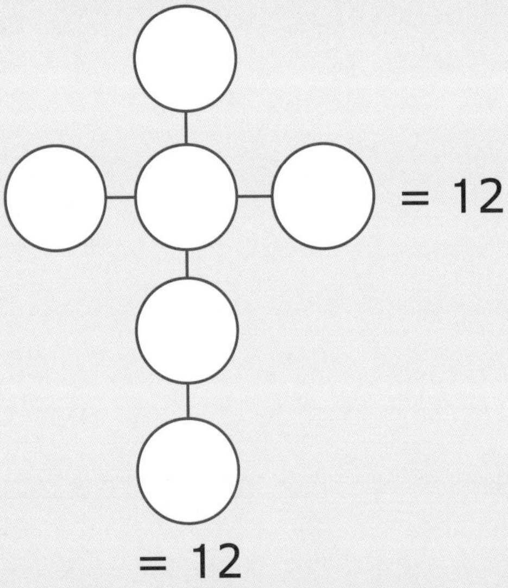

= 12

= 12

Place the numbers 1, 2, 3, 4, 5, and 6 in the six circles making each side of the triangle sum to 10.

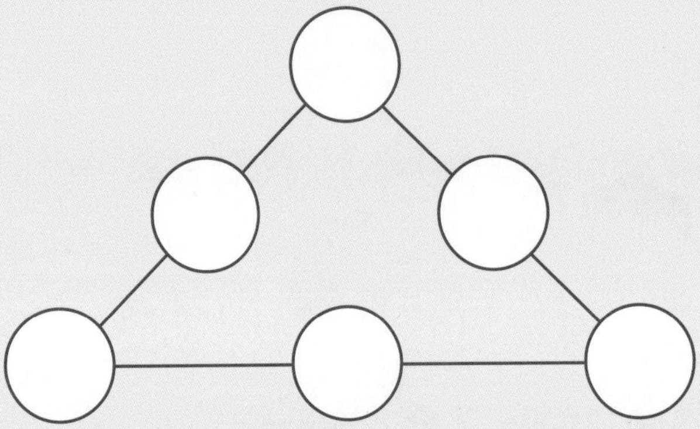

Find the missing number that
makes the number sentence
true. Find answers on the right.

a $2 + 8 = \underline{10}$ $\underline{G}$ A. 8

b $18 - 9 = \underline{\hphantom{00}}$ $\underline{\hphantom{00}}$ B. 81

c $9 \times 9 = \underline{\hphantom{00}}$ $\underline{\hphantom{00}}$ C. 5

d $54 \div 9 = \underline{\hphantom{00}}$ $\underline{\hphantom{00}}$ D. 7

e $9 + \underline{\hphantom{00}} = 16$ $\underline{\hphantom{00}}$ E. 4

f $\underline{\hphantom{00}} - 6 = 13$ $\underline{\hphantom{00}}$ F. 17

g $8 \times \underline{\hphantom{00}} = 32$ $\underline{\hphantom{00}}$ ~~G. 10~~

h $24 \div \underline{\hphantom{00}} = 3$ $\underline{\hphantom{00}}$ H. 29

i $8 + \underline{\hphantom{00}} = 24$ $\underline{\hphantom{00}}$ I. 19

j $27 - \underline{\hphantom{00}} = 10$ $\underline{\hphantom{00}}$ J. 16

k $6 \times \underline{\hphantom{00}} = 30$ $\underline{\hphantom{00}}$ K. 18

l $\underline{\hphantom{00}} \div 3 = 9$ $\underline{\hphantom{00}}$ L. 6

m $\underline{\hphantom{00}} + 7 = 25$ $\underline{\hphantom{00}}$ M. 3

n $\underline{\hphantom{00}} - 9 = 20$ $\underline{\hphantom{00}}$ N. 11

o $\underline{\hphantom{00}} \times 8 = 24$ $\underline{\hphantom{00}}$ O. 9

p $55 \div \underline{\hphantom{00}} = 5$ $\underline{\hphantom{00}}$ P. 27

The remainder (R) is the amount left over when a number cannot be divided evenly.

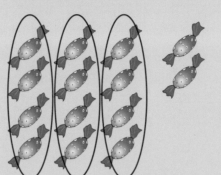

Ricky has 14 pieces of candy to give to 3 friends.

$$\begin{array}{r} 4 \\ 3\overline{)14} \\ -\underline{12} = 4 \times 3 \\ 2 \end{array}$$

$14 \div 3 = 4$ remainder 2

4 is the quotient and 2 is remaining. Write 4 R 2.

Find the quotient and remainder.

a
$$\begin{array}{r} 2 \text{ R } 1 \\ 5\overline{)11} \\ \underline{10} \\ 1 \end{array}$$

b
$4\overline{)13}$

c
$2\overline{)9}$

d
$6\overline{)19}$

e
$7\overline{)20}$

f
$8\overline{)27}$

g
$9\overline{)55}$

h
$3\overline{)29}$

i
$6\overline{)41}$

j
$8\overline{)67}$

k Madison has 16 teddy bears. If she can place 5 teddy bears on each of her 3 shelves, how many will she have left? Write a division sentence and solve.

Find all the quotients, then shade in all the boxes without remainders to find the boat's path to the dock.

Start

$9\overline{)72}$ $\frac{8}{72}$	$5\overline{)45}$	$4\overline{)22}$	$8\overline{)36}$	$9\overline{)56}$
$8\overline{)56}$	$7\overline{)32}$	$8\overline{)54}$	$6\overline{)45}$	$5\overline{)42}$
$7\overline{)42}$	$9\overline{)27}$	$6\overline{)36}$	$8\overline{)64}$	$7\overline{)38}$
$2\overline{)19}$	$8\overline{)63}$	$7\overline{)32}$	$4\overline{)32}$	$4\overline{)39}$
$6\overline{)32}$	$5\overline{)31}$	$9\overline{)36}$	$7\overline{)28}$	$3\overline{)28}$

How many of the division problems had a remainder? _____

How many of the division problems had no remainder? _____

Continue the pattern.

1.

2.

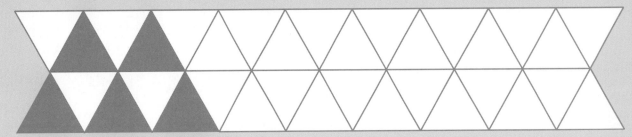

3.

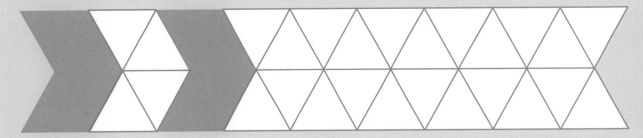

Make your own pattern.

4.

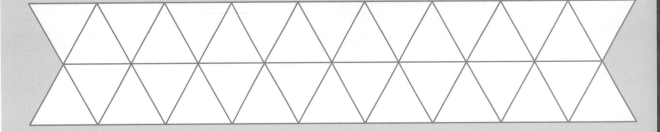

Fill in the missing numbers in the pattern.

1.

2.

3.

4.

5.

Make and describe your own pattern.

6.

Elapsed time is the amount of time that passes from the start of an activity to the end of that activity.

The short hand on the clock is the hour hand.

The long hand on the clock is the minute hand.

Start Time	Elapsed Time	Stop Time
11:55 a.m.	2 hours later	1:55 p.m.
5:00 p.m.	2 hours thirty minutes later	

Start Time	Elapsed Time	Stop Time
8:00 a.m.	4 hours forty minutes later	_____
5:15 p.m.	45 minutes later	_____
12:00 noon	twelve hours later	_____
3:15 p.m	_____	5:01 p.m.

7 days = 1 week

January						
Sun.	Mon.	Tue.	Wed.	Thu.	Fri.	Sat.
			1	2	3	4
5	6	7	8	9	10	11
12	13	14	15	16	17	18
19	20	21	22	23	24	25
26	27	28	29	30	31	

1. What day of the month is January 1st on?

   _____

2. How many days in January?

   _____

3. How many days in March?

   _____

4. How many days in February?

   _____

February						
Sun.	Mon.	Tue.	Wed.	Thu.	Fri.	Sat.
						1
2	3	4	5	6	7	8
9	10	11	12	13	14	15
16	17	18	19	20	21	22
23	24	25	26	27	28	

5. What is the difference between the total number of days in January and February? Write a number sentence for the problem.

   _____

March						
Sun.	Mon.	Tue.	Wed.	Thu.	Fri.	Sat.
						1
2	3	4	5	6	7	8
9	10	11	12	13	14	15
16	17	18	19	20	21	22
23	24	25	26	27	28	29
30	31					

6. On January 4th, Kim went on vacation. If she was gone for 2 months, in what month did she return?

   _____

7. One week and 3 days is the same amount of time as 10 days. Two weeks and 1 day is the same amount of time as _____ days.

8. Beginning February 1st through March 29th, Don practiced tennis every day except March 1st. How many days did he practice?

   _____

   How many weeks did he practice? _____

Use the numbers in the balloons to answer the questions.

1. Which numbers are greater than 572 and

   less than 581? _____

2. Which numbers are greater than 550 and

   less than 580? _____

3. Which number is greater than 580 and

   less than 585? _____

4. Which number is less than 579 and more than 570? _____

5. Write the numbers in the box from least to greatest.

   _____   _____   _____   _____

6. Write the numbers 468, 486, 480, and 488 in order from least
   to greatest.

   _____   _____   _____   _____

7. Write the numbers 110, 111, 101, and 100 in order from least
   to greatest.

   _____   _____   _____   _____

Use <, >, or = to make each number sentence true.

a   549 ⬜ 594   b   844 ⬜ 809

c   696 ⬜ 699   d   987 ⬜ 989

Find the actual answer and the estimated answer by rounding to the nearest tens place. Use the 5-Up Rule.

1   Actual

$$\begin{array}{r} 18 \\ + 45 \\ \hline 63 \end{array}$$

Estimated

$$\begin{array}{r} 20 \\ + 50 \\ \hline 70 \end{array}$$

2   Actual

$$\begin{array}{r} 58 \\ - 29 \\ \hline \end{array}$$

Estimated

$$\begin{array}{r} \\ - \\ \hline \end{array}$$

3   Actual

$$\begin{array}{r} 89 \\ - 51 \\ \hline \end{array}$$

Estimated

$$\begin{array}{r} \\ - \\ \hline \end{array}$$

4   Actual

$$\begin{array}{r} 17 \\ + 91 \\ \hline \end{array}$$

Estimated

$$\begin{array}{r} \\ + \\ \hline \end{array}$$

5   Actual

$$\begin{array}{r} 59 \\ + 49 \\ \hline \end{array}$$

Estimated

$$\begin{array}{r} \\ + \\ \hline \end{array}$$

6   Actual

$$\begin{array}{r} 58 \\ - 41 \\ \hline \end{array}$$

Estimated

$$\begin{array}{r} \\ - \\ \hline \end{array}$$

Find the actual answer and the estimated answer by rounding to the nearest hundreds place. Use the 5-Up Rule.

1   Actual   Estimated

        182   200
      + 450   + 500
        632   700

2   Actual   Estimated

        589
      − 292   − _____

3   Actual   Estimated

        437
      + 89   + _____

4   Actual   Estimated

        175
      − 103   − _____

5   Actual   Estimated

        546
      − 465   − _____

6   Actual   Estimated

        789
      + 987   + _____

Use the drawing on the left to help figure how much should be shaded in on the right for the given amount.

1.

100 cups
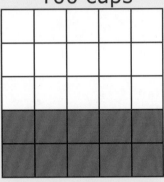

200 cups

2.

1 gallon

½ gallon

3.

10 liters
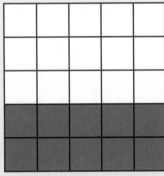

25 liters

4.

3 quarts

1 quart

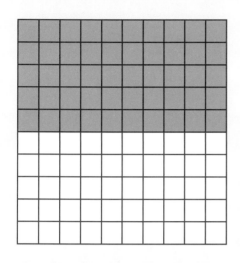

= This square written as a fraction is

$$\frac{50}{100}$$

= This square written in decimal form is

.50

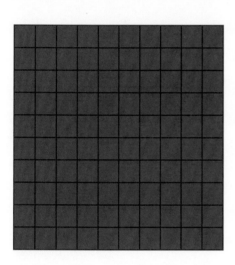

= This square written as a fraction is

$$\frac{100}{100}$$

= This square written in decimal form is

1.00

Write this square as a fraction and in decimal form.

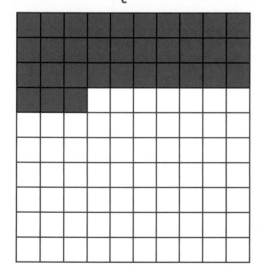

Fraction   Decimal

= _____ = .

Complete each number sentence.

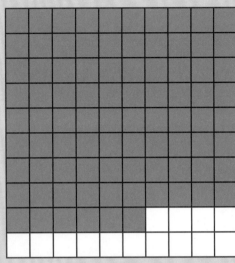

1.

Fraction   ## Decimal

= _____ = [.]

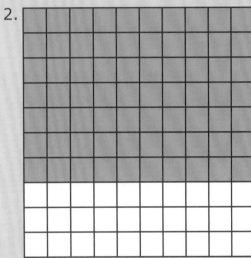

2.

= _____ = [.]

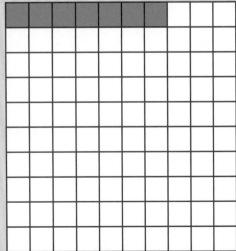

3.

= _____ = [.]

<u>Fraction</u>   <u>Decimal</u>

4. 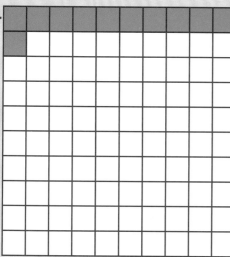   = _____ = ⬜.⬜

5. 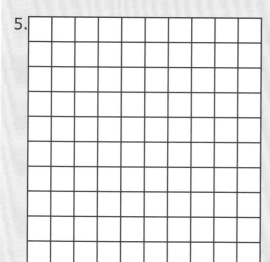   = _____ = ⬜.⬜

6.    = _____ = ⬜.⬜

Complete each number sentence.

1.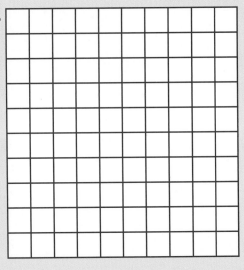

Fraction

Decimal

$= \quad \dfrac{32}{100} \quad = \quad .$

2.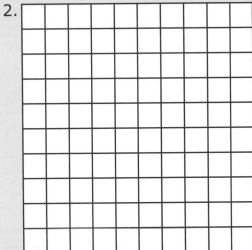

$= \quad \rule{3cm}{0.4pt} \quad = \quad .19$

3.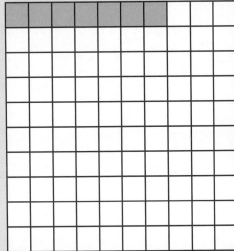

$= \quad \rule{3cm}{0.4pt} \quad = \quad .$

4.

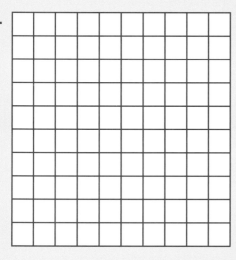

<u>Fraction</u>   <u>Decimal</u>

$= \dfrac{16}{100} =$ [.]

5.

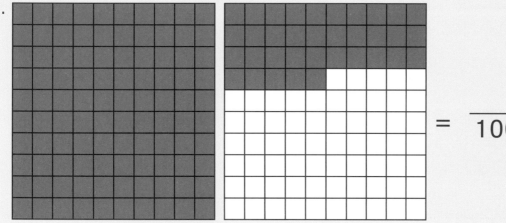

$= \dfrac{}{100} =$ [.]

6.

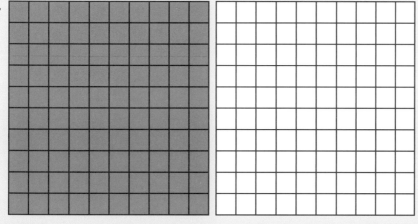

$= \dfrac{166}{100} =$ [.]

Write the missing number.

1. All triangles have _____ sides and _____ angles.

2. All quadrilaterals have _____ sides and _____ angles.

3. All pentagons have _____ sides and _____ angles.

4. All hexagons have _____ sides and _____ angles.

5. All octagons have _____ sides and _____ angles.

1. Draw 2 triangles.

2. Draw 2 quadrilaterals.

3. Draw 2 pentagons.

4. Draw 2 hexagons.

5. Draw 2 octagons.

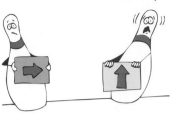

Ordered pairs locate points on a grid. The first number inside the parentheses tells how many spaces to move to the right. The second number tells how many spaces to move up.

The circle is located at (2,6).

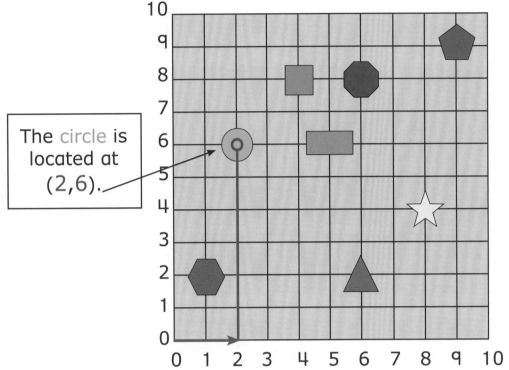

1. The triangle is located at   (_____, _____).

2. The rectangle is located at   (_____, _____).

3. The square is located at   (_____, _____).

4. The pentagon is located at   (_____, _____).

5. The hexagon is located at   (_____, _____).

6. The octagon is located at   (_____, _____).

7. What is located at (8, 4)?   _____

8. The line connecting the hexagon and the triangle is perpendicular to the line connecting

(_____, _____) and (_____, _____).

Find the product. Shade in the boxes with even answers to see a picture.

3 x 7	6 x 4	8 x 2	9 x 1	4 x 5 20	2 x 8	7 x 7
5 x 3	6 x 6	1 x 8	7 x 7	4 x 4	6 x 8	1 x 9
3 x 3	5 x 7	9 x 9	3 x 9	1 x 1	5 x 5	3 x 7
7 x 9	3 x 1	7 x 5	2 x 6	3 x 3	7 x 3	9 x 1
9 x 4	3 x 3	7 x 7	3 x 1	7 x 3	9 x 9	2 x 1
7 x 4	8 x 6	6 x 7	5 x 8	2 x 7	6 x 9	4 x 4

Write a multiplication sentence and solve. Check your answer.

1. How many ears do twenty cats have?   _____

2. How many wheels do three ATVs have?   _____

3. How many toes do four people have?   _____

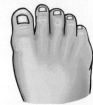

4. This dog found the same number of bones as Fido and
    Spot found. Together, how many have they found?   _____

5. If Bob makes $145 a week,
    how much does he make in five weeks?   _____

6. A company makes 350 brooms a week, how
    many brooms can be made in 8 weeks?   _____

Multiply to find each product, then cross out the answer below.

203	123	516	229	127	200
x 5	x 4	x 3	x 8	x 6	x 7

382	415	283	921	505	812
x 9	x 8	x 4	x 2	x 7	x 9

727	129	235	529	329	127
x 6	x 7	x 4	x 1	x 9	x 5

123	408	219	929	140	709
x 6	x 5	x 4	x 8	x 3	x 2

1,132	762	3,535	1,015	3,320
492	635	1,842	738	7,392
903	7,432	1,400	1,548	4,362
876	529	1,832	2,040	7,308
3,438	420	1,418	940	2,961

A jar contains 3 red marbles, 4 blue marbles, and 6 green marbles. What is the probability of pulling out a red marble?

_3_ out of _13_   or $\dfrac{3}{13}$

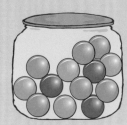

1. A die has 6 sides numbered 1 to 6. If the die is thrown once, what is the probability of rolling the number 2?

_____ out of _____   or   ____

2. A die has 6 sides numbered 1 to 6. If the die is thrown once, what is the probability of rolling an odd number?

_____ out of _____   or   ____

3. If one letter is chosen at random from the word class, what is the probability that the letter chosen is the letter "s"?

_____ out of _____   or   ____   CLASS

4. If a penny is tossed in the air, what is the probability that it will land heads up?

_____ out of _____   or   ____

Bob's TV Watching April 1–7th

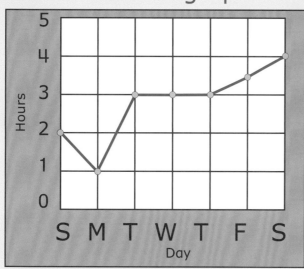

1. On which day did Bob watch the most television? _____

2. On which day did Bob watch the least television? _____

3. How many hours of television did Bob watch that week? _____

4. Estimate how many hours a day you watch television during a week and make a line graph with your results.

Monday: _____ hours   Friday: _____ hours

Tuesday: _____ hours   Saturday: _____ hours

Wednesday: _____ hours   Sunday: _____ hours

Thursday: _____ hours

Estimated TV Watching

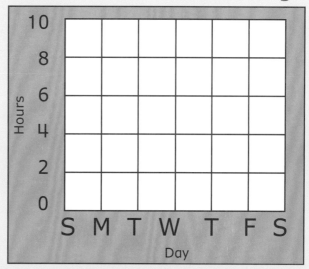

Write a division number sentence and check your answer.

1. Divide 17 butterflies into groups of 5.

____3____ groups with a remainder of ____2____

$$\begin{array}{r} 3 \text{ groups} \\ 5\overline{\smash{)}17} \\ \underline{-15} \\ 2 \text{ left over} \end{array}$$

2. Divide 21 owls into groups of 4.

_____ groups with a remainder of _____

3. Divide 11 roses into groups of 3.

_____ groups with a remainder of _____

4. Divide 34 envelopes into groups of 7.

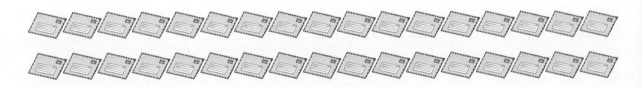

_____ groups with a remainder of _____

5. Divide 45 ants into groups of 6.

_____ groups with a remainder of _____

Division

First, write the
number of 2s in 9.

Second, multiply
4 × 2.

Third, subtract
9 – 8.

Fifth, divide
12 ÷ 2.

Finally, subtract the difference to
see if you have a remainder.

$$\begin{array}{r} 46 \\ 2\overline{)9\,2} \\ -\ 8 \\ \hline 1\,2 \\ -1\,2 \\ \hline \end{array}$$

Fourth, bring down
the next number.

Check: 2 × 46 = 92

First, write the
number of 3s in 7.

Second, multiply
3 × _____.

Third, subtract
7 – _____.

Fifth, divide
_____ ÷ 3.

Finally, subtract the difference to
see if you have a remainder.

$$\begin{array}{r} 3\overline{)7\,2} \\ - \\ \hline \\ - \\ \hline \end{array}$$

Fourth, bring down
the next number.

Check: 3 × ___ = 72

Find the quotient and write the letter of each answer to solve the riddle below.

t
$3\overline{)54}$

l
$4\overline{)252}$

d
$5\overline{)175}$

r
$8\overline{)344}$

y
$6\overline{)510}$

a
$7\overline{)364}$

e
$9\overline{)495}$

s
$8\overline{)752}$

Where can you buy a ruler that is 3 feet long?

$\overline{52}$ $\overline{18}$ $\overline{52}$ $\overline{85}$ $\overline{52}$ $\overline{43}$ $\overline{35}$ $\overline{94}$ $\overline{52}$ $\overline{63}$ $\overline{55}$

Circle the mixed number that matches the picture.

1.  = $\frac{2}{7}$ $\boxed{3\frac{1}{2}}$ $\frac{2}{8}$ 4

2.  = $2\frac{1}{4}$ $2\frac{3}{4}$ $\frac{1}{9}$ $3\frac{3}{4}$

3. = $3\frac{2}{17}$ $3\frac{3}{5}$ $\frac{2}{17}$ $3\frac{2}{5}$

4.  = $1\frac{1}{6}$ $1\frac{1}{5}$ $\frac{2}{17}$ $1\frac{5}{6}$

Circle the fraction that does not belong.

a $\frac{3}{3}$ $\frac{5}{5}$ $\frac{1}{2}$ 1

b $\frac{1}{2}$ $\frac{3}{6}$ $\frac{4}{8}$ $\frac{2}{1}$

c $\frac{1}{3}$ $\frac{4}{8}$ $\frac{2}{6}$ $\frac{3}{9}$

d $\frac{2}{8}$ $\frac{4}{10}$ $\frac{1}{4}$ $\frac{3}{12}$

Write a fraction for each shaded part and
solve the addition or subtraction problem.

1. 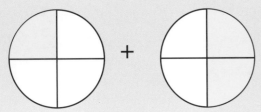 + 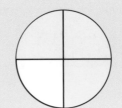 =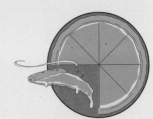

___ ___ ___

2. 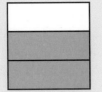 - =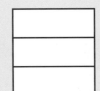

___ ___ ___

3. 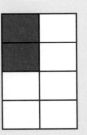 + 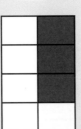 =

___ ___ ___

4.  +  =

___ ___ ___

Customary Units

Measure Length

12 inches (in.) = 1 foot (ft)
3 feet = 1 yard (yd)
5,280 feet = 1 mile (mi)

1 inch

Circle the best measurement for each item.

1. length of a school bus

   40 inches   40 feet   40 yards

2. length of a bed

   75 inches   75 feet   75 yards

3. marathon distance

   26 feet   26 yards   26 miles

4. length of a calculator

   1 inch   5 inches   10 inches

5. length of your arm

   1 inch   1 foot   1 yard

6. distance between Denver and Seattle

   1,023 yards   1,023 miles   1,023 feet

Measure Weight

A slice of bread weighs about 1 ounce.

16 ounces (oz) = 1 pound (lb)

Circle the best measurement for each item.

1. weight of an apple
   3 ounces   3 pounds

2. baby's weight
   6 ounces   6 pounds

3. weight of a truck
   5,000 ounces   5,000 pounds

4. 500 sheets of notebook paper
   5 ounces   5 pounds

Measure Capacity

A school milk carton holds 1 cup.

2 cups (c) = 1 pint (pt)
2 pints   = 1 quart (qt)
4 quarts   = 1 gallon (gal)

5. small dish of ice cream
   1 cup   1 quart

6. small swimming pool water
   5,000 cups   5,000 gallons

7. container of jam
   1 pint   1 gallon

8. gasoline for a truck
   20 quarts   20 gallons

Metric Units

┃┃ 1 centimeter 1	## Measure Length 100 centimeters (cm) = 1 meter (m) 1,000 meters = 1 kilometer (km)

Circle the best measurement for each item.

1. distance between Chicago and Dallas

   1,300 cm   1,300 m   1,300 km

2. length of a shoe

   20 cm   20 m   20 km

3. length of a blue whale

   31 cm   31 m   31 km

4. length of a dollar bill

   15 cm   15 m   15 km

5. length of your arm

   1 cm   1 m   1 km

6. distance from school

   5 cm   5 m   5 km

Draw a picture of an animal that might be 1 centimeter tall.

A paper clip
weighs about 1 gram.

Measure Weight

1000 grams (g) = 1 kilogram (kg)

Circle the best measurement for each item.

1. weight of a nickel

    5 grams   5 kilograms

2. weight of a dog

    28 grams.   28 kilograms

3. weight of a cough drop

    2 grams   2 kilograms

4. weight of a textbook

    2 grams   2 kilograms

Measure Capacity

An eyedropper holds
about 1 milliliter.

1,000 milliliters (mL) = 1 liter (L)

5. liquid in a test tube

    10 mL   10 L

6. water in a pan

    1 mL   1 L

7. soup in a small bowl

    500 mL   500 L

8. large bottle of soda pop

    1 mL   1 L

Measure Capacity

1,000 milliliters (mL) = 1 liter (L)

× 1,000

How many milliliters of liquid are in each tube?

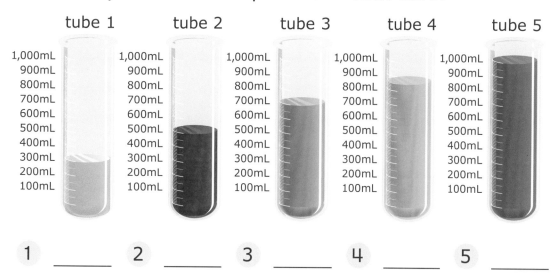

tube 1   tube 2   tube 3   tube 4   tube 5

1 _____ 2 _____ 3 _____ 4 _____ 5 _____

6 How many liters are in tube 5? _____

7 200 mL + _____ = 1 L   8 500 mL + _____ = 1 L

9 100 mL + _____ = 1 L   10 250 mL + _____ = 1 L

11 300 mL + 40 mL = _____   12 15 mL + 25 mL = _____

13 45 mL + 100 mL + 270 mL = _____

14 If tube 1 and tube 3 were emptied into a jar, how many
    total milliliters would be in the jar? _____

    How many liters would be in the jar? _____

15 2000 mL = _____ L   16 8 L = _____ mL

17 3 L = _____ mL   18 10,000 mL = _____ L

19 300 mL + 600 mL + 500 mL + 600 mL = _____ L

Figure the change, then cross out the answer below. Be sure to line the decimals up before you subtract and label your answer.

$$
\begin{array}{r}
\overset{9\ 9}{\$1\cancel{0}.\cancel{0}0} \text{ Paid} \\
-\ \underline{8.51} \text{ Cost} \\
\$\ 1.49 \text{ Change}
\end{array}
$$

	Paid	Cost	Number Sentence	Change
a	$10.00	$2.50	$$\overset{9\ 9}{\$1\cancel{0}.\cancel{0}0}\\ -\ \underline{2.50}\\ \$\ 7.50$$	$7.50
b	$15.00	$1.99		
c	$20.00	$5.09		
d	$5.00	$3.17		

 $7.50 $1.49  $13.01 $14.81 $1.83  $14.91

Paid	Cost	Number Sentence	Change
e $50.00	$7.48		
f $2.00	$.50		
g $5.00	$2.09		
h $10.00	$9.25		
i $4.00	$1.49		

 $2.51 $1.50 $43.52 $42.52 $ .75 $2.91

Figure the change, then cross out the answer below. Be sure to line the decimals up before you subtract and label your answer.

	Paid	Cost	Number Sentence	Change
a	$6.25	$6.20		
b	$10.20	$6.15		
c	$10.05	$6.04		
d	$20.75	$11.50		
e	$50.50	$12.38		

$9.75 $ .05 $38.12 $4.05 $9.25 $4.01

Estimate the length of each line to the nearest half-inch.
Measure and record the actual length to the nearest half-inch.

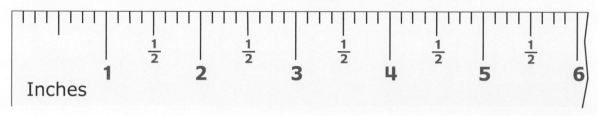

1

2

3

4

5

6

7

8

Line	Estimated Length	Actual Length
1		
2		
3		
4		
5		
6		
7		
8		

Estimate then measure the length of the lines to the nearest centimeter. Label your measurements. Use the results to answer the riddle.

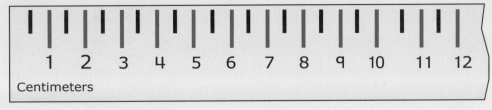

h

m

f

l

a

o

e

t

Line	Estimated (cm)	Actual (cm)
h		
m		
f		
l		
o		
a		
t		
e		

Which months have twenty days?

___   ___   ___   ___   ___   ___   ___   ___   ___
2 cm 10 cm 10 cm   7 cm 8 cm   4 cm 11 cm 1 cm 3 cm

Division

First, write the number of 2s in 9.

Second, multiply 4 × 2.

Third, subtract 9 – 8.

Fifth, divide 12 ÷ 2.

Finally, subtract the difference to see if you have a remainder.

Fourth, bring down the next number.

$$\begin{array}{r} 46 \\ 2\overline{)92} \\ -8 \\ \hline 12 \\ -12 \\ \hline \end{array}$$

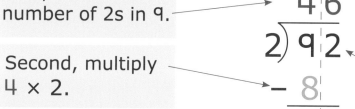

Check: 2 × 46 = 92

Use short division to find the quotient and answer the riddle.

l
$$7\overline{)322}$$

m
$$6\overline{)558}$$

t
$$9\overline{)711}$$

e
$$8\overline{)304}$$

r
$$5\overline{)475}$$

h
$$4\overline{)312}$$

What occurs once in a minute, but never in an hour?

$$\overline{79}\;\overline{78}\;\overline{38}\quad\overline{46}\;\overline{38}\;\overline{79}\;\overline{79}\;\overline{38}\;\overline{95}\quad\overline{93}$$

1. The circus collected $415 from ticket sales. If each ticket costs $5, how many tickets were sold? _____

2. The theatre has 207 seats. If there are 9 seats in a row, how many rows does the theatre have? _____

3. Ricky made a total of $216 for working 8 days. How much did he make each day? _____

Balance Math™

Use the balance scales to solve each problem.

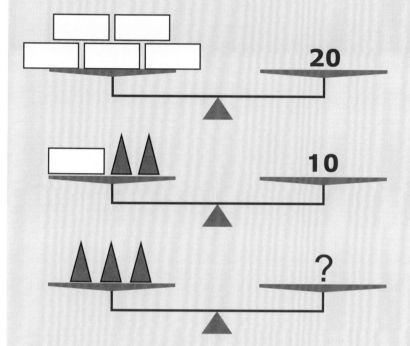

20

10

?

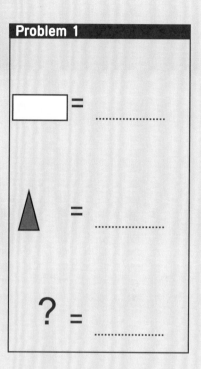

Problem 1

☐ = ...

▲ = ...

? = ...

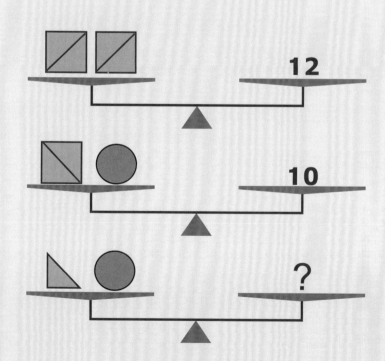

12

10

?

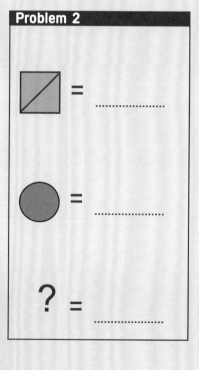

Problem 2

◧ = ...

● = ...

? = ...

*For more activities like this, please see our *Balance Math™ & More!* series.

Write a number sentence to solve each problem.

1. The United States Congress consists of the Senate and House of Representatives. The House of Representatives has 435 voting members, and the Senate has 100. How many members are in Congress altogether?

_____

2. John weighs 101 pounds and Juanita weighs 84 pounds. What is the difference in their weights? _____

3. A box of chocolates has 4 rows. Each row has 8 chocolates. How many chocolates are in the box? _____

4. Altogether 54 students signed up to play basketball. If there are 6 teams, how many students are on each team?

_____

5. At birth, the human body has about 350 bones. By adulthood, some of our bones have fused together to make 206 bones. What is the difference between the numbers of bones a baby has compared to an adult?

_____

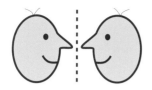

Reflection

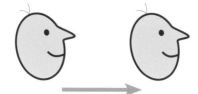

Translation

Rotation

State reflection, translation, or rotation.

1. _____

2. _____

3. _____

4. _____

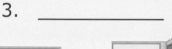

5. _____

6. _____

7. _____

8. _____

51 rounded to the nearest ten is 50.

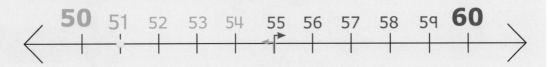

150 rounded to the nearest hundred is 200.

1,300 rounded to the nearest thousand is 1,000.

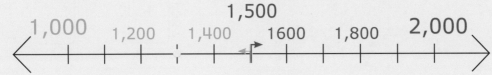

Round to the nearest ten.

a   81   _____

b   11   _____

c   50   _____

d   75   _____

e   99   _____

Round to the nearest hundred.

f   237   _____

g   101   _____

h   850   _____

i   967   _____

j   95   _____

Round to the nearest thousand.

k   8,909   _____

l   8,200   _____

m   5,005   _____

n   9,239   _____

o   949   _____

A **quadrilateral** is a four sided polygon.

Rectangle:    a quadrilateral with 4 right angles and
                        2 sets of parallel sides

Square:    a quadrilateral with 4 right angles,
                        2 sets of parallel sides, and 4 equal sides

Parallelogram:    a quadrilateral with 2 sets of parallel sides
                        and opposite sides and angles are equal

Rhombus:    a quadrilateral with 2 sets of parallel sides
                        and 4 equal sides

Trapezoid: 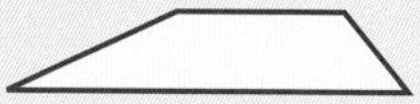   a quadrilateral with 1 set of parallel sides

1. Name three things that a rectangle, square,
    parallelogram, rhombus, and trapezoid have in common.

    _____ _____ _____

2. A square is a rectangle with 4 equal sides.*
    By definition, is a rhombus a parallelogram? _____

3. Fill in the following chart to determine how the
    quadrilaterals are the same and different.
    Write *yes* or *no* in each box if it is something they
    must have.

	4 sides	4 equal sides	1 pair parallel sides	2 pairs parallel sides
rectangle				
square				
parallelogram				
rhombus				
trapezoid				

*In naming, use the most precise term.

Name the quadrilateral and explain why your answer is correct.

1. 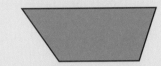 _____

_____

_____

2. _____

_____

_____

Match each quadrilateral with its name.

3. rhombus _____ a.

4. rectangle _____ b.

5. parallelogram _____ c.

6. trapezoid _____ d.

7. square _____ e.

8. quadrilateral _____ f.

Solid Figures

Cube

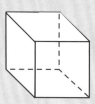

Rectangular prism

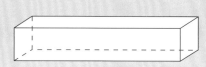

Sphere

Cylinder

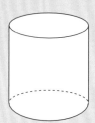

Cone

Square Pyramid

Match each shape above with the closest shape below.

1. Cube = ____

2. Rectangular Prism = ____

3. Sphere = ____

4. Cylinder = ____

5. Cone = ____

6. Square Pyramid = ____

a

b

c

d

e

f

Write a number sentence to solve each problem.

1. The auditorium seats 359 people. If an upcoming concert has sold 193 tickets, how many more tickets can be sold?

_____

2. Jamie bought a pair of jeans for $19, and a shirt for $29. What is the total of her purchases?

_____

3. Tom bought 5 boxes of doughnuts. Each box had a dozen doughnuts in it. Altogether, how many doughnuts did he have?

_____

4. Rob makes $6 per hour mowing lawns. How many hours does he have to mow to earn $54?

_____

5. In the 3rd grade class, there are 17 girls and 8 boys. How many more girls than boys are in the class?

_____

6. Lisa spent $32 for 4 tickets to the show. How much did each ticket cost?

_____

In each problem, cross out the sentence that is not needed to solve the problem. Then solve the problem.

1. Kim was driving 55 miles per hour. She had driven 213 miles of a 320 mile trip. How many miles did she have left to drive on the trip?

   _____

2. George bought 2 bikes at $89 each. He also bought a $69 skateboard. How much did he spend on the bikes?

   _____

3. In 2007, there are 435 representatives and 100 senators in the U.S. Congress. Representative members serve for 2 years, and senator members serve for 6 years. What is the total membership in the U.S. Congress?

   _____

Match the operations.

4. plus = _a_

5. take away = ___

6. quotient = ___

7. product = ___

8. difference = ___

9. sum = ___

10. times = ___

a **+**   b **−**

c **X**   d **÷**

SMARTY PANTS PUZZLES™

The Friday Special!
Free candy bar with every purchase over $10!

Write whether each sentence is true, false, or unknown based on the information on the sign.

_____ 1. Today is Friday and Rob left the store with a candy bar and a bag of groceries so Rob had to spend over $10 at the store.

_____ 2. If you buy $11 worth of candy on Friday, you can choose your own candy bar?

_____ 3. If Tim buys $30 on Friday, the store must give him a free candy bar.

_____ 4. Bonnie spent $25 at the store so she received a free candy bar.

_____ 5. If Linda buys $10 on Friday, the store must give her a free candy bar.

SMARTY PANTS PUZZLES™

Half-Off Sale!

Buy one game, and then get half off your next game.

Write whether each sentence is true, false, or unknown based on the information on the sign.

_____ 1. If you use this sale to buy two games that regularly cost $10 each, you will only pay $10 for both games.

_____ 2. If you use this sale to buy two games that regularly cost $20 each, you will only pay $30 for both games.

_____ 3. This sale does not promise you any savings if you only buy one game.

_____ 4. You must buy both games at the same time to get half-off your next game.

_____ 5. If you buy three games that normally sell for $10 each, the sign guarantees you will save $20.

_____ 6. If you want to buy a $20 game and a $10 game, you could use this sale to save $10.

Answers

Page 1   1. 2;   2. 20;   3. 1;   4. 19;   5. even;
                  6. odd;   7. even;   8. even;   9. even;   10. odd

Page 2   2. one hundred one;   3. two hundred twenty-eight;
                  4. nine hundred fifty-two;   5. sixty-four;   6. six hundred thirty-nine;
                  7. forty-five;   8. one hundred forty-eight

Page 3   Sample checks will vary.

Page 4   2. 2,000 + 300 + 70 + 6;   3. 700 + 6; 4. 300 + 40 + 9;
                  5. 5,000 + 200 + 80;   6. 9,000 + 800 + 60 + 5;   7. 2,000 + 300 + 40 + 1

Page 5   2nd 1,000 + 600 + 60 + 7, one thousand, six hundred sixty-seven;
                  3rd 1,000 + 400 + 80 + 3, one thousand, four hundred eighty-three;
                  4th 1,000 + 400 + 50 + 1, one thousand, four hundred fifty-one;
                  5th 1,000 + 300 + 80 + 1, one thousand, three hundred eighty-one;
                  6th 1,000 + 300 + 60 + 2, one thousand, three hundred sixty-two;
                  7th 1,000 + 200 + 80 + 3, one thousand, two hundred eighty-three;
                  8th 1,000 + 200 + 60, one thousand, two hundred sixty;

Page 6   a. 81;   b. 91;   c. 111;   d. 101;   e. 121;   f. 92;   g. 102;   h. 112;
                  i. 93;   j. 122;   k. 73;   l. 103;   m. 83;   n. 113;   o. 123;   p. 93

Page 7   a. 3, 6, 8, 2, 1, 9, 7, 4, 5;   b. 4, 7, 3, 9, 5, 1, 2, 8, 6;
                  c. 2, 9, 6, 5, 3, 1, 4, 8, 7;   d. 1, 4, 5, 7, 3, 2, 9, 6, 8;
                  e. 9, 2, 7, 1, 6, 8, 4, 3, 5

Page 8   a. 1,019;   b. 655;   c. 1,188;   d. 1,200;   e. 1,211;   f. 1,750;   g. 900;
                  h. 1,079;   i. 942;   j. 901

Page 9   1. 7;   2. 8;   3. 5;   4. 2;   5. 25;   6. 11;   7. 6;   8. 0;   9. 3;   10. 6;
                  11. commutative;   12. associative;   13. zero

Page 10   1. Joel;   2. Rick;   3. $5;   4. Ann, Sue, Joel, and Alex;   5. Rick;   6. Rick

Page 11   1.   2.   3. C;   4. D;   5. B

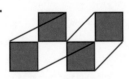

Page 12   c. 80;   a. 20;   s. 50;   u. 30;   o. 10;   n. 400;   t. 200;   f. 300;   h. 700;
                  b. 500; a bunch of ants

Page 13   a. 113 (A), 110 (E);   b. 125 (A), 120 (E);   c. 98 (A), 100 (E);
                  d. 324 (A), 330 (E);   e. 118 (A), 120 (E);   f. 64 (A), 70 (E);
                  g. 934 (A), 900 (E);   h. 1,881 (A), 1900 (E);   i. 448 (A), 400 (E);
                  j. 130 (A), 100 (E);   k. 1,022 (A), 1000 (E);   l. 323 (A), 300 (E)

Page 14   1. 44 & 93; 2. More than one correct answer; sample answer:
          (29 + 11; 30 + 10 = 40). 3. 20+10+10+10+20+20=90

Page 15   8 + 8 + 8 = 24 gallons

Page 16   1. 700 + 30 + 5; 2. Seven hundred thirty-five

Page 17   1. 34 + 39 = 73; 2. 689 + 160 = 849; 3. Answers will vary.

Page 18   1. 21 − 14 = 7; 2. $69 − 43 = $26; 3. Answers will vary.

Page 19   More than one correct answer; sample answers:

Page 20   More than one correct answer; sample answers:

Page 21   1-2 More than one correct answer; sample answers:

1.  ; 2. ; 3. , 2; 4. 4

Page 23   1. $.75; 2. $1.20; 3. $1.35; 4. $2.35; 5. $2.50

Page 24   2. $1.12; 3. $1.25; 4. $3.00; 5. $.27; 6. $3.01

Page 25   7. $10.01; 8. $1.01; 9. $5.00; 10. $10.25; 11. $5.05; 12. $11.01

Page 26   a. $4.48; b. $4.78; c. $4.99; d. $5.97

Page 27   e. $6.77; f. $8.50; g. $7.98; h. $9.98

Page 28      2, 4, 6, 8, 10, 12, 14;
          1, 3, 5, 7, 9, 11, 13;
          1, 2, 4, 7, 11, 16, 22, 29, 37;
          1, 1, 2, 3, 5, 8, 13, 21, 34, 55

Page 29 $.50 (A), $1.00 (E); $1.45 (A), $1.00 (E);
          $2.50 (A), $3.00 (E); $1.49 (A), $1.00 (E)

Page 30   1. 37, 121, 152, 152, 72;   2. 102, 159, 55, 151, 123;
          3. 102, 137, 120, 156, 156; 4. 120, 127, 137, 191, 155

Page 31   21, 23, 44, 32, 70, 21, 35; k. 22; i. 34; h. 23; c. 31; s. 15; t. 29;
          o. 18; e. 16; cookie sheets

Page 32   a. >; b. >; c. <; d. >; e. >; f. <; g. >; h. <; i. =; j. <;
          k. <; l. >; m. <; n. =; o. <

Page 33   a. 114; b. 112; c. 272; d. 334; e. 123; f. 477; g. 150; h. 412;
i. 486; j. 323; 112, 114, 123, 150, 272, 323, 334, 412, 477, 486

Page 34

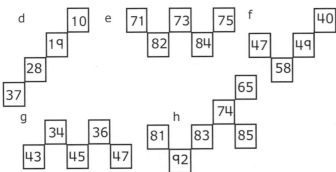

Page 35   5, A=6; 2, B=17; 3, C=11; 8, D=15; 2, E=16; 7, F=9; 9, G=18;
5, H=25; 12, I=8; 5, J=14; 5, K=7; 12, L=10; 4, M=5; 11,
N=19; 6, O=13; GOOD JOB

Pages 36-37

a	1			2
b	2			2
c		4		1
d	1	1		2
e		4	2	

;

f	3		1	
g	3	2		4
h	4			
i	2		3	2
j	2	3		1

Pages 38-39   b. $.41 < $.65; c. $.27 < $.71; d. $.38 = $.38; e. $.86 < $.93;
f. $.57 > $.47; g. $.76 = $.76; h. $.52 < $.98

Page 40   triangle; triangle; octagon; quadrilateral; pentagon; quadrilateral
More than one correct answer; sample answer: 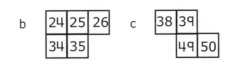, hexagon

Page 41   1. A, B, F, G; 2. D, E; 3. C, H; More than one correct answer,
sample answer: [triangles figure].

Page 42   Estimated lengths may vary. Actual lengths are as follows: 1. 9cm;
2. 14cm; 3. 12cm; 4. 1cm; 5. 3cm; 6. 10cm; 7. 2cm

Page 43   The result will always be a multiple of 9.

Page 44   a. 3 in.; e. 1 in.; r. 5 in.; l. 6 in.; y. 4 in., o. 7 in.; you rule

Page 45   1. dog; 2. fish; 3. 3 gerbils; 4. More than one correct answer;
sample answer:

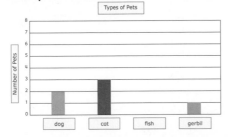

Page 46   parallelogram; rhombus; trapezoid. More than one correct answer; sample answer:

Page 47   1. 60 – 10 = 50; 2. 60 – 10 = 50; 3. 200 – 100 = 100;
           4. 400 – 200 = 200; 5. 800 – 700 = 100

Page 49   2. eight o-five, 8:05; 3. nine, 9:00; 4. 10:35 - 10:05 = thirty minutes

Page 50   b. 113; c. 189; d. 619; e. 211; f. 219; g. 111;
           h. 317; i. 541; j. 216; k. 125; l. 118; m. 381; n. 612; o. 125

Page 51   1.   2.

           3.   4.

           5.   6.

Page 52   a. 8, 9, 10; b. 12345, 123456, 1234567; c. 29, 37, 46; d. 31, 36, 41;
           e. 5, 5, 5; f. 94, 93, 92; g. 16, 17, 19; h. 19, 21, 23; i. 5, 5, 6, 6;
           j. 20, 32, 44

Page 53   1. e; 2. a; 3. c; 4. i; 5. b; 6. d; 7. f; 8. g; 9. h

Page 54   a. 8; b. 9; c. 3; d. 7; e. 6; f. 5; g. 15; h. 2; i. 1; j. 4; k. 11;
           l. 12; m. 10; n. 13; o. 14; seal

Page 55   3 × 5 = 15; 2 × 4 = 8; 3 × 8 = 24; 3 × 2 = 6; 2 × 9 = 18;
           5 × 1 = 5; 3 × 7 = 21; 3 × 5 = 15; 4 × 10 = 40; 2 × 6 = 12

Page 56   12 and 12; 20 and 4; 12 and 4; 2 and 9; 21 and 3, 21;
           3 and 3; 5 and 1, 5; 5 and 5, 25; 24 and 4,6

Page 57   2 × 5 = 5 + 5 = 10; 3 × 3 = 3 + 3 + 3 = 9;
           4 × 4 = 4 + 4 + 4 +4 = 16; 7 × 3 = 7 + 7 + 7 = 21;
           2 × 9 = 9 + 9 = 18; 5 × 5 = 5 + 5 + 5 + 5 + 5 = 25;
           6 × 1 = 1 + 1 + 1 + 1 + 1 + 1 = 6; 4 × 6 = 6 + 6 + 6 + 6 = 24

Page 58   a. 15, 15, 16, 18, 40, 28; b. 36, 30, 20, 35, 24, 24; c. 12, 30, 28, 12, 45, 0;
           d. 20, 24, 28, 32, 36, 40; e. 25, 30, 35, 40, 45, 50

Page 59   a. 10, 10, 7, 7, 15; b. 36, 16, 21, 12, 8; c. 27, 14, 24, 6, 24;
           d. 6, 27, 18, 8, 20

Page 60   a. 63, 42, 63, 48, 12, 14; b. 56, 36, 49, 36, 35, 18;
           c. 24, 30, 7, 0, 63, 12; d. 30, 36, 42, 48, 54, 60; e. 35, 42, 49, 56, 63, 70

Page 61   a. 40, 40, 72, 64, 81, 48; b. 27, 56, 8, 35, 12, 16; c. 36, 24, 45, 32, 9, 0;
           d. 40, 48, 56, 64, 72, 80; e. 45, 54, 63, 72, 81, 90

Page 62   a. 16, 28, 6, 36, 6, 0; b. 40, 36, 6, 45, 16, 28; c. 20, 54, 56, 81, 64, 42;
           d. 49, 36, 18, 32, 24, 10; e. 9, 0, 48, 54, 56, 35

Page 63
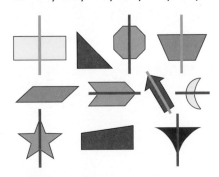

Page 64

Page 65   1. 6;   2. 100;   3. 5;   4. 2;   5. 50;   6. 6;   7. 20;   8. 0;   9. 20;
           10. 4; 11. associative; 12. identity; 13. commutative

Page 66
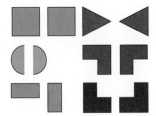

Page 67   More than one correct answer; sample answers:
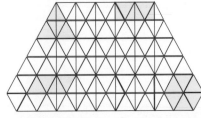
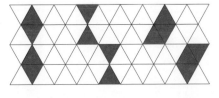

Page 68   1. March 20; 2. February 16; 3. March 8; 4. March 28;
           5. eight weeks six days; 6. 48 days; 7. 4 weeks

Page 69   1. 2011; 2. 36 months; 3. 15 years old; 4. 9 years 2 months;
           5. 10 years old; 6. 18 months

Page 70   1. 7 inches; 2. 3 yards; 3. 12 feet   4. 8 inches; 5. 700 miles; 6. 2
           inches; 7. 10 feet; 8. 100 yards

Page 71   1. black and brown; 2. blue and red;
           1. blue, vertical; 2. green, horizontal

Page 72   MOTHEMATICS

Page 73   a. $9.62, $5.63, $13.47, $6.19, $1.01; b. $6.64, $6.09, $8.47, $11.29, $6.73;
           c. $8.24, $6.59, $3.28, $7.22, $11.44; d. $4.82, $10.42, $23.64, $16.17, $8.54

Page 74   2. $4.25; 3. $4.31; 4. $3.50; 5. $17.75; 6. $19.25; 7. $19.31

Page 75   1. even; 2. odd; 3. even; 4. odd; 5. odd; 6. even; 7. odd; 8. odd;
9. even; a. 31, odd; b. 30, even; c. 24, even; d. 42, even;
e. 81, odd; f. 32, even; g. 250, even; h. 39, odd; i. 156, even

Page 76   1. 90°F; 2. 30°F; 3. 50°F; 4. 350°F; 5. 40°F

Page 77   1. 32°C; 2. 1°C; 3. 10°C; 4. 180°C; 5. 3°C

Page 78   1. 2 pints; 2. 2 pints; 3. 2 gallons; 4. 2 quarts; 5. 1 quart

Page 79   1. 400 mL; 2. 10mL; 3. 500 mL; 4. 3 L; 5. 2 L; 6. 1000 L; 7. 10 mL; 8. 2 L

Page 80   More than one correct answer; sample answers:

Page 81   1. blue; 2. yellow; 3. no

Page 82   1. yellow, blue, red; 2. heads, tails; 3. green; 4. 1 in 8, 5 in 8, 2 in 8

Page 83   1. ; 2. ; 3. ; 4. ; 5. ; 6.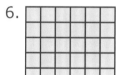

Page 84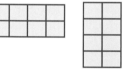

Page 85   ; ;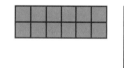

Page 86   1. factors; 2. less than; 3. addends; 4. difference; 5. equal;
6. product; 7. greater than; 8. sum

Page 87   1. 35; 2. 20; 3. 6, 12, 18; 4. 12, 24, 36; 5. 24

Page 88   1. 3; 2. 5; 3. 22; 4. 22 – 8 = 14; 5. 22 – 5 – 3 = 14

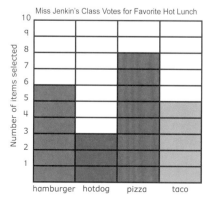

Page 89   1. 3 groups of 6 = 18, 6 + 6 + 6 = 18, 3 × 6 = 18;

                    2. 4 groups of 3 = 12, 3 + 3 + 3 + 3 = 12, 4 × 3 = 12;

                    3. 2 groups of 7 = 14, 7 + 7 = 14, 2 × 7 = 14

Page 90   1. 4 people; 2. 3 flowers

Page 91   1. 3 guitars; 2. 6 pieces of candy;

                    3. $.25 + $.25 + $.25 + $.25 = $1.00

Pages 92-93 1. 8 ÷ 4 = 2 groups; 2. 15 ÷ 5 = 3 groups; 3. 12 ÷ 3 = 4 groups;

                    4. 12 ÷ 4 = 3 groups; 5. 16 ÷ 8 = 2 groups; 6. 21 ÷ 7 = 3 groups

Page 94   b. 3, ; c. 5, ; d. 4, ;

                e. 3, 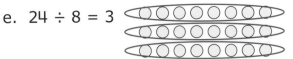; f. 6, ; g. 2,

                h. 14 ÷ 7 = 2; i. 15 ÷ 5 = 3; j. 6 ÷ 2 = 3; k. 20 ÷ 5 = 4

Page 95   a. 8 ÷ 2 = 4; b. 9 ÷ 3 = 3; ; c. 16 ÷ 4 = 4,

                ; d. 25 ÷ 5 = 5,

                e. 24 ÷ 8 = 3

Page 96   a. 61; b. 67; c. 19; d. 36; e. 26; f. 77; g. 18; h. 69; i. 38; j. 62;

                k. 404; l. 191; m. 356; n. 167; o. 59; p. 307; q. 168; r. 91;

                s. 177; t. 626; u. 99; v. 46; w. 199; x. 378; y.h 297; launch

Page 97   9 ÷ 3 = 3; $3\overline{)12}^{\,4}$; 4 ÷ 2 = 2; $4\overline{)12}^{\,3}$; 15 ÷ 5 = 3; $6\overline{)18}^{\,3}$;

                14 ÷ 7 = 2; $10\overline{)20}^{\,2}$; 25 ÷ 5 = 5; $9\overline{)18}^{\,2}$; 16 ÷ 4 = 4 ; $3\overline{)24}^{\,8}$;

                14 ÷ 2 = 7; $7\overline{)21}^{\,3}$; 15 ÷ 3 = 5; $8\overline{)16}^{\,2}$; 20 ÷ 5 = 4; $9\overline{)27}^{\,3}$

Pages 98-99 1. 8 ÷ 2 = 4, 4 × 2 = 8;   2. $8\overline{)24}^{\,3}$, 3 × 8 = 24;

                3. 16 ÷ 4 = 4, 4 × 4 = 16; 4. 20 ÷ 5 = 4, 4 × 5 = 20;

                5. 20 ÷ 4 = 5, 4 × 5 = 20

                                            20   15   10   5

Page 100   a. 10 ÷ 2 = 5; b. $8\overline{)24}^{\,3}$; c. 28 ÷ 7 = 4; d. $5\overline{)20}^{\,4}$; $\frac{-5}{15}$; $\frac{-5}{10}$; $\frac{-5}{5}$; $\frac{-5}{0}$

Page 101   E=2; A=3; U=4; W=7; Y=5; N=1; O=8; I=9; R=6; YOU ARE A WINNER.

Page 102   a. 345, 6,504, 364, 2,324, 9,952; b. 440, 408, 125, 1,266, 9,848;

                c. 337; d. 5,216; e. 7,878; f. 764

Page 103   r. 2; y. 8; l. 1; b. 9; a. 4; t. 5; e. 7; i. 6; h. 3; a. 4; b. 9; y. 8;

                the library

Page 104

6 × 8 = 48	4 × 7 = 28	5 × 9 = 45
8 × 6 = 48	7 × 4 = 28	9 × 5 = 45
48 ÷ 8 = 6	28 ÷ 7 = 4	45 ÷ 9 = 5
48 ÷ 6 = 8	28 ÷ 4 = 7	45 ÷ 5 = 9
6 × 7 = 42	2 × 8 = 16	3 × 9 = 27
7 × 6 = 42	8 × 2 = 16	9 × 3 = 27
42 ÷ 7 = 6	16 ÷ 8 = 2	27 ÷ 9 = 3
42 ÷ 6 = 7	16 ÷ 2 = 8	27 ÷ 3 = 9

Page 105

3 × 5 = 15	5 × 4 = 20	7 × 3 = 21
5 × 3 = 15	4 × 5 = 20	3 × 7 = 21
15 ÷ 3 = 5	20 ÷ 5 = 4	21 ÷ 7 = 3
15 ÷ 5 = 3	20 ÷ 4 = 5	21 ÷ 3 = 7
4 × 3 = 12	5 × 6 = 30	8 × 3 = 24
3 × 4 = 12	6 × 5 = 30	3 × 8 = 24
12 ÷ 3 = 4	30 ÷ 5 = 6	24 ÷ 3 = 8
12 ÷ 4 = 3	30 ÷ 6 = 5	24 ÷ 8 = 3
9 × 2 = 18	7 × 4 = 28	5 × 8 = 40
2 × 9 = 18	4 × 7 = 28	8 × 5 = 40
18 ÷ 2 = 9	28 ÷ 4 = 7	40 ÷ 5 = 8
18 ÷ 9 = 2	28 ÷ 7 = 4	40 ÷ 8 = 5

Page 106   1. d; 2. g; 3. a; 4. f; 5. b; 6. e; 7. c; 8. h

Page 107 $\frac{1}{2}$, $\frac{1}{3}$, $\frac{2}{4}$, $\frac{1}{2}$, $\frac{3}{8}$, $\frac{1}{5}$, $\frac{2}{3}$

Page 108   1. $\frac{1}{5}$; 2. $\frac{4}{5}$; 3. $\frac{3}{10}$; 4. $\frac{1}{10}$; 5. $\frac{6}{10}$

Page 109
1. There are 3 brown squares out of 3 brown squares = $\frac{3}{3}$ = 1

2. There are 4 purple parts out of 4 purple parts = $\frac{4}{4}$ = 1

3. There are 6 pink parts out of 6 pink parts = $\frac{6}{6}$ = 1

4. More than one correct answer; sample answer: $\frac{7}{7} = \frac{8}{8} = \frac{9}{9} = \frac{10}{10} = \frac{100}{100} = 1$

Page 110 $\frac{2}{3}$ = $\frac{4}{6}$; $\frac{3}{4}$ = $\frac{6}{8}$; $\frac{2}{4}$ = $\frac{4}{8}$

Page 111   a. $\frac{2}{8}$, $\frac{2}{6}$, $\frac{6}{9}$; b. $\frac{6}{8}$, $\frac{15}{24}$, $\frac{3}{8}$; c. $\frac{8}{20}$, $\frac{12}{20}$, $\frac{5}{30}$

Page 112   1. $\frac{1}{2}$, $\frac{3}{4}$, $\frac{3}{8}$, $\frac{5}{6}$;   2. $\frac{2}{4}$, $\frac{1}{4}$, $\frac{1}{2}$, $\frac{7}{12}$;   3 and 4. More than one correct answer; sample answer: ;

Page 113   1. $\frac{3}{7}$;   2. $\frac{1}{7}$;   3. green and pink;   4. More than one correct answer; sample answer: .

Page 114   1. $\frac{1}{2}$;   2. $\frac{1}{3}$, $\frac{2}{3}$;   3. $\frac{1}{4}$, $\frac{2}{4}$, $\frac{3}{4}$;   4. $\frac{1}{5}$, $\frac{2}{5}$, $\frac{3}{5}$, $\frac{4}{5}$;

5.

Page 115

Page 116   a. 10, 10, 12, 12, 15, 15;   b. 8, 8, 35, 35, 40, 40;
c. 42, 42, 45, 45, 7, 7; d. 28, 28, 24, 24, 21, 21

Page 117   a. 2, 1, 5, 4, 3; b. 1, 4, 2, 3, 5; c. 2, 1, 3, 5, 4; d. 6, 9, 8, 7;
e. 9, 7, 8, 6; f. 6, 9, 8, 7; a-c are 1 through 5, d-f are 6 through 9.

Page 118   a-e. ; g. hundreds; h. ones; i. tens;
k. 4000 + 800 + 70 + 6;
l. 3000 + 400 + 60 + 7; m. 8000 + 700 + 3;
o. seven thousand, two hundred thirteen

Page 119   c. <; d. <; e. <; f. >; g. >; h. >; i. <; j. >; k. =;
l. >; n. 39, 41, 48; o. 300, 398, 401; p. 29, 48, 52, 76

Page 120   2. one hour; 3. one hour and 15 minutes;
4. one hour and 5 minutes; 5. Kansas City to New Orleans

Page 121   a. 2 weeks; b. 2 years; c. 21 days; d. 4 weeks; e. 12 months; f. 28 days;
g. <; h. >; i. >; j. >; k. =; l. =; m. >; n. <; o. =; p. <

Page 122   1. October 22; 2. August 13; 3. December 6; 4. August 1;
5. September 11; 6. July 21; 7. September 18; 8. September 24

Page 123   a. 6, 7, 8, 9, 10;   b. 12, 14, 16, 18, 20; c. 21, 24, 27, 30, 33;
d. 28, 32, 36, 40, 44; e. 30, 35, 40, 45, 50; f. 36, 42, 48, 54, 60;
g. 42, 49, 56, 63, 70; h. 48, 56, 64, 72, 80; i. 54, 63, 72, 81, 90;
j. 60, 70, 80, 90, 100; k. 66, 77, 88, 99, 110;
l. 72, 84, 96, 108, 120; m. 13, 19, 22, 28;   n. 12, 17, 32, 37

Page 124 3; 6; 9; 12; 15; 18; 21; 24; 27; 30; 33; 36; 39; 42; 45; 48; 51; 54; 57; 60; 63; 66; 69; 72; 75; 78; 81; 84; 87; 90; 93; 96; 99; diagonal lines

Page 125 4; 8; 12; 16; 20; 24; 28; 32; 36; 40; 44; 48; 52; 56; 60; 64; 68; 72 ; 76; 80; 84; 88; 92; 96; 100; diagonal lines

Page 126

							25
		325	300				50
		350	275			100	75
		375	250	225		125	
			400		200	175	150
			425				
	475	450					
	500						

Page 127 a. >; b. <; c. =; d. >; e. =; f. >; g. =; h. =; i. >; j. <; k. =; l. <

Page 128 $\frac{2}{8} = \frac{1}{4}$; ⊘ = ⊘; $\frac{3}{4} = \frac{6}{8}$; ⊘ = ⊘;

$\frac{1}{2} = \frac{4}{8}$; ⊘ = ⊘; $\frac{8}{8} = \frac{2}{2}$; ⊘ = ⊘

Page 129 More than one correct answer for drawings; sample answers:

⊘ $= \frac{2}{8}$

$\frac{2}{4}$; ⊘ $= \frac{4}{8}$

$\frac{2}{8}$; ⊘ $= \frac{1}{4}$

$\frac{3}{4}$; ⊟ $= \frac{6}{8}$

$\frac{1}{4}$; ⊡ $= \frac{2}{8}$

$\frac{2}{8}$; ▦ $= \frac{4}{16}$

Page 130 $\frac{4}{8}$

Page 131 Lee $\frac{3}{8}$, Brenda $\frac{2}{8}$, Mia $\frac{6}{8}$, Will $\frac{1}{8}$

Pages 132–133 2. $\frac{9}{12}$ ▦; 3. $\frac{4}{16}$ ▦; 4. $\frac{5}{6}, \frac{10}{12}$ ▦; 5. $\frac{1}{8}, \frac{3}{24}$ ▦;

6. $\frac{2}{8}, \frac{4}{16}$ ▦; 7. $\frac{1}{2}, \frac{4}{8}$ ⊘; 8. $\frac{1}{4}, \frac{5}{20}$ ⊛

Page 134   1.  , <; 2.  , <; 3. , >;

4. 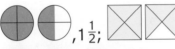 , =; 5. $\frac{1}{8}$, $\frac{2}{8}$, $\frac{3}{8}$; 6. 0, $\frac{1}{2}$, 1

Page 135   1. Jim; 2. Tom ($\frac{3}{8}$ of raspberry);

3. Tom ($\frac{3}{8}$ of raspberry), Jason ($\frac{1}{2}$ raspberry);

4. Jim and Jason ($\frac{1}{4} + \frac{1}{4} = \frac{1}{2}$)

Pages 136-137   1. $1\frac{1}{2}$; 2. $1\frac{1}{3}$; 3. $1\frac{2}{4}$; 4. $2\frac{2}{6}$; 5. $2\frac{1}{2}$;

6. $2\frac{1}{2}$; 7. $3\frac{2}{3}$; 8. $1\frac{5}{8}$; 9. $2\frac{5}{6}$; 10. 3

Page 138    , $1\frac{1}{2}$; , $1\frac{3}{4}$; , $2\frac{1}{5}$; , $2\frac{1}{2}$;

 , $3\frac{1}{2}$; , $1\frac{7}{8}$;

, $3\frac{1}{4}$;

Page 139   2. , $\frac{4}{5}$; 3. , $\frac{7}{10}$

Page 140 $\frac{2}{4} + \frac{1}{4} = \frac{3}{4}$; $\frac{1}{4} + \frac{1}{4} = \frac{2}{4}$; $\frac{5}{8} + \frac{2}{8} = \frac{7}{8}$;

$\frac{1}{8} + \frac{5}{8} = \frac{6}{8}$; $\frac{1}{4} + \frac{1}{4} + \frac{1}{4} = \frac{3}{4}$; $\frac{2}{6} + \frac{1}{6} + \frac{1}{6} = \frac{4}{6}$

Page 141 $\frac{2}{3}$ and $\frac{1}{3}$; $\frac{1}{5}$ and $\frac{2}{5}$; $\frac{1}{4}$ and $\frac{3}{4}$; $\frac{2}{6}$ and $\frac{3}{6}$

Page 142   1. $\frac{1}{3}$; 2. , $\frac{2}{5}$; 3. , $\frac{7}{10}$

Page 143 $\frac{3}{8}$, ; $\frac{3}{4}$, ; $\frac{5}{8}$, ; $\frac{4}{8}$, ; $\frac{3}{16}$, ;

$\frac{1}{4}$, ; $\frac{1}{3}$, ; $\frac{5}{16}$,

Pages 144-145   1. 3,684 miles; 2. 1,992 miles; 3. 2,160 miles; 4. 4,236 miles;
5. 3,058 miles; 6. 5,111 miles; 7. between 10 and 11 days

Pages 146-147   1. 140 calories; 2. 90 calories; 3. 310 calories; 4. 96 calories;
5. French Fries and Hamburger; 6. 407 calories

Pages 148-149 Order of addends in number sequences may vary. 2. 17; 3. 12; 4. 15, 32; 5. 36, 15, 36; 6. 52, 69; 7. 69, 83 – 14 = 69; 8. 41, 76 – 35 = 41; 9. $50 – $21 = $29; 10. 5, 5 + 6 = 11; 11. 10, 10 + 11 = 21; 12. 22, 17 + 22 = 39; 13. 9, 9 + 14 = 23; 14. 19; 15. 75, 25; 16. 12; 17. 25, 25 + 25 = 50; 18. 29, 43 + 29 = 72; 19. 18, 45 + 18 = 63; 20. $45 – $10 = $35

Page 150 a 11; b 4; c 39; d 17; e 12; f 9; g 47; nice belt

Page 151
$6 \div 3$ means how many threes in six (2);
$8 \div 4$ means how many fours in eight (2);
$6 \div 2$ means how many twos in six (3);
$9 \div 3$ means how many threes in nine (3);
$10 \div 5$ means how many fives in ten (2);
$12 \div 4$ means how many fours in twelve (3);
$14 \div 7$ means how many sevens in fourteen (2);
$15 \div 3$ means how many threes in fifteen (5)

Page 152 $8 \div 4$, ; $9 \div 3$, ; $16 \div 4$, ; $12 \div 6$, ; $15 \div 5$, ; $10 \div 2$, ; $18 \div 9$, ; $21 \div 7$, ; $14 \div 2$,

Page 153 $2\overline{)8}^{\,4}$; $5\overline{)15}^{\,3}$; 12; $6\overline{)12}^{\,2}$; fours, 16, $4\overline{)16}^{\,4}$; threes, 18, $3\overline{)18}^{\,6}$

Page 154 $3 \times 5 = 15$, ; $5\overline{)20}^{\,4}$, ; $3 \times 7 = 21$, ; $32 \div 8 = 4$, ; $5 \times 5 = 25$, ; $6\overline{)24}^{\,4}$, ; $9\overline{)27}^{\,3}$, ; $18 \div 6 = 3$,

Page 155 Mike = $3\frac{1}{2}$ pieces; Ramone = 2 pieces; Tim = $1\frac{1}{2}$ pieces; Butch = 1 piece

Page 156 1. $10\overline{)50}^{\,5}$; 2. $7\overline{)56}^{\,8}$; 3. $4\overline{)36}^{\,9}$; 4. $3\overline{)18}^{\,6}$

Page 157 5. $3\overline{)27}^{\,9}$; 6. $4\overline{)24}^{\,6}$; 7. $5\overline{)30}^{\,6}$; 8. $9\overline{)54}^{\,6}$; 9. $45 \div $5 = $9

Page 158 a. $8 \div 2 = 4$ so $2 \times 4 = 8$;   b. $15 \div 5 = 3$ so $5 \times 3 = 15$; c. $24 \div 6 = 4$ so $4 \times 6 = 24$; d. $32 \div 8 = 4$ so $8 \times 4 = 32$; e. $21 \div 3 = 7$ so $3 \times 7 = 21$; f. $42 \div 7 = 6$ so $7 \times 6 = 42$; g. $27 \div 3 = 9$

Page 159 $4 + 4 + 4 = 3 \times 4$; $9 + 9 = 2 \times 9$; $5 \times 3 = 3 + 3 + 3 + 3 + 3$;

$6 + 6 + 6 = 3 \times 6$; $5 \times 4 = 4 \times 5$; $7 + 7 + 7 = 3 \times 7$;

$8 + 8 + 8 + 8 = 4 \times 8$; $5 + 5 + 5 + 5 + 5 = 5 \times 5$

Page 160   1-3. More than one correct answer; sample answer: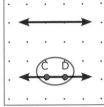

4. Point C and Point D

Page 161   1. 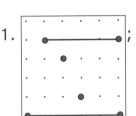 ; 2. 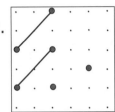 ; 3. 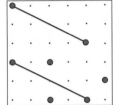 ;

4. More than one correct answer; sample answer: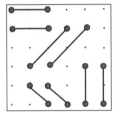

5.

Page 162   More than one correct answer; sample answer:

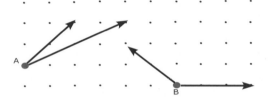

Page 163   1. 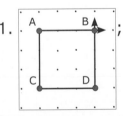 ; 2. all figures have right angles except;

1st row: triangle & circle; 2nd row: parallelogram;

3rd row: half circle

Page 164   right, acute, obtuse; acute, acute, obtuse; obtuse, obtuse, acute

Page 165   More than one correct answer; sample answers: A 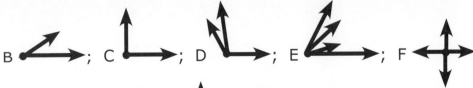 ;

B   ; C   ; D   ; E   ; F

Page 166   1.  ; 2.   ; 3. Answers will vary.

Page 167

4	4	4	Rectangle
5	5	1	Pentagon
3	3	0	Equilateral-Triangle
3	3	1	Right Triangle
4	4	0	Parallelogram
6	6	0	Hexagon
4	4	0	Trapezoid
4	4	4	Square

Page 168   a. 240, 280, 200, 210, 540, 120; b. 160, 360, 150, 180, 320;
c. 5,600, 4,000, 900, 600, 2,100

Page 169   Cam, 1 piece; Maria, 3 pieces; Liz, 5 pieces; Pam, 6 pieces

Pages 170-171 1. $20 \div 4 = 5$ $4 \times 5 = 20$;   2. $21 \div 7 = 3$ $7 \times 3 = 21$;

3. $32 \div 8 = 4$ $8 \times 4 = 32$,   4. $45 \div 9 = 5$ $9 \times 5 = 45$;

5. $18 \div 6 = 3$ $6 \times 3 = 18$;   6. $72 \div 8 = 9$ $8 \times 9 = 72$;

7. $3 \div 1 = 3$ $1 \times 3 = 3$;   8. $40 \div 5 = 8$ $5 \times 8 = 40$;

9. $27 \div 3 = 9$ $3 \times 9 = 27$;

10. $3\overline{)12}^{\,4}$; 11. $10 \div 2 = 5$; 12. $2\overline{)6}^{\,3}$

Page 172   a. 3, 8, 5, 7, 1; b. 4, 4, 4, 6, 4; c. 1, 9, 7, 5, 6;
d. 4, 1, 6, 8, 7; e. 4, 9, 7, 2

Page 173   1. $24 \div 6 = 4$ (first picture) ;
2. $21 \div 3 = 7$ (middle picture)

Page 174   1. 10 units, 16 units, 8 units;
2. 8 units, 12 units, 14 units, 10 units; 3. 26 units

Page 175   1. ; 2. ; 3. ; 4.

Page 176   1. 12 cm; 2. 14 cm; 3. 12 cm; 4. 17 cm

Page 177   1. p = 12 cm; 2. p = 12 cm; 3. Drawings will vary.

Page 178   1. 2 square units, 6 square units, 8 square units;
2. 3 square units, 5 square units, 6 square units, 4 square units

Page 179   a. 12 square units; b. 12 square units;   c. 8 square units;
d. 8 square units;   e. 9 square units;   f. 9 square units;
g. 40 square units; h. 20 square units; i. 24 square units

Page 180   P = 8 cm, A = 3 square cm;   P = 14 cm, A = 12 square cm;
P = 12cm, A = 7 square cm;   P = 14 cm, A = 6 square cm;

, ; Multiply the length times the width.

Page 181   The drawings should match the book.

Page 182   1. 1 pound; 2. 1 ounce; 3. 8 pounds; 4. 130 pounds; 5. 5 ounces; 6. 4,000 pounds; 7. 5 pounds; 8. 2 ounces; 9. 1 ounce; 10. 4 pounds

Page 183   1. 2 grams; 2. 1 kilogram; 3. 5 grams; 4. 82 kilograms; 5. 8 kilograms; 6. 1,800 kilograms; 7. 100 grams; 8. 2 kilograms; 9. 45 grams; 10. $1\frac{1}{2}$ kilograms; 11. 3 kilograms;   12. $\frac{1}{2}$ gram

Page 184   Answers will vary.

Page 185   1. 18, 81; 2. 36, 63; 3. 159, 195, 519, 591, 915, 951; 4. 348, 384, 438, 483, 834, 843; 5. 112, 121, 211

Page 186   a. 12, 14, 32, 7, 18, 36, 10;   b. 4, 64, 24, 27, 40, 18, 24; c. 35, 16, 15, 20, 49, 81, 0;   d. 9 , 24, 48, 54, 56, 3, 18; e. 25, 16, 63, 36, 0, 3, 64;   f. 12, 20, 14, 56, 45, 42, 54

Page 187   a. 5, 16, 18, 28, 36, 24, 12;   b. 25, 54, 56, 2, 24, 32, 12; c. 49, 64, 9, 10, 42, 45, 0;   d. 4, 16, 35, 28, 30, 9, 25; e. 63, 0, 5, 64, 72, 12, 32;   f. 1, 8, 48, 42, 18, 42, 24

Page 188   1. Favorite Color; 2. 35 students; 3. yellow, green, orange, red, blue; 4. 6 students

Page 189

```
  $ 12      $ 17
  x  4      x  5
     8        35
+ 40      + 50
  $ 48      $ 85
```

Pages 190-191   1. 371; 2. 225; 3. 368; 4. 448; 5. 135; 6. 166; 7. 747; 8. 280; 9. 259; 10. 284; 11. 776; 12. 228

Page 192

5	3	3
4	4	4
3	5	5
2	6	6

Page 193   1. Favorite Ice Cream; 2. 5 students; 3. 7 students; 4. 4 + 3 + 5 + 7 = 19 students; 5. 7 − 4 = 3 students

Page 194   1. red; 2. black;   3. black card, red card;   4. 1 out of 6 ($\frac{1}{6}$);

5. 1 out of 6 ($\frac{1}{6}$);   6. 5 out of 6 ($\frac{5}{6}$)

Page 195   1. 7 + 8 = 15 years;   2. 8 − 3 = 5 years;   3. 7 + 8 = 15 years;
4. 8 − 7 = 1 year;   5. 11 − 8 = 3 years;   6. 16 − 7 = 9 years;
7. 21 − 8 = 13 years; 8. 7 − 1 = 6

Pages 196-197   2. $ 8, $8+8+8=$24;   3. $ 17, $17+17+17=$51;
 x 3   x 3
 $ 24   21
 + 30
 $ 51

4. $ 15, $15+15+15+15+15=$75; 5. $ 15, $15+15+15+15+15+15=$90;
x 5   x 6
25                                    $90
+ 50
$ 75

6. $ 17, $17+17+17+17+17+17=$102; 7. $ 8, $8+8+8+8+8+8=$48;
x 6   x 6
$102 $48

8. $ 8, $8+8+8+8+8+8+8+8=$64;
x 8
$64

9. $ 17, $17+17+17+17+17+17+17+17+17=$153;
x 9
$153

10. $ 15, $15+15+15+15+15+15+15+15+15=$135
x 9
$135

Page 198   2. 24 ÷ 4 = 6 groups;   3. 72 ÷ 9 = 8 groups; 4. 36 ÷ 6 = 6 groups;
6. 6 ÷ 2 = 3 groups;   7. 6 ÷ 3 = 2 groups

Page 199   e 168; t 84; c 249; y 229; i 134; r 172; l 248; electricity;
t 352; e 574; d 248; y 286; a 116; r 336; s 276; yesterday

Page 200   5 + 5 + 5 = 15, 3 × 5 = 15; 6 + 6 + 6 + 6 + 6 = 30, 5 × 6 = 30;
3 + 3 + 3 + 3 + 3 + 3 = 18, 6 × 3 = 18; 9 + 9 + 9 + 9 = 36, 9 × 4 = 36;
8 + 8 + 8 + 8 + 8 + 8 + 8 + 8 = 64, 8 × 8 = 64; 2 + 2 + 2 + 2 + 2 + 2 = 12,
2 × 6 = 12; 7 + 7 + 7 + 7 + 7 = 35, 7 × 5 = 35; 1 + 1 + 1 + 1 + 1 + 1 = 6,
6 × 1 = 6; 0 + 0 + 0 + 0 = 0, 4 × 0 = 0

Page 201 $6; $12; $18; $24; $30; $36; $42; $48; $54; $60; $66;
$72; $78; $84; $90; $96; $102; $108; $114; $120; $126;
$132; $138; $144; $150, $156, $162; $168; $174; $180

Page 202   2. 5 + 3 + 6 = 14 animals; 3. 6 ÷ 2 = 3 squirrels;
4. 4 × 5 =20 deer; 5. 12 + 16 = 28 wildflowers and pine cones;
6. 16 − 12 =4 more pine cones; 7. 12 ÷ 3 = 4 wildflowers

Page 203   2. 40 ÷ 8 = 5 pages;   3. 6 × 8 = 48 pencils; 4. 7 × 8 = 56
stickers; 5. 4 × $8 = $32; 6. and 7. Answers will vary.

Page 204   1. Test E; 2. Test A; 3. 3, 4, 6, 7, 9; 4. 9 – 3 = 6 problems correct;
5. 3 + 4 + 6 + 7 + 9 = 29 problems

Page 205   1. 6 children; 2. 19 children; 3. 37 students;

4. 19 – 4 = 15 children;

Page 206   2. square; 3. circle; 4. moon; 5. (9,9); 6. (1,4); 7. (5,5)

Page 207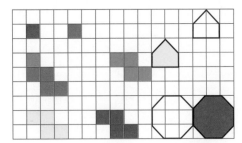

Page 208   , a; 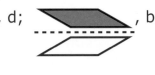 , c;   , d;   , b

Page 209   e. 149; w. 210; r. 131; c. 842; a. 929; u. 118; s. 211; o. 1,136,
b. 171; p. 846; i. 465; g. 833; l. 95;   t. 574; h. 657;
with a cowculator

Page 210   a. 71;   b. 135; c. 386; d. 116; e. 136; f. 78;   g. 302; h. 199;
i. 176; j. 207; k. 148; l. 12;   m. 211; n. 399; o. 621; p. 495;
q. 102; r. 90 ; s. 81;   t. 291; u. 223; v. 229; w. 111; x. 640

Page 211   a. 16, 21, 24, 45, 6, 9; b. 40, 49, 30, 12, 18, 24;
c. 126, 224, 315, 343, 747, 344;
d. 1080, 3432, 4350, 5649, 3604, 5607

Page 212   1. 4 × 6 = 24, 24 ÷ 4 = 6;   2. 3 × 6 = 18, 18 ÷ 3 = 6;
6 × 4 = 24, 24 ÷ 6 = 4;   6 × 3 = 18, 18 ÷ 6 = 3;
3. 5 × 8 = 40, 40 ÷ 5 = 8;   4. 9 × 2 = 18, 18 ÷ 9 = 2;
8 × 5 = 40, 40 ÷ 8 = 5;   2 × 9 = 18, 18 ÷ 2 = 9

Page 213   a. 6; b. 15; c. 20; d. 8; e. 9; f. 6; g. 40; h. 72; i. 12; j. 20;
k. 18; l. 12

Page 214   C and D are right angles. A, E and F are acute angles.
B is an obtuse angle. G and I are congruent triangles.
A square has 4 congruent sides.

Page 215   Scalene Triangle has no congruent sides (brown triangle);
Isosceles Triangle has 2 congruent sides (orange triangle);
Equilateral Triangle has 3 congruent sides (red triangle);
Right Scalene Triangle has a right angle with no congruent sides (pink);
Right Isosceles Triangle has a right angle with 2 congruent sides (gray)

Page 216   1. All figures are polygons except the circle and half circle.
   All the four-sided figures are quadrilaterals.

   2. ◣◢ ; 3. ▭ ; 4. No; 5. Yes

Page 217   P; T; none; P; P; none; No, because a trapezoid has <u>just</u> one pair of parallel sides and a parallelogram has two.

Page 218   1.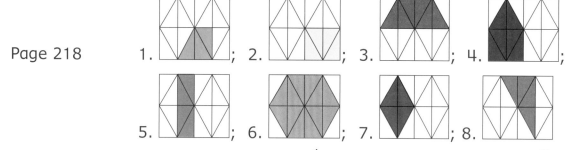

   5. ; 6. ; 7. ; 8.

Page 219   2. 1 out of 7 are blue, $\frac{1}{7}$;   3. 2 out of 7 are yellow, $\frac{2}{7}$;

   4. 1 out of 7 are green, $\frac{1}{7}$; 5. 1 out of 8 are pink, $\frac{1}{8}$

Page 220   b. $\frac{4}{8}$, ; c. $\frac{4}{6}$, ; d. $\frac{6}{8}$, ; e. $\frac{3}{12}$, ; f. $\frac{6}{10}$,

Page 221   a. <; b. >; c. >; d. <; e. >; f. <; g. >; h. =; i. <; j. =;
   k. <; l. <; m. >; n. =; o. =

Page 222   1. 12; 2. 18; 3. 12; 4. 8; 5. 72

Page 223   Estimates will vary. 1. 1 inch; 2. 4 inches; 3. $5\frac{1}{2}$ inches;

   4. $2\frac{1}{2}$ inches; 5. 5 inches

Page 224   a $\frac{1}{4}$; e $1\frac{1}{2}$; c $2\frac{7}{8}$; m $3\frac{3}{8}$; d 4; i $5\frac{1}{8}$; l $5\frac{3}{4}$; decimal

Page 225   1. intersecting lines; 2. parallel lines; 3. right angle; 4. acute angle

Page 226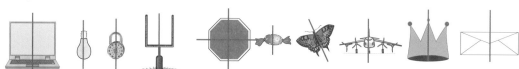

Page 227   1. $3.92; 2. $3.82; 3. $2.22; 4. $3.35; 5. $1.70; 6. $1.75

Pages 228-229   a. $2.75; b. $1.65; c. $3.20; d. $4.50; e. $3.10; f. $3.25;
   g. $7.50; h. $3.40; i. $1.75; j. $5.00; k. $5.10

Pages 230-231   1. sandwich, hamburger; 2. sandwich, taco, pizza;
                 3. sandwich, hamburger, soup;
                 4. 2 hamburgers, sandwich, taco, soup;
                 5. 3 sandwiches; pizza;
                 6. sandwich, taco, hamburger, pizza, soup

Page 232   a. $2.75, $2.92, $3.92, $4.75, $1.52; b. $1.55, $.33, $7.30,
                 $3.64, $1.09; c. $2.47, $2.95, $4.59, $4.21, $1.75; $3.25; $2.90;
                 $8.31; $.86; $7.56; $.50

Page 233   a. 5/6,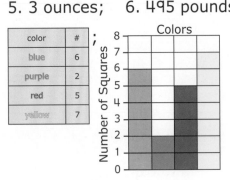

c. 3/4, ... ; d. 7/10, ...

Page 234   a. 3/6 (1/2), ... , ... , ... ; b. 1/8, ... , ... , ... ;

c. 1/4, ... , ... , ... ; d. 3/10, ...

Page 235   a. 320, 270, 420; b. 450, 140, 120; c. 480, 400, 70; d. 240,
                 630, 720; e. 160, 360, 180

Page 236   a. 600, 1,000, 1,800; b. 6,400, 4,900, 2,400;
                 c. 2,400, 8,100, 200; d. 7,200, 4,500, 4,200;
                 e. 720, 4,800, 3,500; f. 200, 5,600, 5,400

Page 237   a. 168, 336, 100, 216, 747, 378; b. 142, 83, 608, 273, 310, 174;
                 c. 462, 152, 504, 256, 176, 406; d. 224, 232, 200, 249, 133, 156

Page 238   1. 6 inches;   2. 6 feet;   3. 1,700 miles;   4. 1 foot;
                 5. 3 ounces;   6. 495 pounds;   7. 15 gallons;   8. 1 cup

Page 239

color	#
blue	6
purple	2
red	5
yellow	7

Colors graph — Number of Squares: blue 6, purple 2, red 5, yellow 7

Page 241   Choices will vary.

Page 242   1. 800 km;   2. 2 m;   3. 17 cm;   4. 2,000 kg;
                 5. 1 g;   6. 250 mL;   7. 10 l;   8. 22 cm

Page 243

°C	°F
100°	212°
95°	203°
90°	194°
85°	185°
80°	176°
75°	167°
70°	158°
65°	149°
60°	140°
55°	131°

°C	°F
50°	122°
45°	113°
40°	104°
35°	95°
30°	86°
25°	77°
20°	68°
15°	59°
10°	50°
5°	41°
0°	32°

1. 68°F; 2. 35°C; 3. 32°F; 4. 100°C;
5. 180°F

Pages 244-245 1. 7 square units; 2. 10 square units; 3. 9 square units;
4. 15 square units; 5. area = length × width in square units;
6. ; Drawings will vary.

Pages 246-247 1. 12 units; 2. 14 units; 3. 14 units; 4. 16 units; 5. 14 units;
6. The label should be units not square units (area);
7. Drawings will vary. (rectangles with sides, 3 by 2, 1 by 4, $1\frac{1}{2}$ by $3\frac{1}{2}$)

Page 248 1. January 6; 2. April 6; 3. March 24; 4. 12 days; 5. Feb.;
6. April 25; 7. 59 days; 8. 90 days (A); 9. 48 days (A)

Page 249 1. E; 2. N; 3. V; 4. E; 5. L; 6. O; 7. P; 8. E; ENVELOPE

Pages 250-251 1. cube, cylinder, rectangular prism; 2.-7. More than one correct
answer; sample answers: 2. box of crackers; 3. barrel; 4. ball;
5. top of witch's hat; 6. Jack in the box; 7. Pyramids in Egypt;
8. sphere; 9. cylinder; 10. cube

Page 252 1. 7, 8;   2. 16, 51;   3. 35, 23;   4. 9, 65; 5. 8, 4;
6. 6, 36; 7. 26

Page 253 a-e

5	2	4	7
	1	7	9
		8	2
8	4	2	7
1	6	0	5

; g. thousands; h. tens; i. ones;
k. 7000 + 200 + 60 + 9;
l. 600 + 90 + 3; m. 8000 + 10 + 7

Page 254 b. 4 + 5 – 3;   c. 5 + 7 – 3;
d. 3 + 4 + 5 + 7; e. 4 + 7 – 5 + 3;   f. 3 + 7 – 4 – 5;
g. 4 + 5 + 7 – 3; h. 5 + 7 – 3 – 4;   i. 7 – 5 + 4 – 3

Page 255 six thousands, four hundreds, two tens, three ones;
nine thousands, three hundreds, five tens, zero ones;
eight thousands, zero hundreds, six tens, zero ones;
seven thousands, six hundreds, six tens, six ones;
four thousands, five hundreds, zero tens, one ones;
three thousands, two hundreds, one tens, two ones;
one thousands, eight hundreds, three tens, nine ones

Page 256 ; 1. .1 or $\frac{1}{10}$; 2. .7 or $\frac{7}{10}$; 3. .9 or $\frac{9}{10}$;
4. .5 or $\frac{5}{10}$ $\left(\frac{1}{2}\right)$

Page 257 a. 17, 19, 21; b. 88, 86, 84; c. 40, 45, 50; d. 71, 81, 91; e. 24, 27, 30; f. 5, 5, 5; g. 64, 81, 100; h. 34, 55, 89; i. 68, 77, 86; j. 256, 512, 1024; k. 18, 20, 21; l. 20, 15, 10; m. 63, 72, 81; n. 16, 20, 20

Page 258 1. ; 2. ; 3. ; 4. ;

5. ; 6. *The number in each rectangle is determined by the addition of the adjacent rectangles above it.

Page 259

Page 260 1. right angle;   2. acute angle; 3. obtuse angle; 4. acute angle;
5. obtuse angle; 6. acute angle; 7. right angle;   8. acute angle;

9. ;   10. ;   11.

Page 261 Shading will vary.

Page 262
```
     15
     90
 + 600
   705
```

Page 263 a. 660, 5,768, 1,132, 2,712; b. 1,080, 1,332, 472, 816;
c. 4,736, 6,468, 640, 2,046

Page 264 a. 3,514, 2,132, 7,614, 6,272; b. 916, 4,228, 2,289, 1,032;
c. 2,005, 789, 4,508, 714

Page 265 2. 20 ÷ 4 = 5 tables 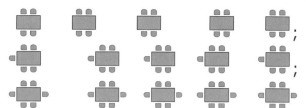 ;
3. 25 ÷ 5 = 5 tables ;
4. 30 ÷ 6 = 5 tables

Page 266

250	90	160	1,010	1,750
200	75	140	910	1,500
150	60	120	810	1,250
100	45	100	710	1,000
50	30	80	610	750
0	15	60	510	500

Page 267

89	131	164	1,100	33
32	129	132	1,011	32
26	121	102	1,010	29
11	102	43	1,001	21
9	91	24	111	11

Pages 268-270 Answers will vary.

Page 271 1. Friday; 2. 80-65=15 degrees; 3. Friday; 4. Monday;
5. Monday, Wednesday; 6. 100 candy bars

Page 272 2. 6,000 + 50 + 9; 3. 5,000 + 700 + 20;
4. 8,000 + 100 + 70 + 3; 5. 3,000 + 200 + 10 + 6;
6. 5,000 + 100 + 40 + 3

Page 273 2. 7,345; 3. 6,503; 4. 8,350; 5. 720; 6. 2,461; 7. 8,411;
8. 1,426; 9. 4,306; 10. 379;
a. seven hundred one; b. five thousand, two hundred forty-three;
c. one thousand, six hundred; d. nine thousand, one hundred
    forty-seven; e. six thousand, eighteen

Page 274 2. 9; 3. 7; 4. 4; 5. 13; 6. 35; 7. 6; 8. 18; 9. 100; 10. 0

Page 275 a. 16 < 17; b. 16 < 24; c. 30 > 21; d. 17 < 25; e. 9 > 8;
f. 71 > 49; g. 32 > 25; h. 6 = 6; i. 50 < 60; j. 34 < 36

Page 276 g. 147; i. 137; b. 183; e. 155; r. 198; a. 85; o. 104; v. 146;
l. 122; t. 161; h. 142; m. 204; w. 1317; s. 1270; p. 1160;
wow have I got problems

Page 277 a. 389; b. 63; c. 212; d. 84; e. 207; f. 83; g. 143;
h. 185; i. 78; j. 480; k. 374; l. 501; m. 100; n. 58;
o. 206; p. 72; q. 191; r. 192; s. 87; t. 18; u. 284;
v. 182; w. 91; x. 68

Page 278 b. 348; c. 558; d. 54; e. 171; f. 306; g. 322; h. 98;
i. 448; j. 376; k. 498 l. 142; m. 891; n. 468; o. 783;
p. 66 q. 110; r. 644; s. 539; t. 640

Page 279   a. 5, 50, 500; b. 3, 30, 300; c. 4, 40, 400; d. 2, 20, 200; e. 4, 40, 400; f. 2, 20, 200; g. 400; h. 10; i. 7; j. 10; k. 80; l. 300

Page 281   1. translation or reflection; 2. rotation; 3. translation or reflection; 4. reflection; 5. translation; 6. rotation

reflection   rotation

7.   8.   Drawings of rotation may vary

Page 282   1. (2,2); 2. (9,8); 3. (9,2); 4. (3,8); 5. yellow; 6. blue; 7. (2,2) & (9,2) or (3,8) & (9,8); 8. (9,2) & (9,8)

Page 283   Pictures should match. 3. 4.

Pages 284-285   2. 9 cm; 3. 3 cm; 4. 13 cm; 5. 15 cm; 6. 2 cm; 7. 10 cm; 8. 4 cm;

Page 286   o. 4; g. $2\frac{1}{2}$; m. 2; t. $3\frac{1}{2}$; e. 6; s. $4\frac{1}{2}$; p. 5; a. 1; postage stamp

Page 287   1. Red; 2. Gray; 3. Black; 4. 30 3rd graders; 5. Tuesday; 6. Friday; 7. Monday & Wednesday

Pages 288-289   Answers will vary.

Page 290   1. 40 ft; 2. 24 in.; 3. 44 yd; 4. 38 in.; 5. 60 ft; 6. 30 yd; 7. 240 ft

Page 291   1. 8 square units; 2. 12 square units; 3. 9 square units; 4. 18 square units; 5. 15 square units; 6. 24 square units; 7. 7 square units; 8. 13 square units;

Pages 292-293   1.

nickels	1	2	3	4	5	6	7
pennies	5	10	15	20	25	30	35

;

2.

dimes	1	2	3	4	5	6	7
nickels	2	4	6	8	10	12	14

;

3.

100 pennies =	1 dollar
20 nickels =	1 dollar
10 dimes =	1 dollar
4 quarters =	1 dollar

;

4. 1 dollar, 1 quarter, 2 dimes, and 2 pennies;
5. 2 dollars, 3 quarters, 2 dimes, and 4 pennies

Page 294   a. $11.39; b. $3.75; c. $8.60; d. $7.25; e. $14.00; f. $.60; g. $10.98; h. $2.86; i. $2.50; j. $5.50; k. $5.10, >; l. >, $9.50; m. $6.00, <; n. $2.50, =, $2.50

Page 295   1. $3.99 + $1.49 = $5.48; 2. $20 − $5.48 = $14.52; 3. $8.08 - $5.75 = $2.33

Page 296   Number placement will vary.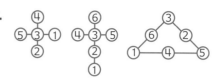

Page 297   b. O; c. B; d. L; e. D; f. I; g. E; h. A; i. J; j. F; k. C; l. P;
m. K; n. H; o. M; p. N

Page 298   b. 3 R1; c. 4 R1; d. 3 R1; e. 2 R6; f. 3 R3; g. 6 R1; h. 9 R2; i. 6
R5; j. 8 R3; k. 16 ÷ 5 = 3 R1

Page 299

8	9	5R1	4R4	6R2
7	4R4	6R6	7R3	8R2
6	3	6	8	5R3
9R1	7R7	4R4	8	9R3
5R2	6R1	4	4	9R1

Remainders = 15 problems;
No remainders = 10 problems

Page 300   1. [striped triangle pattern]; 2. [triangle pattern];
3. [triangle pattern]; 4. Drawings will vary.

Page 301   1. 2, 4, 6, 8, 10, 12, 14;   2. 1, 3, 5, 7, 9, 11;
3. 90, 100, 110, 120, 130;   4. 100, 95, 90, 85, 80;
5. 1, 2, 4, 7, 11, 16;   6. Drawing and description will vary.

Pages 302-303   7:30 p.m.; 12:40 p.m.; 6:00 p.m.; 12:00 am midnight; one
hour forty-six minutes later

Page 304   1. Wednesday; 2. 31 days; 3. 31 days; 4. 28 days;
5. 31 − 28 = 3 days; 6. March; 7. 15 days; 8. 8 weeks = 56 days

Page 305   1. 578, 579, 580; 2. 578, 579; 3. 581; 4. 578;
5. 578, 579, 580, 581; 6. 468, 480, 486, 488;
7. 100, 101, 110, 111; a. <; b. >; c. <; d. <

Page 306   1. 63, 70; 2. 29, 30; 3. 38, 40; 4. 108, 110;
5. 108, 110; 6. 17, 20

Page 307   1. 632, 700; 2. 297, 300; 3. 526, 500; 4. 72, 100;
5. 81, 0; 6. 1,776, 1,800

Page 308   1. [grid]; 2. [grid]; 3. [grid]; 4. [grid]

Page 309   1. $\frac{33}{100}$ = .33;

Pages 310-311   1. $\frac{86}{100}$ = .86;   2. $\frac{70}{100}$ = .70; 3. $\frac{7}{100}$ = .07; 4. $\frac{11}{100}$ = .11;
5. $\frac{1}{100}$ = .01;   6. $\frac{61}{100}$ = .61;

Pages 312-313   1. .32;   2. $\frac{19}{100}$;   3. $\frac{7}{100}$ = .07;

4.  .16;   5. $\frac{135}{100}$ = 1.35;   6. 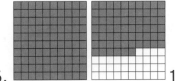 1.66

Page 314   1. 3 sides and 3 angles;   2. 4 sides and 4 angles;
3. 5 sides and 5 angles;   4. 6 sides and 6 angles;
5. 8 sides and 8 angles

Page 315   More than one correct answer; sample answers:

Page 316   1. (6,2);   2. (5,6);   3. (4,8);   4. (9,9);
5. (1,2);   6. (6,8);   7. star;   8. (6,2) and (6,8)

Page 317

3 x7 = 21	6 x4 = 24	8 x2 = 16	9 x1 = 9	4 x5 = 20	2 x8 = 16	7 x7 = 49
5 x3 = 15	6 x6 = 36	1 x8 = 8	7 x7 = 49	4 x4 = 16	6 x8 = 48	1 x9 = 9
3 x3 = 9	5 x7 = 35	9 x9 = 81	3 x9 = 27	1 x1 = 1	5 x5 = 25	3 x7 = 21
7 x9 = 63	3 x1 = 3	7 x5 = 35	2 x6 = 12	3 x3 = 9	7 x3 = 21	9 x1 = 9
9 x4 = 36	3 x3 = 9	7 x7 = 49	3 x1 = 3	7 x3 = 21	9 x9 = 81	2 x1 = 2
7 x4 = 28	8 x6 = 48	6 x7 = 42	5 x8 = 40	2 x7 = 12	6 x9 = 54	4 x4 = 16

Picture: a smiling face

Page 318   1. 40 ears; 2. 12 wheels; 3. 40 toes;
4. 12 bones; 5. $725; 6. 2,800 brooms

Page 319   1,015, 492, 1,548, 1,832, 762, 1,400;
3,438, 3,320, 1,132, 1,842, 3,535, 7,308;
4,362, 903, 940, 529, 2,961, 635;
738, 2,040, 876, 7,432, 420, 1,418

Page 320   1. 1 out of 6 or $\frac{1}{6}$;   2. 3 out of 6 or $\frac{3}{6}$;
3. 2 out of 5 or $\frac{2}{5}$;   4. 1 out of 2 or $\frac{1}{2}$

Page 321   1. Saturday; 2. Monday; 3. $19\frac{1}{2}$ hours; 4. Line graph will vary.

Page 322   2. 5 groups with a remainder of 1;

3. 3 groups with a remainder of 2;

4. 4 groups with a remainder of 6;

5. 7 groups with a remainder of 3

Page 323
$$3\overline{)72}$$
$\underline{-6}$
12
$\underline{-12}$
; Second 3×2; Third $7 - 6$; Fourth bring down 2; Fifth $12 \div 3$; Finally remainder 0; Check $3 \times 24 = 72$

Page 324   t. 18; l. 63; d. 35; r. 43; y. 85; a. 52; e. 55; s. 94;

at a yard sale

Page 325   2. $2\frac{1}{4}$; 3. $3\frac{2}{5}$; 4. $1\frac{5}{6}$;

a. $\frac{1}{2}$; b. $\frac{2}{2}$; c. $\frac{4}{8}$; d. $\frac{4}{10}$

Page 326   1. $\frac{1}{4} + \frac{2}{4} = \frac{3}{4}$;   2. $\frac{2}{3} - \frac{1}{3} = \frac{1}{3}$, ;

3. $\frac{2}{8} + \frac{3}{8} = \frac{5}{8}$, ;   4. $\frac{1}{2} + \frac{1}{2} = \frac{2}{2}$ or 1,

Page 327   1. 40 feet; 2. 75 inches; 3. 26 miles;
4. 5 inches; 5. 1 yard;   6. 1,023 miles

Page 328   1. 3 ounces; 2. 6 pounds; 3. 5,000 pounds; 4. 5 pounds;
5. 1 cup; 6. 5,000 gallons; 7. 1 pint; 8. 20 gallons

Page 329   1. 1,300 km; 2. 20 cm; 3. 31 m; 4. 15 cm; 5. 1 m; 6. 5 km;
pictures will vary.

Page 330   1. 5 grams; 2. 28 kilograms; 3. 2 grams; 4. 2 kilograms;
5. 10 mL; 6. 1 L; 7. 500 mL; 8. 1 L

Page 331   1. 300 mL; 2. 500 mL; 3. 700 mL; 4. 850 mL; 5. 1,000 mL;
6. 1 L; 7. 800 mL; 8. 500 mL; 9. 900 mL; 10. 750 mL;
11. 340 mL; 12. 40 mL; 13. 415 mL; 14. 1,000 mL, 1 L;
15. 2 L; 16. 8,000 mL; 17. 3,000 mL; 18. 10 L; 19. 2 L

Pages 332-333   b. $15.00 − 1.99 = $13.01; c. $20.00 − 5.09 = $14.91;
d. $5.00 − 3.17 = $1.83;   e. $50.00 − 7.48 = $42.52,
f. $2.00 − .50 = $1.50;   g. $5.00 − 2.09 = $2.91;
h. $10.00 − 9.25 = $.75;   i. $4.00 − 1.49 = $2.51

Page 334   a. $6.25 − 6.20 = $.05;   b. $10.20 − 6.15 = $4.05;
c. $10.05 − $6.04 = $4.01; d. $20.75 − 11.50 = $9.25,
e. $50.50 − 12.38 = $38.12

Page 335	Estimated lengths will vary. 1. 6 inches; 2. 3 inches; 3. 5 inches; 4. 4 inches; 5. 1 inch; 6. 2 inches; 7. 2 inches; 8. 1 inch
Page 336	Estimated lengths will vary. h. 11; m. 3; f. 8; l. 10; o. 7; a. 2; t. 4; e. 1; all of them
Page 337	l. 46; m. 93; t. 79; e. 38; r. 95; h. 78; the letter m
Page 338	1. 83 tickets; 2. 23 rows; 3. $27 per day
Page 339	▢ = 4; ▲ = 3; ? = 9; ◪ = 6; ● = 4; ? = 7
Page 340	1. 435 + 100 = 535 members; 2. 101 – 84 = 17 pounds; 3. 4 × 8 = 32 chocolates; 4. 54 ÷ 6 = 9 students; 5. 350 – 206 = 144 bones
Page 341	1. rotation; 2. reflection; 3. translation; 4. translation; 5. rotation; 6. reflection; 7. rotation; 8. translation
Page 342	a. 80; b. 10; c. 50; d. 80; e. 100; f. 200; g. 100; h. 900; i. 1,000; j. 100; k. 9,000; l. 8,000; m. 5,000; n. 9,000; o. 1,000

Page 343   1. quardrilaterals or 4 sides, 4 angles, 1 pair of parallel sides;
            2. yes; 3.

	4 sides	4 equal sides	1 pair parallel sides	2 pairs parallel sides
rectangle	yes	no	yes	yes
square	yes	yes	yes	yes
parallelogram	yes	no	yes	yes
rhombus	yes	yes	yes	yes
trapezoid	yes	no	yes	no

Page 344	1. parallelogram, quadrilateral with 2 pairs of parallel sides and opposite angles equal; 2. trapezoid, quadrilateral with one pair of parallel sides; 3. d; 4. c; 5. a; 6. e; 7. b; 8. f
Page 345	1. a; 2. d; 3. e; 4. f; 5. b; 6. c
Page 346	1. 359 – 193 = 166 tickets; 2. $19 + $29 = $48; 3. 5 × 12 = 60 doughnuts; 4. 54 ÷ 6 = 9 hours; 5. 17 – 8 = 9 more girls; 6. 32 ÷ 4 = $8
Page 347	1. Kim was driving 55 miles per hour. 107 miles; 2. He also bought a $69 skateboard. $178; 3. Representative members serve for 2 years, and senator members serve for 6 years. 535 members; 5. b; 6. d; 7. c; 8. b; 9. a; 10. c
Page 348	1. unknown (He may have spent less than $10 but bought the candy bar.); 2. unknown (The sign did not say you could pick your candy bar.); 3. true; 4. unknown (Did she spend the money on Friday?); 5. false (The sign said "over" $10.)
Page 349	1. false (Cost will be $10 + $5 = $15); 2. true (Cost will be $20 + $10 = $30); 3. true; 4. unknown; 5. false; 6. true